LIFE IN THE
VICTORIAN
HOSPITAL

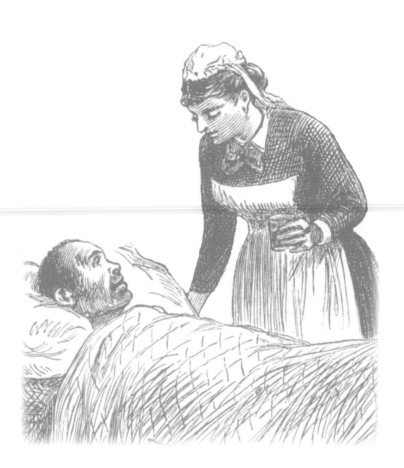

LIFE IN THE
VICTORIAN
HOSPITAL

MICHELLE HIGGS

The History Press

First published 2009

The History Press
The Mill, Brimscombe Port
Stroud, Gloucestershire, GL5 2QG
www.thehistorypress.co.uk

British Library Cataloguing in Publication Data.
A catalogue record for this book is available from the British Library.

ISBN 978 0 7524 4804 6

Typesetting and origination by The History Press
Printed in Great Britain

Invoice
To: William Pearce
          46 Briscoe Road
          Hoddesdon, Hertfordshire En11 9DG
          019924444346

Deliver
To: William Pearce
          46 Briscoe Road
          Hoddesdon, Hertfordshire En11 9DG
          019924444346

Stock Code /ISBN	Description	Qty	Price	Total
9780752448046	Life In The Victorian Hospital	1	£4.99	£4.99
9781852855031	Poisoned Lives	1	£6.99	£6.99

Sub Total	£11.98
VAT	£0.00
Royal Mail UK First Class	£0.00
Total	£11.98
INTERNET Tendered	£11.98
Change Due	£0.00

VAT GD 182

Contents

Acknowledgements

While writing this book, I received help and advice in locating information and illustrations from a number of different sources. I would like to express my gratitude to the following:

The staff of Birmingham Archives and Heritage Service; Glamorgan Record Office; Gloucestershire Archives; Great Ormond Street Hospital NHS Trust & Kingston University; Gwent NHS Trust; Gwent Record Office; Centre for Kentish Studies; Kent & Medway NHS & Social Care Partnership Trust; Lancashire Record Office; the University of Aberdeen Special Archives; Wiltshire and Swindon Archives; Alistair Tough of the NHS Greater Glasgow and Clyde Board Archives; Fiona Watson of the Northern Health Services Archives in Aberdeen; Alan Humphries of the Thackray Museum in Leeds; Dr Ian Paterson of the Northern General Hospital in Sheffield; Kevin Towers of the West London Mental Health NHS Trust; Dr Paul P. Davies; Paul Arnold; Gareth Edwards and Yvonne Goulding.

Special thanks are due to Dr Sue Hawkins of the Historic Hospital Records Project for her feedback and advice on the Children's Hospitals chapter, to Ava Connelly for helping with my research in Glasgow and to Ellie Thomas for giving a nurse's perspective on Victorian medical treatments.

I am extremely grateful to the K. Blundell Trust, administered by the Society of Authors, for providing me with a generous grant, without which I could not have undertaken research in Scotland and Wales.

I would also like to thank the following people who were so generous with their time and their research:

Benjamin Caine, Rina Callingham, Geoff Couling, Paula Couling, Wendy Fitzpatrick, Lisa Gregg, Caroline Haycock, Carl Higgs, Christopher J. Hogger, Lyn and Alan Howsam, David Rawdon, Jill Reeves, Stuart Reid, John Royle, Prue Stokes, Richard Waddy and Louise Williams.

Finally, I would like to thank my husband Carl for his unstinting support, and my family and friends for their encouragement during the writing of this book.

Illustrations

Introduction

The era of the Victorian hospital was one of cash-strapped institutions, deadly hospital infections, surgical advances and medical discoveries. Through it all, life-threatening diseases were no respecter of class, affecting rich and poor alike.

However, the medical treatment for such diseases differed significantly, depending on the patient's social class. The wealthy still received private medical treatment at home or, later in the nineteenth century, in a practitioner's consulting room. The middle classes might pay for their treatment but could also frequent one of an increasing number of specialist hospitals. The working classes who were just above the poverty line could get free treatment from charitable general hospitals or dispensaries. For the abject poor who were receiving poor relief, their only option was to seek treatment at the workhouse infirmary.

Whatever medical treatment was received, it made a difference if:

> ... the sick person was male or female; young or old; confronted with minor, serious, shameful, or life-threatening illness ... was rich or poor; trusted his doctor or not; was in a hospital, outpatient department, doctor's surgery or at home; was educated or not; was seeing the neighbourhood practitioner or a high-powered specialist; was in the hands of a 'good' doctor or not.[1]

During the Victorian period, there was a huge growth in the number and type of hospitals to cater for the increasing population. A bewildering array of medical facilities were available including voluntary hospitals, poor law infirmaries, specialist and children's hospitals, hospitals for infectious diseases, dispensaries, cottage hospitals, convalescent homes and lunatic asylums. However, at first there was no real advantage to going into a Victorian hospital for treatment as they offered 'little beyond the domiciliary capabilities of a physician or surgeon'.[2]

A patient entering hospital for treatment at the end of Queen Victoria's reign would have experienced a much higher standard of care than was available at the beginning. Increased medical knowledge and surgical skills led to more accurate diagnoses and targeted treatment, addressing the causes of disease, rather then just the symptoms. A better understanding of the transmission of deadly hospital diseases such as erysipelas, pyaemia and hospital gangrene, along with antiseptic and aseptic techniques, dramatically cut mortality rates in hospital. Scientific innovations such as anaesthetics and artery clamps increased the range of operations surgeons could safely and successfully perform. Above all, it could be argued that better training of nurses, with whom patients had the most contact, significantly improved the care a patient could expect in hospital.

Aberdeen Royal Infirmary. (Private collection)

Chapter 1

The Hospitals of the Eighteenth Century

Until the eighteenth century, there were no medical hospitals in Britain outside London.[1] This was largely because the great majority of religious hospitals, which were established by the end of the fourteenth century, were closed after the dissolution of the monasteries. There had been 500 such institutions in England alone.[2]

Before 1720, London's only hospitals were St Bartholomew's and St Thomas's, founded in 1123 and c.1215 respectively, and re-established as secular facilities, plus Bethlem, England's only lunatic asylum. Eighteenth-century Britain saw a gradual founding of general hospitals across the country, established for the deserving poor on a secular basis and funded by charity.

Five more hospitals were opened in London: the Westminster (1720), Guy's (1724), St George's (1733), The London (1740) and The Middlesex (1745). By the beginning of the nineteenth century, London's hospitals treated over 20,000 patients a year.[3]

Many Scottish hospitals also had eighteenth-century origins. Edinburgh's Royal Infirmary was set up in 1729 with Aberdeen establishing its own infirmary ten years later. In the last quarter of the eighteenth century other Scottish cities followed their example, including Dumfries (1776), Glasgow (1794) and Dundee (1798).

In England, most major cities established hospitals between 1730 and 1800, including Winchester and Bristol (1736), York (1740), Exeter (1741), Bath (1742), Northampton (1743), Manchester (1752), Birmingham (1779) and Sheffield (1792).[4] By 1800, 'every sizeable town' had a hospital.[5]

It was not until the early nineteenth century that general hospitals were established in Wales, which is perhaps indicative of the smaller size of eighteenth-century Welsh towns and their propensity for the use of dispensaries. Although it was a relatively small town, Carmarthen had a dispensary as early as 1807.[6] Swansea's Infirmary was founded in 1814 followed by Cardiff in 1837, Aberystwyth in 1838 and Carmarthen in 1846. The infirmaries in Swansea, Cardiff and Aberystwyth developed from dispensaries founded in 1808, 1822 and 1821 respectively.

Some hospitals were founded by individual benefactors, the most famous example being Thomas Guy and Guy's Hospital in London. In Elgin, Scotland, Dr Gray's Hospital was founded and endowed by Dr Alexander Gray, a surgeon for the East India Company, who amassed 'a considerable personal fortune' during the time he spent working in Bengal.[7] Other hospitals, such as the Royal Devon and Exeter, were established by 'local groups of concerned citizens'.[8]

Unlike the earlier hospices and religious-based hospitals, these new hospitals were not built for paupers. They were founded to serve the 'industrious poor, and, in particular, the urban poor'.[9] The managers of the Glamorgan and Monmouthshire Infirmary, later known as the Cardiff Royal Infirmary, clarified exactly who the hospital was meant to treat. The objective of the institution was 'to afford medical relief to the labouring classes and mechanics, who, while in the enjoyment of health and strength, are enabled to maintain themselves and families in decency and comfort, but who, when suffering from disease or accident, become objects of real concern and sympathy'.[10]

The exact type of 'industrious poor' each hospital aimed to treat depended on the area in which it was situated. For example, the London, founded in 1740, was set up to help 'in particular, the manufacturers and merchant seamen together with their families'.[11] With the city's close association with the slave trade, it is unsurprising that Bristol's General Hospital, set up in 1737, was founded to treat those engaged in this industry 'using part of the personal fortune of one man actively involved in it, John Elbridge, a Quaker and collector of customs'.[12] The clientele of Liverpool's first hospital, founded in 1749, was inextricably linked with trade in the city's port.

Gray's Hospital, Elgin (postmarked 1908).

In common with general hospitals, the first specialist hospitals had their foundation in the eighteenth century. London's charitable Lock Hospital, which catered exclusively for venereal cases, opened in 1746. Venereal disease had been previously thought of as a just punishment for sins, and it has been argued that the opening of hospitals like the Lock was 'a sign of a changing climate of opinion'.[13] The founders of hospitals for sufferers of venereal disease were taking the Enlightenment view that 'relief of suffering was the duty of humanity'.[14]

Despite this more charitable point of view, it could be difficult to secure funding for a hospital treating venereal diseases. Glasgow's Lock Hospital, founded in 1805, could not generate enough income from its subscribers and 'needed grants from the parish authorities to keep it open'.[15] In Edinburgh, subscribers were even less forthcoming and the city's Lock Hospital, established in 1835, had to close after just twelve years.[16]

London's first lying-in or maternity hospitals were opened in the mid-eighteenth century.[17] They included the British (1749), the City (1750), the General (1752) and the Westminster (1765).[18] Glasgow's Lying-in Hospital, opened in 1792, was connected with the university.[19] These maternity hospitals guaranteed much-needed bed-rest to impoverished women and allowed unmarried mothers 'to deliver their illegitimate babies with no questions asked'.[20]

Lying-in hospitals were to fall victim to high death rates of mothers and babies from puerperal fever, but, for the medical profession, they provided an environment where 'students could practise obstetric skills'.[21]

Eighteenth-century hospitals provided medical treatment, food, shelter and time for convalescence. They treated accidents and emergencies and restricted themselves to 'routine complaints likely to respond to rest and treatment' such as winter bronchitis or ulcerated legs.[22] Those with infectious diseases were usually excluded from the general hospitals because they could not be cured, and admitting them would only lead to further outbreaks of disease. The exception was in Scotland, where the voluntary general hospitals vigorously adhered to the principle of accepting all cases which needed medical treatment, with separate wards for fever and smallpox patients.

In the eighteenth and early nineteenth centuries, 'there were no medical procedures exclusive to hospitals: you could be operated upon on the kitchen table, and you gave birth at home'.[23]

Chapter 2

General Voluntary and Endowed Hospitals

At the beginning of Queen Victoria's reign, there were two kinds of general hospital available to the industrious poor: voluntary and endowed. It is unlikely that patients would have perceived any difference between the two, which related to the funding of each type of hospital.

The vast majority of Victorian general hospitals were voluntary, funded by charity. It was always a challenge to meet the running costs, in terms of food, drugs, dressings, medical sundries and wages, not to mention the maintenance of the buildings.

The administrators of every voluntary hospital faced the same daily challenge: that of balancing the books. They had to generate their income from a number of different sources including regular subscriptions, church collections, bequests from wills, ad hoc donations from individuals and businesses, and the staging of charitable events.

Endowed hospitals such as Guy's and Dr Gray's were funded with large legacies which, if invested wisely, provided a regular source of income for the hospital. With the increase in population and demand for medical services, by the last quarter of the nineteenth century, most endowed hospitals had to supplement their investment income from other sources, for instance by opening wards for paying patients. Until then, these favoured few hospitals had the luxury of being able to pick and choose the cases they treated, without being bound to recommendations from subscribers.

Subscriptions and subscribers

Voluntary general hospitals throughout Britain operated the subscription system which provided funds for the hospital and dictated who could receive medical treatment. Under this system, wealthy members of the local community paid an annual sum, which entitled them to recommend a set number of in- or out-patients to the hospital per year. The precise number which could be recommended depended on the value of the subscription, and a sliding scale was published in hospitals' annual reports.

Subscriptions varied across the country. For instance, at Birmingham's General Hospital, annual subscriptions started at 10s 6d, which entitled subscribers to recommend three out-patients only. The scale had nine levels with the top subscription of £5 5s 0d entitling subscribers to recommend two in-patients and six out-patients every year.[1] At the Royal South Hants Infirmary in Southampton, subscribers could recommend 'one in-patient or three out-patients per year for each guinea subscribed'.[2]

At many hospitals, if the annual subscription was sufficiently high, usually one guinea or more, this entitled the subscriber to become a governor of the hospital for one year. Subscribers could also pay a single sum to become a life governor of the hospital. At the South Hants Infirmary, the cost was £21.[3]

Recommendations by subscribers were sometimes known as 'letters', 'tickets' or in Scotland, a 'line'. Although subscriptions were a vital source of income, they were only ever sufficient to subsidise the cost of care for patients.

It was important to encourage subscribers to renew their subscriptions each year. In their Annual Report for 1848, the managers of the Cardiff Royal Infirmary addressed their subscribers directly: 'Your Medical Officers by your means go among people whom you may never see, and into houses which you may never enter, to alleviate the amount of human misery, of which you can have no experience.'[4]

This address was designed to tug at the subscribers' hearts (and their purse strings), but it also clearly demonstrates the wide gulf in social class between the subscribers and the patients.

Grenoside Hospital Parade in aid of Sheffield hospitals, 1908. (Courtesy of Grenoside & District Local History Group)

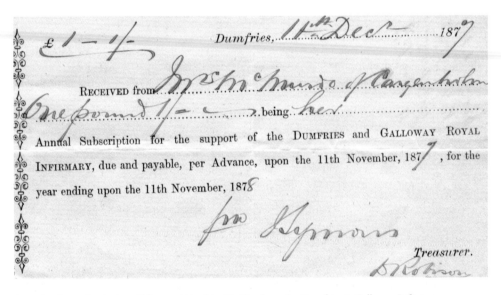

A receipt for a subscription of £1 1s paid by Mrs McMurdo to the Dumfries & Galloway Infirmary, 11 December 1877.

Fund-raising

In the Victorian period, it was always easier to raise funds for 'children and young adults than old people, for acute disease rather than chronic, for the 'worthy' poor than the residuum, for physical than mental disorders'.[5]

The role of the hospital treasurer was vital in ensuring that funds kept coming in. His work was 'part accountant and part publicist'.[6] A good treasurer could increase his hospital's income by emphasising the numbers of patients successfully treated and cured in the local press and in annual reports. By the same token, a fraudulent collector could prove disastrous to a hospital's annual income if he disappeared with the collection.

The Royal South Hants Infirmary is an example of a typical Victorian voluntary hospital. In 1855, the hospital's total income was £2,473. This was broken down into various sources of income: '36 per cent (£883 8s 6d) came from subscriptions; 25 per cent (£613 14s 11d) from donations and approximately 30 per cent (£742) from investment income. The remainder was made up of legacies, payments by patients and employers, and by the sale of slops from the hospital kitchen.'[7] As a comparison, the 'hotel' costs of the hospital, which included the provision of beds, linen and food to patients, 'were never less than 53 per cent of total expenditure annually'.[8] In 1858, these costs amounted to over £1,345.[9]

Bequests

Bequests were an important source of income to hospitals, often left by grateful former patients or generous benefactors. Thomas Darbey, described as a gentleman of Sedgley in Staffordshire, died in 1863 aged sixty-three. The son of a shoemaker, he had become wealthy during his lifetime and was a proprietor of land and houses. He had no family and left numerous bequests to charities including the sum of £300 to the South Staffordshire General Hospital and Dispensary at Wolverhampton. The money was for 'the charitable uses of the said Hospital'. A condition of the bequest was that Thomas Darbey's executors should have 'the privilege of recommending the same number of in or out patients to the said Hospital as a subscriber or donor of the above amount or value may have'.

As a wealthy gentleman, it is highly unlikely that Thomas Darbey ever had treatment at the South Staffordshire General Hospital and Dispensary himself, but it is quite possible that he was treated in his own home by a consultant working at the hospital. He died of 'Malignant disease of Bladder and Prostate', also known as prostate cancer.[10]

Charitable events

Once the general hospitals were established in their local communities, they became a focus for fund-raising through charitable events. These were often annual affairs, such as summer fêtes, music festivals and galas, prompting much civic pride. The success of such events depended largely upon the calibre of the committees which organised them and, in the second half of the nineteenth century, ladies' committees sprang up across the country to galvanise support for their local hospitals.

In Birmingham, the musical festivals in support of the city's General Hospital became famous in their own right. The first concert was started in 1768 and 'had become a triennial event by 1784'.[11]

'The Great Lawn and Tent, Chelsea Hospital.' (*The Illustrated London News*, 20 June 1846)

At The Hospital for Sick Children in Great Ormond Street, the Annual Festival Dinner was a vital component of the institution's annual fund-raising efforts. With eminent speakers such as Charles Dickens, Oscar Wilde and members of the Royal Family, this one event 'could raise almost half the Hospital's total income'.[12]

Other forms of income

Church collections were a significant form of income for many hospitals, especially in Scotland. In 1867, the Aberdeen Royal Infirmary received a total of £954 1s 1d from church collections, with various amounts from the Established Church, the Free Church, the Episcopal Churches and the United Presbyterian and other churches. In the same year, the hospital received just £85 from subscriptions and £84 in donations from public bodies and works.[13]

Like the hospitals in ports at Bristol, Liverpool and London, Southampton's Royal South Hants Infirmary provided hospital and accident facilities for both passengers and crew members of the numerous ships which docked there. It is no coincidence that 'P&O was a "Life Governor" of the RSH and paid £21 each year through its agent, Captain Engledue, who was also appointed Vice-President of the Infirmary'.[14] The company also made donations to the hospital and regularly took collections on board its ships for the hospital's benefit.

The endowing of hospital beds, either for a fixed term or in perpetuity, was particularly effective for raising funds for children's hospitals. From 1868, The Hospital for Sick Children in Great Ormond Street introduced a scheme under which wealthy benefactors could sponsor individual beds, 'following an example set by the children's magazine *Aunt Judy*'.[15]

Sometimes a hospital building itself could be a source of income. Bristol's General Hospital, established in 1832, quickly outgrew its first premises and a new building was erected between 1856 and 1857, which included an out-patient department for 300 patients. The new building itself provided an income for the hospital because the basement was designed as 'warehousing for the nearby harbour'.[16]

Gifts in kind, not just money, were frequently received from members of the local community. This might include clothing, linen, books and magazines, toys or specific medical equipment.

The Hospital Saturday Fund

Organised workmen's collections to support local hospitals began in Birmingham in 1846 when an Artisans' Fund was founded by Mr S. Bradley to benefit the Queen's Hospital in Birmingham. The hospital treated a large number of workplace accidents and in the following year local workers contributed almost £1,000 to its funds.[17] From the 1850s, there were similar schemes in place in other towns, the largest of which supported the Glasgow and North Stafford infirmaries. During the 1870s, the Artisans' Fund at the Queen's Hospital was developed into the Hospital Saturday Fund, 'led by influential inhabitants, including one of the hospital's surgeons, Sampson Gamgee'.[18]

The Hospital Saturday Fund was a formal organisation controlled by workers elected from the workshops. It encouraged workers to contribute a small weekly sum of money and was so named because Saturday was usually the day when the week's wages were paid.

In 1874, £258 was raised in street collections and £5,000 in workshops. By 1890, the respective sums had increased to £5,096 and £15,237. The funds were distributed according to 'the work, economy and efficiency of the different institutions'.[19]

The Queen's Hospital in Birmingham quickly benefited from the Fund, the first evidence of this being an additional wing opened in 1873. As a direct result of the Fund, by 1875 the governors were able to make the hospital a free institution so that patients did not need letters of recommendation from subscribers to be treated.[20]

Critics of the scheme included the *British Medical Journal*, which believed the Hospital Saturday Fund's penny-a-week scheme was 'a dangerous precedent' arguing that it 'will be essentially provident and will establish a moral if not a legal claim' to treatment.[21] It has been argued that the worker who contributed a penny a week to the Hospital Saturday Fund assumed 'that this entitled him and his family to use its facilities and so increased demand'.[22]

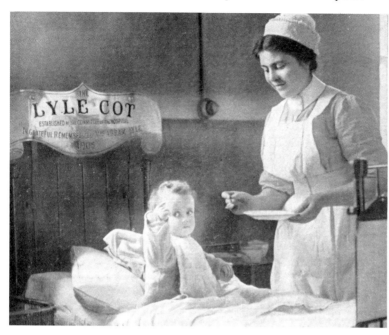

A Memorial Cot at the
**QUEEN'S
HOSPITAL FOR
CHILDREN.**

**Hackney Road, Bethnal
Green, London, E.2.**

The child's arm is held up
by a splint for purposes
of surgical treatment.

The Hospital and its
Branch at Bexhill, the
Little Folks Home,
have 170 beds, and cost
£35,000 a year to main-
tain. Only **£1,500** of this
is provided by endow-
ments.
Patron :
H.M. Queen Alexandra.
President:
H.R.H. The Duke of York
Chairman:
**Colonel Lord Wm. Cecil,
C.V.O.**
*Chairman of Little Folks
Home Committee :*
Sir Arthur Spurgeon, J.P.
*T. Glenton-Kerr,
Secretary.*

A Memorial Cot at the Queen's Hospital for Children (n.d.).

The Hospital Sunday Fund

Operating at the other end of the social scale, the Hospital Sunday Fund was aimed at raising money from the middle classes. It began in the 1850s and was organised through co-ordinated collections at church services. By 1873, a central organisation had been set up to 'stimulate the raising of money and rationalise its distribution'. In its first year, it collected £27,000; by 1889 the annual sum collected had increased to £41,700.[23] The Council of the Hospital Sunday Fund distributed the money according to the 'needs and merits' of each institution.[24]

In 1897, the Prince of Wales' Hospital Fund for London was set up, which was a development of the original Hospital Sunday Fund. After Edward became King, it became the King Edward's Hospital Fund. This fund 'successfully capitalised on the popularity of royalty and spearheaded centralised charitable giving in London for half a century'.[25]

Voluntary general hospitals after 1860

By the mid-1860s, there were two free hospital services: the charitable voluntary hospitals and the poor law infirmaries funded from rates. It was said that the public was 'lavishing princely munificence on the splendid institutions which ostensibly supply the national hospital requirements' but 'ignored the *real hospitals of the land*'.[26]

Voluntary hospitals originally carried 'the stigma of charity',[27] but after 1860 demand for their services increased dramatically. This was largely because hospitals began to offer treatments 'beyond the scope of GP or informal care'.[28]

In exchange for such sophisticated treatment, the Victorian hospital became the place where 'disease could be displayed to students on what became standard ward rounds: being charity cases, the patients could not complain'.[29] The morgue also provided valuable material for research and the training of students.[30] Under the terms of the 1832 Anatomy Act, medical students were allowed to use dead paupers for dissection purposes. It has been argued that the passing of this Act 'made the poor less willing to receive treatment in hospitals, for fear they would be experimented on and dissected'.[31]

However, the main reason for passing the Act was to curtail the actions of so-called 'bodysnatchers' or grave-robbers, who stole corpses from newly dug graves to meet the demand by medical schools for anatomical specimens to study and dissect. This practice was carried out in Edinburgh and London, but

'Hospital Saturday.' (*The Illustrated London News*, 22 July 1893)

not in Aberdeen or Glasgow.[32] Matters came to a head in 1818 when Burke and Hare turned to murder as a way of increasing the number of corpses they supplied to Edinburgh University.[33]

The voluntary hospitals were supported by charity and staffed by 'unpaid and able, and often fashionable, part-time consultants' while the poor law infirmaries were maintained out of the rates and staffed by paid full-time doctors 'of no particular standing'.[34] The voluntary hospitals could legally transfer their patients, usually chronic cases, to poor law infirmaries which had to take paupers. This they did increasingly from the 1880s, especially in London, retaining the interesting cases and getting rid of 'those they did not want [in order] to make room for the next batch of accidents and acute sick'.[35]

By the end of the nineteenth century, the challenge of funding general voluntary hospitals was far greater, given the increase in the number of patients treated, the burgeoning staff on roll and the accommodation needed to house them, plus the maintenance and expansion of most hospitals. In 1898, the drugs, dressings and medical sundries at The London cost £10,252 and 'the various dressings alone, the wools, lint, gauze etc., cost ...£3,500'.[36] The Annual Dispensary Account gives some insight into the sundries used at the London, which must have been similar in other large, city hospitals: 'Carbolic acid, 4,600 lbs; glycerine, 2,856 lbs; olive oil, 200 gallons; strapping, 15,608 yards; tow [a type of disposable dressing], 95 cwt. 74 lbs; absorbent cotton wool, 10,533 lbs; Blaud's pills [iron tablets],672 lbs; lemons, oranges etc. 7,800.' Anaesthetics included 'ether, 189 lbs; chloroform, 292 lbs' plus cocaine.[37]

Bed provision

Between 1861 and 1911, the provision of hospital beds almost tripled[38] but voluntary hospitals failed to meet the demands of a growing population. In 1861 in England and Wales, there were 230 voluntary hospitals offering 14,800 beds. However, 5,200 of these beds were in London hospitals and one eighth of the total number was provided by specialist institutions. This represents a combined figure of 0.7 beds per 1,000 population.[39] At the same time, there were 50,000 beds in poor law institutions.

In Scotland in 1891, there were 6,000 beds in voluntary hospitals, 4,500 in poor law institutions and just 1,500 in public health institutions. Twenty years later, this had increased to 10,500 voluntary beds, 6,900 poor law beds and 7,900 beds in public health institutions.[40] In Glasgow, the provision of beds in voluntary hospitals was half that provided in Edinburgh at 1.6 and 3.1 beds per 1,000 population respectively. By comparison, the average beds per 1,000 population in the English provinces was only 1.06.[41]

Patients could be turned away from a hospital simply because all the beds were full, or worse, if a dire financial situation had forced the hospital to close certain wards. The London served one and a half million people in the East End and was the largest hospital in Britain and 'with a single exception, the largest in Europe'.[42] By the end of Queen Victoria's reign, it had 776 beds, 300 nurses and 'a great medical staff', treating almost 200,000 patients per year. Even with so many beds, The London still had to turn people away. One doctor commented: 'If we had two thousand beds, we could fill them all and keep them full. We are constantly obliged to patch up and send home cases that ought to come in, but which we cannot receive for want of room'.[43]

Hospital design

The most common Victorian hospital design was the corridor plan with numerous wards leading off a central corridor. City hospitals built to this plan included the Westminster, Bath, Hull, Manchester and many others.[44] Some other hospitals including the Middlesex, St George's, Reading and Leicester were built with a 'H-shaped' interior corridor.[45]

In the 1860s, only a few hospitals were built on the favoured pavilion plan, including St Bartholomew's and the London Fever Hospital. Some smaller hospitals were designed with one 'pavilion', including the Charing Cross Hospital and the Ipswich Hospital.[46] The new Gothic-style Leeds Infirmary, built in 1864–68 to replace an earlier hospital, was 'one of the largest early pavilion-plan hospitals' with accommodation for 296 patients.[47]

Florence Nightingale was an outspoken advocate of pavilion wards, which had windows on both sides for cross-ventilation, and allowed for easier 'surveillance of patients by the nursing staff'.[48] This lack of patient privacy in favour of nursing sightlines is 'an appropriate reminder that patients mostly came from lower classes'.[49] In her book *Notes on Hospitals*, Miss Nightingale argued that the essentials for the 'health of hospitals' were 'fresh air, light, ample space and subdivision into separate buildings'.[50] This sub-division was required to prevent dirty air from transmitting from one ward to another. It was believed that large quantities of air were beneficial to health so 'patients were constantly exposed to continuing draughts of ... chilly and dirty air'.[51]

When it was re-built in 1868–71 opposite the Houses of Parliament, St Thomas's Hospital in London, which was home to the Nightingale School for training nurses, was 'by far the largest pavilion-plan general hospital, providing beds for 600 patients'.[52] There were six adjacent ward pavilions and 'a ventilated lobby separated [each] ward from the sanitary facilities to prevent smells, which were believed to harbour disease, from entering the ward'.[53]

Chapter 3

Specialist Hospitals

In addition to the general hospitals, patients could also seek treatment in the growing number of specialist hospitals. As many of these institutions made a charge for their services, they had a different clientele from voluntary hospitals. The fees charged were less than those of elite medical practitioners and they were 'free of the stigma of charity' which blighted the voluntary general hospitals.[1] For this reason, they became particularly popular with the middle classes.

The specialist institutions 'partly created their own demand'.[2] They included fever and maternity hospitals as well as those for the ear, nose and throat, the chest, skin diseases and mental illnesses. Most specialist hospitals met needs 'which the patient could recognise for himself'.[3] This was because the names of the hospitals described the diseases they treated, for example, St Mark's in London was originally called the 'Benevolent Dispensary for the Relief of the Poor Afflicted with Fistula, Piles and other Diseases of the Rectum and Lower Intestines'.[4] Like St Mark's, many of the new specialist hospitals began as out-patient dispensaries before developing in-patient facilities.[5]

By 1860, London had at least sixty-six specialist hospitals and dispensaries including the Royal Hospital for Diseases of the Chest (1814), the Brompton Hospital (for tuberculosis, 1841), the Royal Marsden

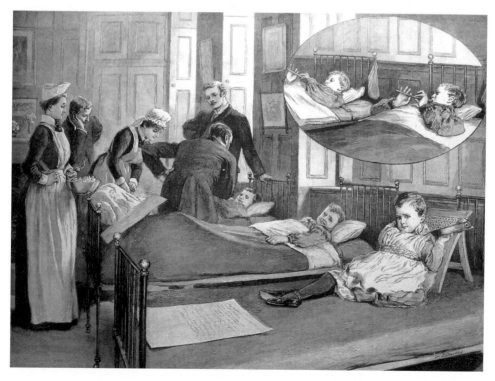

'The Alexandra Hospital for Children with Hip Disease: The Schachnar Ward – The Morning Round.' (*The Graphic*, 11 October 1890)

'The Hospital for Consumption and Diseases of the Chest at Brompton.' (*The Illustrated London News*, 24 June 1865)

Hospital (for cancer, 1851), the Hospital for Sick Children, Great Ormond Street (1852), and the National Hospital (for nervous diseases, 1860).[6]

In Glasgow and Edinburgh in the same period, the following specialist hospitals were founded: Glasgow Eye Infirmary (1824), Edinburgh Eye, Ear, Nose and Throat Hospital (1834) and the Edinburgh Hospital for Sick Children (1860). Glasgow's Royal Hospital for Sick Children did not open until 1883.

It has been argued that 'the professional disease of blocked promotion'[7] helped to create a large number of Victorian specialist hospitals. Ambitious doctors could more easily 'cultivate a reputation for special skill in treating one particular condition'.[8]

For example, Birmingham's Orthopaedic Hospital was established in 1817 by George Freer, a 'local surgeon with a national reputation'.[9] Dispensing from a building in New Street, the hospital was originally called 'The Institution for the Relief of Hernia, Club Feet, Spinal Diseases, and all Bodily Deformities'. It expanded, moving first to Great Charles Street and then, in 1855, to Newhall Street. The first cases 'were not adult workers disabled by their industrial employments, but local children born with malformed limbs'.[10] The hospital's aim was to 'transform disabled children into productive citizens'. It undertook very few operations until the last quarter of the nineteenth century because it was concentrating on children with softer bones, and there was no need to resort to surgery to treat them.[11]

Hospitals for incurables

In 1850, *Household Words*, edited by Charles Dickens, lamented the fact that there was no large hospital for incurables, 'for the help of those who of all others most require succour, and who must die, and do die in thousands, neglected, unaided'.[12] At the time, there were a few small charities for incurables across the country such as an asylum in Leith for a few females afflicted with incurable diseases, and there were a few places in general hospitals which took incurables such as the cancer ward of the Middlesex and 'the ward for seven incurable patients in the Westminster'.[13]

Dickens quoted the case of a poor servant girl afflicted with 'a disease to which the domestics of the middle classes, especially, are very liable – white swelling of the knee'. When she presented herself at a hospital, she was told that an operation would be 'certain death' and therefore she was incurable, and could not be admitted. With no relations to call on for help, the girl '[crawled] back to a miserable lodging, she lay helpless till her small savings were exhausted. Privations of the severest kind followed; and despite the assistance of some benevolent persons who learnt her condition when it was too late, she died a painful and wretched death'.[14] Charles Dickens called this situation 'a marvellous oversight of benevolence'.[15]

When Guy's Hospital was reserved for the acute sick, there was just one hospital in London for chronic cases: the relatively small Royal Hospital for Incurables at Putney. Founded in 1854, it was funded by public subscription with accommodation 'far from adequate to meet the needs of this type of patient'.[16] Provision for incurables still remained inadequate and by 1890 it catered for just thirty-eight men and 180 women.[17]

Eye hospitals

At the beginning of the nineteenth century, the first eye hospitals were founded 'partly because of the heavy incidence of trachoma in soldiers returning from the Napoleonic Wars'[18] and partly because of the high concentration of eye ailments in most industrial regions.

The London Eye Dispensary, which became Moorfields, was opened in 1805. Between 1808 and 1832, nineteen more eye infirmaries were established in the provinces 'by an English public that valued its sight above all other senses'.[19] By 1866, there were six eye hospitals in London, although there were seven ophthalmic departments in the general hospitals.[20] Birmingham's Eye Hospital opened in 1823, catering for patients from the industrial working classes, particularly those who had been injured in the workshops of the various metal and glass trades.[21]

Women's hospitals

In the 1840s, with the emergence of gynaecology as a precise science, specialist women's hospitals started to appear in London and quickly spread to the provinces. The Jessop Hospital for Women in Sheffield, opened in 1864, was just one example. It was established specifically to 'attend cases of midwifery and diseases particular to women'.[22]

Birmingham's Women's Hospital started off as a dispensary in 1871 but quickly provided four free and four paying beds for in-patients. It catered for women 'suffering from diseases of the pelvic organs regardless of their social backgrounds'. Operations were carried out in three temporary wards or sheds in the garden next door to the hospital, which it was hoped would reduce the risk of infection.[23]

Although the first ovariotomies took place in the 1850s, it was not until the late 1860s and early 1870s that they became accepted as a standard surgical procedure. Between 1871 and 1877, the death rate for ovariotomies at Birmingham's Women's Hospital varied greatly between 30 per cent and 100 per cent.[24] After moving to a larger hospital with twenty-one beds but still performing operations in wards in the garden, the surgeons, Lawson Tait and Thomas Savage, had reduced the death rate for ovariotomies from 20 per cent to 9 per cent by 1881. The hospital's average death rate was also 9 per cent 'despite the performance of more than 120 abdominal sections annually'. This death rate continued to decline, reaching 1.4 per cent in 1892.[25]

Birmingham's Women's Hospital was pioneering in helping to expand the roles of women in medicine locally. It was the first in the city to appoint a female practitioner with Louisa Atkins becoming house surgeon in 1872, succeeded by Mary Pechey in 1875. It was also the first in the city to appoint a female dispenser in 1872 'largely because this proved to be cheaper than appointing a man to the job'.[26] Women were also present on the managerial board of the hospital, with a rule which stated that 'half of the managing board's 18 members be women'.[27]

Criticism of specialist hospitals

Although payments were encouraged in cottage hospitals which were controlled by general practitioners, similar payments were criticised in hospitals controlled by specialists. In the eyes of the general practitioners, such payments amounted to undercutting because there was no reason for a patient to pay for a non-specialist opinion from a general practitioner when he could pay the same price for a specialist opinion.[28]

Some specialist hospitals charged their out-patients 1s or 2s 6d for 'advice', a service which attracted 'some better-off patients who would not have attended at a general hospital'.[29] These included teachers, clerks and tradesmen who could not afford to pay a guinea for a private consultation with a physician or surgeon.

Children's and women's hospitals usually took payments from patients. For instance, the women's hospital in London's Soho Square charged sums 'varying from half-a-guinea per week to three guineas per week'.[30] It introduced a uniform charge of two guineas after 1877. Pay beds were also available at the London Fever Hospital.

Specialist hospitals were criticised by many doctors 'as a matter of principle'[31] while others resented the reduction in 'teaching material' and private practice. The governors of general hospitals were opposed to specialist hospitals because they lost out on charitable funds which would otherwise have been donated to them.

The *British Medical Journal* joined the debate in 1853 arguing that 'Half the special hospitals [were] founded in the grossest self-seeking on the part of some individual … An energetic surgeon makes up his mind to step to fame and fortune by means of bricks and mortar.'[32]

By 1860, when it was proposed to set up a Hospital for Stone and Diseases of the Urinary Organs (St Peter's Hospital), a protest movement was organised including 'all the leading figures and representative bodies of medicine'.[33] In 1863, *The Lancet* launched an attack on 'this rampant evil of over-weening specialism'.[34] It commented: 'Next may come a Quinine Hospital, an Hospital for Treatment by Cod Liver Oil, by the Hypophosphates, or by the Excrement of Boa-Constrictors.'[35]

Many of the general hospitals amended their rules so that no member of medical staff could work in a specialist hospital. Walter John Coulson was a surgeon at St Mary's Hospital and was also on the staff at the new St Peter's Hospital. When given an ultimatum by the general hospital, he chose to leave St Mary's.[36] By 1889, only thirty-one out of an estimated 195 medical staff in London general hospitals 'did not hold some office in a special hospital as well'.[37]

The smaller specialist hospitals such as St Mark's and the Skin Hospital at Blackfriars appealed for subscriptions 'without offering any rights to subscribers in return for their money'.[38] Using this method of funding, the doctors retained the right to select the patients. Other specialist hospitals employed secretaries to raise funds while older specialist hospitals such as the Brompton Hospital for Diseases of the Chest still used the traditional methods of 'selling life governorships with the right to give subscribers' tickets for sums of thirty guineas or less'.[39]

Specialist departments in general hospitals

In response to the increasing number of specialist hospitals, many general hospitals, particularly in London, opened their own special departments. Guy's had an ophthalmology department with in-patient and out-patient facilities by 1831, and departments for obstetrics and gynaecology by 1842. A skin disease clinic was started in 1851 and another for aural diseases in 1862.[40]

By 1869, St Bartholomew's had a full ophthalmology department and by 1880, there were 'special clinics for diseases of the throat and skin, and for orthopaedics, obstetrics and gynaecology'.[41] The ophthalmic ward at St Thomas' was opened in 1851. The London had departments for obstetrics in 1853, for ear, nose and throat in 1866 and for orthopaedic cases in 1875.

Chapter 4

Dispensaries

If a patient had been refused treatment at a voluntary hospital, he or she could always turn to the local dispensary. The first free dispensaries started in London and Scotland in the late eighteenth century. Between 1770 and 1850, they provided 'a more important institutional form of healthcare for the urban poor' than the voluntary hospital.[1]

Dispensaries might be founded by generous benefactors or instigated by concerned businessmen or those from the medical profession, such as the dispensary in Haverfordwest which was established by three physicians 'for administering advice and medicines to the sick poor'.[2]

Provident dispensaries

The free charitable dispensaries were replaced from the middle of the nineteenth century by new provident dispensaries which operated on a subscription basis. Patients could take advantage of their services if they had made a regular weekly contribution to the scheme, usually a penny a week.[3] They also provided cover for dependants. Provident dispensaries did not ordinarily provide for charity cases but those in receipt of poor relief could usually receive treatment by an arrangement with the guardians or relieving officers.[4]

The dispensary at Fir Vale Infirmary, Sheffield. (With permission of the Waddy family)

Scottish dispensaries

There were no provident dispensaries on the English model in Scotland, with Perth being one of the few cities to attempt to set up such a service. The Perth Dispensary had been founded in 1819 to 'vaccinate, give medicine and obstetric care when necessary to the poor'[5] with just over 300 patients treated annually up to 1832. However, the directors of the dispensary were concerned that 'not all the patients were really deserving of this charity'.[6] In 1834, in an attempt to solve this problem, it was decided to open the Perth Self-Supporting Dispensary, aimed specifically at those who were earning a regular wage. In return for a subscription of a penny a week, workers could get medical treatment. This new dispensary was run alongside the free dispensary and in the next three years, perhaps unsurprisingly, the number of workers contributing to it 'numbered 31, 9 and lastly only 4, while the original free dispensary increased its work'.[7] Both dispensaries were closed when the Perth Royal Infirmary opened in 1838.[8]

Glasgow and Edinburgh both had a number of dispensaries serving the poor. Edinburgh's second dispensary, the New Town Dispensary which opened in 1815, 'pioneered home visitation of the poor'.[9] A third free dispensary in Edinburgh was run by the Edinburgh Medical Mission Society, which had realised that 'free medical treatment was highly successful in promoting evangelism'.[10] Patients at the Mission 'gathered at a certain hour, a service was held' and the patients were then treated.[11] Medical students gained valuable training experience while working at the Mission.

There were a number of short-lived dispensaries in Glasgow including the Western Public Dispensary which, at its peak, employed four medical officers 'seeing 1,000 patients per year'.[12] The city also had missionary dispensaries such as the Glasgow Medical Mission, 'which dispensed advice, medicines and scripture'.[13]

In Aberdeen, the General Dispensary and the Royal Infirmary operated according to an arrangement, under which the Dispensary treated out-patients living within a specified boundary, and the Infirmary treated those out-patients who lived further away outside the boundary. Staff from the Dispensary, as was common in Scotland, visited patients at home when necessary.[14]

Treatments provided by dispensaries

Dispensaries were generally an urban phenomenon but they provided a valuable service to the working classes. In Stockton-on-Tees in 1861, the dispensary treated over 13 per cent of the population. Dispensaries were staffed by general practitioners, sometimes salaried and sometimes on a voluntary basis, which allowed them to offer 'professional diagnosis and prescription services, as well as dispensing medicines'.[15]

In larger dispensaries where doctors received salaries, there was less 'bottle doctoring' 'which relied upon product sales rather than medical knowledge'.[16] In some dispensaries, the effect of the cheap medicines on offer was dubious to say the least.

Dispensaries were sometimes used by local authorities to address particular problems. The cities of Manchester and Leicester suffered with high infant mortality rates of around 200 per 1,000 births. In the 1870s, the local authorities for both cities provided 'diarrhoea medicines free to the artisan and poorer classes'[17] through the dispensaries in the hope that it would cut the number of infant deaths. This was a large-scale operation and, for example, in Leicester between 10 July and 30 September 1878, 'more than 3,000 people, half of them children, were treated for diarrhoea'.[18] Diarrhoea was always more prevalent and more dangerous during the summer months.

Decline of dispensaries

It was only when the work of the out-patients departments in voluntary hospitals was expanded that the dispensaries became less important. However, at most Scottish hospitals there was a dispensary attached, analogous with an out-patients department, many of which operated a 'district department' which involved visiting the poor in their homes.[19]

Many dispensaries, originally for out-patients only, developed into full-scale hospitals. The Scarborough Dispensary was established in 1852 as a charity for poor patients, who were treated as out-patients or, if they were too sick to attend, on a home-visit basis.[20] By the 1860s, it became apparent that serious accident cases could not be treated properly because of the lack of in-patient facilities. Two rooms were fitted out as dedicated accident wards and were opened in 1866.[21]

Chapter 5

Children's Hospitals

In the early to mid-nineteenth century, there was a growing demand for specialist children's hospitals as children were frequently turned away from general hospitals because of 'the likelihood of their transmitting fevers into these institutions'.[1] The Salop Infirmary's rule of 1859 regarding children was common to most general hospitals. 'No child under seven years of age (except in extraordinary cases, such as fractures, stone, or where couching, trepanning or amputation is necessary)' could be admitted.[2]

At first, it was believed that children's hospitals would be 'both cruel and impracticable'[3], in part because of the enforced separation of a child from its mother and family. However, evidence of high mortality rates in children demonstrated a distinct need for medical institutions to treat them.

In the Victorian period, there were a large number of infectious diseases which could be fatal for children. Whooping cough accounted for two-fifths of deaths among children under five[4] while scarlet fever was particularly virulent among children aged four to eight[5]. Measles, affecting both adults and children, 'never killed less than 7,000 people a year'[6] in the whole of the nineteenth century. As in adults, tuberculosis was a major killer of children.

Diphtheria joined this list of killer diseases from the mid-nineteenth century onwards. By the 1870s, half of deaths from diphtheria occurred in children under five and 'of the rest, four-fifths were between five and thirteen'.[7] Even if these serious diseases were not fatal, they could leave a child with 'permanent and debilitating physical damage'.[8] The painful, crippling, bone diseases so prevalent in nineteenth-century children were usually due to a form of tuberculosis. In children, stomach disorders such as diarrhoea, dysentery and enteritis were also major killers, indicative of polluted water supplies and a general lack of hygiene.[9]

Children in general hospitals

In January 1843, an inquiry into English and Welsh hospitals revealed that there were only twenty-six patients under the age of ten 'suffering from Diseases peculiar to their age'.[10] The inquiry also revealed that there were 'only 136 children under the age of ten years in the London general hospitals'.[11] Presumably, the majority of these 136 children were not suffering from diseases which were particular to children. In any case, in spite of these low figures, large numbers of children were being treated for ailments in poor law infirmaries, which were completely separate from the general hospitals.

The usual practice when children were admitted to general hospitals was to put the girls and young boys in female adult wards and the older boys in male adult wards. Under this arrangement, in Florence Nightingale's view, the patients 'often became the child's best protector and nurse'.[12]

Where children were admitted to general hospitals, it was usually for surgery cases including 'treatment for accidents, for abscesses, frequently of tuberculous origin but labeled as scrofular at that time, for removal of bladder stones, or with disabilities, such as hare-lip, that could be relieved by surgery'.[13] At this time, The London refused admission to all children under the age of seven except those requiring 'amputation' or 'cutting for stone'.[14]

The first children's hospital in Britain

In Liverpool, a specialist children's dispensary was founded in 1851 but it did not offer in-patient facilities until 1858. The Hospital for Sick Children in Great Ormond Street, London was the first children's hospital in Britain to provide accommodation for in-patients. It opened in 1852 for children between the ages of two and twelve suffering from diseases:

> ...peculiar to, or modified in some important respect by their early age...Infants and children under two years of age are not generally eligible for admission as inpatients, it being undesirable on account of their

tender age to separate them from their mothers. Such young children, however, are eligible as outpatients and, under special circumstances…may be received into the hospital with or without their mother.[15]

Researchers at Kingston University have compiled this history of the founding and early years of The Hospital for Sick Children in Great Ormond Street:

> *Originally set up in a mansion house at no. 49 Great Ormond Street, The Hospital for Sick Children had ten beds, later increased to twenty. Its founder, Dr Charles West, had worked at the Universal Dispensary for Children and Women in Waterloo Road and recognised the need for a children's hospital with in-patient facilities, as was available in France and Germany. He had three ambitions for the new hospital: 'the provision of healthcare to the children of the poor, the encouragement of clinical research in paediatrics, and the training of paediatric nurses'.[16]*
>
> *By 1858, the hospital was able to purchase the neighbouring house at no. 48 and increase the number of beds from 20 to 75. In 1860, the hospital treated 384 in-patients and 6,833 out-patients. By 1870, these figures had increased to 691 and 12,221 respectively.[17]*
>
> *It became apparent that the original two houses providing accommodation for the hospital 'had become cramped and over-intensively used, and were a danger from poor sanitation and over-crowding'. In 1875, a new purpose-built 100 bed hospital was erected on the site of the gardens of the original houses which became known as 'The Hospital in the Garden'.[18]*

Increase in children's hospitals

After the Hospital for Sick Children in Great Ormond Street opened, children's hospitals were established in Norwich (1853) and Manchester (1855). In Manchester, the hospital developed from the Dispensary for Children, which 'by the 1840s was treating 2,000 patients annually'.[19] Patients of the dispensary were visited in their own homes if it was considered necessary. The custom of home visiting was continued when the dispensary became a hospital, and 'persisted at the end of the century when most other paediatric hospitals had given up outside assistance as unnecessary and financially burdensome'.[20]

In the 1860s, a further eleven children's hospitals were established. The Edinburgh Hospital for Children was opened in 1860 followed by five other hospitals in the provinces: Birmingham (1861), Bristol (1866), Gloucester (1867), Brighton (1868) and Nottingham (1869). In London, five more children's hospitals were opened: the Victoria Hospital for Children (1866), the North Eastern Hospital, Hackney (1867), the Hospital for Hip Diseases in Childhood (1867), the East London Hospital, Shadwell (1868) and the Evelina Hospital (1869).[21]

At least half the children treated as hospital in-patients in the early 1860s 'were in the eight London and provincial children's hospitals'.[22] By 1888, there were thirty-eight hospitals in Britain exclusively for children.[23]

Like other specialist hospitals, some, but not all, of Britain's children's hospitals were established 'mainly due to the initiative of individual physicians seeking professional advancement rather than the expression of a perceived community need'.[24]

Birmingham is an excellent example. The city's first children's hospital was established in the old eye infirmary in 1861 as a sixteen-bed facility. Its founder, Thomas Pretious Heslop, had worked in Birmingham's main institutions including the General Hospital and Queen's Hospital, and was 'frustrated with his career in the months leading up to the charity's foundation'.[25] Perhaps as a result of this, the hospital's rules stated that 'all medical appointments came with restricted tenures in order that sought-after openings would regularly appear, and thereby allow more than a select group the benefit of the hospital's clinical material'.[26]

There was an immediate demand for the Birmingham Children's Hospital's services with almost 8,000 children being treated in 1863.[27] This was remarkable given that the hospital only had twenty-two beds in 1865. In 1868 a new out-patient building was opened to keep in- and out-patients separate 'to prevent the spread of infectious diseases'.[28] By 1870, the number of beds had risen to forty, accommodated in a building which had previously been a lying-in hospital. A year later, the hospital had fifty-five beds.

Birmingham's Children's Hospital was one of the first in the city to pioneer convalescent homes after 'a permanent battle with hospital fevers'. Other hospitals in the city followed suit, with the General opening the Jaffray Hospital in 1885 specifically for this purpose.[29]

When Aberdeen's Royal Hospital for Sick Children was first planned, it was originally hoped to provide 'in addition to wards for treatment of the sick, a day ward or nursery, where children suffering

Left: Sidney Jones, a patient at the Hospital for Sick Children in London. (Museum & Archive Service, Great Ormond Street Hospital for Children NHS Trust)

Below: 'The East London Hospital for Children.' (*The Illustrated London News*, 27 April 1872)

from want of fresh air, suitable food and proper attention could be received…'[30] However, this plan could not be carried out, probably because of a lack of financial support. The hospital opened in 1877 as a 'modest institution' with fourteen cots and there was an immediate demand for the service it provided. In the first year, 100 children were admitted to the hospital as in-patients and 1,059 were treated as out-patients.[31]

Admission procedures to children's hospitals

Most children's hospitals operated their admission procedures along the same lines as voluntary general hospitals. They were funded by subscriptions and potential patients needed a letter of recommendation from a subscriber. As in the general hospitals, this rule was relaxed if a child was brought in as an accident or emergency.

At The Hospital for Sick Children in Great Ormond Street, patients with subscribers' letters were to be given priority but 'acutely sick children without recommendation could also be admitted from out-patients at the discretion of the medical attendant'.[32]

At first, most children's hospitals admitted medical cases in far greater numbers than surgical cases, knowing that the latter could be dealt with by a general hospital. For example, the Hospital for Sick Children in Edinburgh did not have a surgical ward until 1887 because surgical cases were routinely admitted to the Edinburgh Royal Infirmary.[33]

After the 1870s, when major surgery became safer, the surgeons of children's hospitals started to attempt more complicated operations such as cleft palates, and elective operations 'such as osteotomy to straighten legs deformed by the ever ubiquitous disease of rickets'.[34]

Researchers at Kingston University have compiled this typical surgical case from the medical records of a Great Ormond Street patient:

> *Sydney (or Sidney) Jones was the son of a boot and shoe manufacturer in Upper Holloway, London. He was admitted to The Hospital for Sick Children on 13 June 1873 when he was just eight years old, 'under the recommendation of Miss Wood (probably the woman who became matron several years later)'. Sydney had disease of the right knee and, in common with many children with the same affliction, he was probably suffering from 'a tubercular infection of his knee joint'. As the disease was well advanced, it was decided to amputate his leg at thigh level. Although this was a serious operation, it was a success and Sydney was pronounced fully recovered and discharged to the hospital's own convalescent home at Highgate on 4 September. He was finally discharged 'well' after three weeks on 2 October. Despite his ordeal as a child, Sydney went on to marry and have children, and worked as a clerk to a builder, and later as a skilled craftsman working in cabinet and pianoforte making.[35]*

Chapter 6

Poor Law Infirmaries

For the abject poor, those with infectious diseases and those afflicted with chronic illnesses, admittance to a voluntary hospital was not usually permitted. Poor law infirmaries were the only option. Before the reforms of the 1860s, these hospitals, which were part of the workhouse (or poorhouse in Scotland), were unhygienic and insanitary, and staffing levels were woefully inadequate to properly care for the patients.

In England and Wales, under the principles of the workhouse test, it was always intended that conditions in poor law infirmaries should be 'worse than those in the voluntary hospitals'.[1] In 1840, only £150,000 out of a total Poor Law expenditure of £4.5 million was spent on medical services[2], largely because the guardians of poor law unions were under constant pressure to keep the rates low. With little investment in improving sanitation, furnishings or staffing levels, overworked medical officers and nurses struggled on to provide the best care they could.

Living conditions

General hygiene in poor law infirmaries 'left much to be desired'.[3] The floors of the Huddersfield poor law infirmary were described by the medical officer as 'filthy. I don't think they had been washed down throughout the hospital, from the time of its being opened …'.[4] It was said there was a 'superficial veneer of hygiene' in most workhouses, particularly 'a special air of *bescrubbedness*, rather a powerful odour of soap and water, about the wards of the workhouse infirmaries'.[5]

At all workhouses, there was a general lack of toilet facilities. Few workhouses provided lavatory paper because 'a very large proportion of the poor' were not in the habit of using it.[6] There were 'number-less instances' of closets being blocked with 'old towels, dusters and dishcloths – and leaves of Holy Scripture'.[7]

The Halifax Poor Law Infirmary (postmarked 1905)

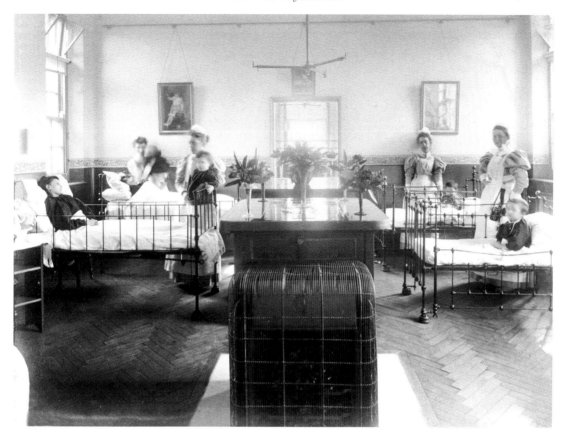

The children's ward at Fir Vale Infirmary, Sheffield. (With permission of the Waddy family)

Bathing facilities were also lacking and only one London workhouse was found to have sufficient baths attached to the sick wards.[8] The number of towels available was 'most inadequate' with a ration of one towel for every twenty-four to thirty-one inmates at Paddington Workhouse.[9] Soap was also rationed because 'it might readily be wasted'.[10]

Sufferers of venereal and skin diseases were housed in the dreaded 'foul' wards, which were frequently in a worse condition than the wards of the main infirmary. Charles Dickens described the foul wards of Wapping Workhouse: 'They were in a building monstrously behind the time – a mere series of garrets and lofts … and only accessible by steep and narrow staircases, infamously ill adapted for the passage upstairs of the sick or downstairs of the dead.'[11]

Furnishings

The beds in poor law infirmaries were 'generally not fit for their purpose'.[12] At a Bristol workhouse, a visitor observed that 'The same rough beds (generally made with one thin mattress laid on iron bars) which are allotted to the rude able-bodied paupers, are equally given to the poor, emaciated bed-ridden patient…'.[13]

Country workhouses were more likely to provide feather beds but 'the rugs varied very much, but generally they were of cotton, and, with the blankets, were often very old and thin'.[14] In London, there were significant differences in the quality of sheets between various workhouses. At St James', the sheets were 'faded, worn or ragged' articles and at Marylebone 'three sheets are appropriated to each bed and one is changed weekly'.[15]

In 1867, it was reported that the Dudley Union poor law infirmary lacked '…that air of comfort and convenience which should be found in sick wards'.[16] There was also 'a want of chairs and other furniture'[17] and the ground floor was made of brick, which it was believed would be too cold for patients.

Staffing

Before the 1860s, poor law infirmaries or sick wards were run by the resident medical officer, but were still under the superintendence of the workhouse master and matron. Visitors to union workhouses across England and Wales all commented on the lack of paid nurses to tend to the sick. Where there was a paid nurse, unpaid paupers were used to supplement the nursing staff. At this point, nurses were not trained in either voluntary hospitals or poor law infirmaries.

Reforms of the 1860s

The appalling conditions in London poor law infirmaries were highlighted by a report published by *The Lancet* between 1865 and 1866. This led to the founding of the Association for Improving London Workhouse Infirmaries in 1866 and an official government inquiry of the same year, carried out by two inspectors, Mr Farnall and Dr Smith, appointed by the Poor Law Board.[18]

Mr Farnall concluded that only one of London's workhouses was 'sufficient for the purpose to which it was dedicated', based on the assumption that each patient should be provided with 'not less than 1,000 cubic feet of air'. At the time, the Poor Law Board required that inmates should have 500 cubic feet per resident 'but even this low standard was not enforced in many sick wards'.[19]

The inquiries led directly to the passing of the Metropolitan Poor Law Amendment Act of 1867, which allowed London poor law unions to set up infirmaries separate from the workhouse. By 1882, London had six fever hospitals, four asylums and twenty infirmaries.[20] This new legislation did not apply to workhouses outside London but it did start to affect 'the way in which infirmaries were built around the country'.[21]

These new infirmaries were managed separately from the workhouse 'with a resident medical superintendent in charge of medical staff'.[22] The pauper patients would undoubtedly have benefited from this new system. Under the previous arrangement, the medical officers managed the infirmaries in conjunction with the masters and matrons, who had no medical background and were charged with keeping expenditure low.

Like the new voluntary hospitals, from the 1860s onwards the majority of new workhouse infirmaries were built to a pavilion design with separate ward blocks, pairs of windows opposite each other to provide cross-ventilation and two fireplaces to aid the circulation of air.[23]

After the 1860s

After the reforms of the 1860s, poor law infirmaries were no longer exclusively for paupers. People needing hospital treatment living in the parishes which the unions served began to be admitted straight into the poor law infirmaries. In fact, 'roughly one-third of Poor Law infirmary entrants were non-paupers'.[24]

In London, the best poor law hospitals 'were reckoned to rival voluntary institutions'.[25] In 1888, a Select Committee of the House of Lords was told that:

> … in consequence of the excellence of the treatment in these infirmaries and their separation from the workhouses, the poor are so ready to resort to them that there is a tendency to regard them as a kind of 'state hospital', entrance into which does not imply that the patient is a pauper.[26]

The MP Arthur Pell, who was a governor of Guy's Hospital and a poor law guardian for forty-six years, told the same committee that he considered 'the infirmary of St-George's-in-the-East to be as perfect in its way as any hospital in London'.[27]

In England and Wales, outdoor medical relief was phased out in 1871. This valuable form of medical aid had supported 300,000 people in 1860 alone.[28] After 1871, there was increasing pressure on the voluntary hospitals, dispensaries and sick clubs as the poor sought other ways to get medical treatment.

A national census of sick paupers in 1896 revealed that 58,550 patients were being treated in 'separate infirmaries' and other 'wards for the sick'. The term 'separate infirmary' was used for 'institutions ranging in size from a Birmingham infirmary with 1,300 beds to a building in Church Stretton containing 4 infirm patients'.[29] Of these patients, 22,100 were in 'separate infirmaries' with 36,450 sick in the general mixed workhouses.[30]

The inadequacy of many English and Welsh poor law infirmaries was mirrored by those in Scotland. Although legislation had been passed in 1845 which allowed parishes to appoint medical officers to serve the poorhouses, by the 1890s almost 10 per cent of parishes 'still relied upon payments to GPs for specific visits or services for paupers…'.[31] However, the Scottish poor law did introduce the first national nurse training system in 1885,[32] so theoretically patients in poorhouse wards should have experienced a better standard of nursing care than in England and Wales.

There were fewer poorhouses in Scotland than the number of workhouses for the population in England and Wales. For this reason, it was more common for the poor to receive medical relief in their homes than to be admitted to the poorhouse. By 1868, there were sixty poorhouses in Scotland and 'one person in every twenty-four of the Scottish population was receiving poor relief: only one in fourteen of these was in a poorhouse'.[33]

Into the twentieth century

In the larger towns and cities where poor law infirmaries were managed separately from the workhouse, conditions were undoubtedly an improvement on those experienced by paupers in the mid-nineteenth century. These new purpose-built poor law infirmaries were 'modern … with salaried medical staffs, trained nurses and all the latest apparatus of a hospital'.[34] By the 1890s, the West Bromwich Union infirmary could accommodate 250 patients[35] and had a trained head nurse with five under-nurses and two night-nurses to assist her. The fact that the infirmary was a distinct department made it 'popular with the poorer stratum of society, for in case of illness the poor will willingly go to the Infirmary, whereas they would indignantly refuse to go to the Workhouse itself…'[36]

Despite the reforms of poor law infirmaries, conditions 'continued to be determined at a local level', particularly in the smaller workhouses. Three hundred rural infirmaries still 'lacked surgical equipment and basic medical supplies'.[37] As late as the mid-1890s in rural Wales, it was noted that the small workhouses had very few inmates who, in any case, were 'accustomed to an exceedingly simple and primitive style of life'.[38] It is hardly surprising that the guardians of these small poor law unions were reluctant to provide trained nurses or expensive, modern medical equipment.

The lack of nurses, trained or otherwise, remained a thorny issue, and one which would have had a profound effect on the patients in poor law infirmaries. In the 1890s in East Anglia workhouses, it was reported that 'Not infrequently a single paid nurse was in charge of thirty or forty patients, and this meant that almost everything for the sick had to be done by pauper inmates. They had nothing to gain if they did the duty assigned to them well, nothing to lose if they did it badly … most of them were not disposed to take much trouble in attending to helpless old folk requiring assistance…'.[39] By 1901, only one fifth of rural infirmaries had appointed a superintendent nurse.[40]

It was not only in rural areas where improvements were still to be made. In 1895–96, Ernest Hart who had been a member of the original Lancet Commission, supervised a survey of provincial workhouses and 'was shocked to find that in many cases conditions were as bad as those he had witnessed in 1866'.[41] In one workhouse he found that the sick were 'lying on plank beds with chaff mattresses about three inches thick between their weary bodies and the hard uneven planks. One paralysed woman had a spring bed with a chaff mattress over the springs… Some idiots and imbeciles share the wards with these patients'.[42]

The care and provision in Scottish poorhouses was also 'inadequate'[43] at the turn of the century. Until the 1890s, poorhouse provision did not extend to the unemployed.[44] However, by the end of the nineteenth century, it became more common for the sick poor to be admitted to the poorhouse on medical grounds, rather than receiving treatment in their own homes.[45]

Chapter 7

Hospitals for Infectious Diseases

Fever hospitals were inspired by the pioneering work of John Haygarth, a physician to the Chester Infirmary.[1] In the 1770s, he surveyed the whole of the city, noting that the densely populated suburbs where the poor lived were most affected by epidemics, and that contagious fevers spread easily from person to person in insanitary conditions.

During a fever epidemic in 1783, Haygarth was permitted by the governors of the hospital to turn an attic room into a fever ward. Here, victims were taken 'immediately when they fell ill, and nursed in circumstances in which a free flow of fresh air prevented spread to other patients or staff at the Infirmary'.[2] The experiment was a success and this encouraged fever hospitals in other towns and cities to be set up in the 1790s and 1800s. Also known as 'Houses of Recovery', fever hospitals were established in industrial places such as Manchester, Liverpool, Stockport, Newcastle and Leeds, as well as London.

These hospitals adopted similar nursing and medical procedures for treating fever victims, including 'fresh air, clean bedclothes, cold water baths, special diet, and purgatives'.[3] Preventive measures included removing the patient as soon as possible plus the provision of clean clothes, soap and whitewash for the walls for his family.

Treatment in the 'Houses of Recovery' was free and no letters of recommendation were required. Patients with any contagious fever, except smallpox, could be admitted and most patients were diagnosed with 'typhus', 'low', 'continued' or 'spotted' fever or erysipelas.[4]

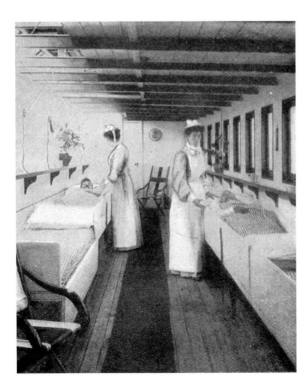

'The Fight with Smallpox: Hospital Ships in the Thames – The Starboard Ward of the Saloon Hospital on Board the "Geneva Cross".' (*The Illustrated London News*, 1 March 1902)

Infectious cases in general hospitals

In the first half of the nineteenth century, many general hospitals continued to admit infectious cases. This included the Westminster, St Bartholomew's, St Thomas', The London, the Nottingham General Hospital, Manchester Royal Infirmary, Sheffield General Infirmary and Newcastle Infirmary. Some hospitals treated these cases in separate wards, while in others they were treated in the same wards as the other patients.

In Scotland, fever cases were usually admitted to separate wards of the general hospitals, but there was still a risk of spreading infection when supposed 'convalescents' mixed with the other patients. Sixty-seven-year-old John Mackie, a mason from Aberdeen, had undergone a successful lithotrity operation at the city's Royal Infirmary in August 1840. However, he 'caught typhus fever from the convalescents in the airing ground, and died of the fever…'.[5]

In May 1850, five boys with the surname of Smith were admitted to the Aberdeen Royal Infirmary from Pork Lane in the city as fever cases. They were either all brothers, or closely related. Seven-year-old George and four-year-old Christopher were first to be admitted on 18 May, followed two days later by James and Robert who were fourteen and twelve respectively. Lastly, Simon aged eleven was admitted on 22 May. All five boys left the hospital in mid-June, all cured.[6]

By 1860, the practice of treating infectious cases in general hospitals started to decline, largely because 'the wisdom of accommodating [them] … was increasingly being questioned…'.[7]

Specialist hospitals for infectious diseases

The fashion for specialist hospitals did not extend to the treatment of infectious diseases, even though such diseases were 'the great killers of the poor and the main menace for the rich'.[8] In London, there remained just one hospital for fever cases and another for smallpox cases.[9]

Only a handful of specialist hospitals were founded to cater for patients with infectious diseases, rather than fever. The Brompton Hospital for Consumption and Diseases of the Chest in London was founded in 1841 by a layman, Philip Rose, who 'found it impossible to gain admission to any general hospital for one of his employees who had tuberculosis'.[10] These early hospitals for consumption advocated 'a dry, warm atmosphere with closed windows, rest and sedation and a limited diet with little or no meat'.[11] By the end of the nineteenth century, verandas, balconies and sun-baths were 'standard features of TB sanatoria'[12] and also in many general hospitals as the open-air treatment for tuberculosis became generally accepted.

Legislation to prevent infectious diseases

In Britain, legislation came into force in 1853 for the compulsory vaccination of infants against smallpox. By 1871, specific measures were introduced to enforce the earlier Act through inspection. Vaccination, used in tandem with notification, isolation and disinfection, 'succeeded in eradicating smallpox as an indigenous disease in Britain after 1885'.[13]

The Sanitary Act of 1866 and the Metropolitan Poor Act of 1867 allowed for the setting up of much-needed isolation hospitals where patients with infectious diseases could be treated. In London, these hospitals were intended for the poor until 1887, when the service was extended to the middle classes. Again, these isolation hospitals suffered the stigma of charity, but by 1900 London's chain of infectious diseases hospitals came to be valued 'for the care they offered to patients, and to relieve households of the complex rituals of isolation and disinfection on which the public health authorities insisted for such cases'.[14]

These Metropolitan Asylums Board hospitals were linked by a network of horse-drawn and river ambulances, with six ambulance stations adjoining the hospitals 'such that most of London was within three miles of a station'.[15]

The vehicles themselves were designed so they could be 'thoroughly cleaned to prevent infection'.[16] Each of the six ambulance stations 'contained a house for the superintendent and housekeeper (married couple), sleeping quarters for staff, kitchen, mess, stores, coach-smith's forge, stabling for fifteen horses, coach houses, omnibuses and an accident cart'.[17] During the smallpox epidemics of 1871–72 and 1880–81, the Metropolitan Asylums Board had to borrow hulks moored on the Thames to use as floating hospitals.[18] As the new fever hospitals admitted children, they 'relieved the paediatric hospitals of much of their former responsibility, particularly with cases of scarlet fever'.[19]

The Combination Hospital, Greenock (postmarked 1919).

In Scotland, the Public Health (Scotland) Act of 1867 gave local and sanitary authorities the power to provide hospitals for the isolation and treatment of infectious cases. Gradually, separate fever hospitals were built. Interestingly, Aberdeen's first such hospital, the City Hospital opened in 1874, was designed with asepsis in mind as it was originally 'built of concrete – both walls and floor – without any wooden floors or linings, so that wards could without damage have literally been hosed out if required.'[20]

Between 1840 and 1880, scarlet fever was the chief cause of death among infectious diseases and accounted for between 4 per cent and 6 per cent of all deaths.[21] By 1900, scarlet fever was surpassed first by measles, then by diphtheria, both of which outstripped smallpox.[22]

The passing of the Infectious Diseases Notification Act in 1889 led to a significant increase in provincial hospitals for infectious diseases. Under the terms of the Act, general practitioners were required by law to notify their Medical Officer of Health of all infectious cases and, if necessary, such patients could be forcibly removed to an isolation facility. The long list of notifiable diseases included smallpox, cholera, diphtheria, membranous croup, erysipelas, scarlatina or scarlet fever, typhus, typhoid, enteric fever, relapsing fever, continued fever, or puerperal fever.

In order for the isolation system to work, it had to be provided free of charge to patients. The legislation affected the whole of Britain and by 1891, around a quarter of the 1,600 sanitary authorities provided some form of hospital for infectious diseases. The standard of these services varied from 'the model hospital at Walker-on-Tyne [to] … a wooden shed with its space for 40 beds forming a portion of the hospital provision at Preston'.[23] Local authorities which had not already set up an isolation hospital could be ordered to do so under the terms of the 1893 Isolation Hospitals Act.

In London by the 1890s, over 70 per cent of all 'fever' cases were catered for as public health status patients in a local authority isolation facility.[24] By 1893, there were reported to be 'excellent isolation hospitals'[25] at Bournemouth, Portsmouth, Poole, Weymouth, Winchester, Fareham, Calne, Havant, Catherington and other places. However, many important centres were 'without any accommodation whatever for infectious diseases, and the omission of the sanitary authorities to avail themselves of the powers with which they are invested entails a most serious responsibility upon themselves, and constitutes a danger to the public health.'[26]

The Medical Officer of Health's Report for 1893 for the county of Cheshire pointed out that the provision of hospitals for infectious diseases was woefully inadequate '…to meet the requirements of an area with a population of about 550,000…'.[27] He added that '…the provision is even more inadequate than it looks on paper. Some are not kept in readiness when patients leave, some though in use during 1893 may have since been abandoned, pulled down or let as cottage accommodation…'.[28] In Cheshire in 1893, 4,863 cases of infectious disease were notified but only 690 (14.1 per cent) received any kind of treatment.[29] By 1900, most provincial cities had fever facilities, often with separate accommodation for smallpox cases, but rural areas still lagged behind.

Chapter 8

Cottage Hospitals

Despite the increasing number of voluntary hospitals, there were still large areas of the country which were situated at an impractical distance from their nearest hospital. There were also hospitals which were so overstretched that they regularly had to turn away people who needed medical treatment.

Hospitals in the community

The solution for these communities was the cottage or 'village' hospital. Cottage hospitals were run for the benefit of local communities by general practitioners who were willing to provide medical treatment for the poor for a small fee.[1] As these hospitals charged for their services, they were aimed at the working classes who could afford to pay, not the abject poor who could get treatment at a poor law infirmary.

The first cottage hospital in Britain was opened in 1859 by the gifted surgeon Albert Napper, at Cranleigh, Surrey. The village was around thirty-five miles away from the nearest voluntary hospital, St Thomas' in London, and around eight miles from the nearest poor law infirmary at Guildford.[2] Although Cranleigh's cottage hospital was 'no more than a two-up two-down'[3] and there were only between four and six beds, Albert Napper recorded that the first hundred patients treated there had complaints which included 'compound fracture of both bones in the leg, extensive cicatrix from a burn, chronic pneumonia of both lungs, multiple injuries, amputation of fingers in a boy…'.[4]

By 1865, there were eighteen cottage hospitals and, fifteen years later, there were 180.[5] Some cottage hospitals were started with donations from philanthropists, while others were funded by local subscribers.

The Cottage Hospital, Tenbury (postmarked 1907).

For instance, at Weston-super-Mare a hospital 'was started by the working classes with subscriptions of 1*d* per week'.[6]

The founding of cottage hospitals could cause controversy in a local community, especially where the local voluntary hospital perceived the new institution to be a threat to its survival. Any new medical facility would be competing for donations in that area. Concerns were raised when the Accrington & District Cottage Hospital was opened in 1898 specifically for people living in the districts of Accrington, Church, Clayton-le-Moors and Oswaldtwistle, where there was 'no provision for the prompt treatment of cases of accident'.[7] In 1894, the districts sent 151 in-patients and 684 out-patients to be treated at the Blackburn Infirmary, their nearest voluntary hospital. The year before the hospital opened, the districts had raised £610 for the Blackburn Infirmary in 'Hospital Saturday' collections and £73 on 'Hospital Sunday'. This was a significant sum but the administrators of the cottage hospital pointed out that it would derive some of its income from payments by patients, although it acknowledged the infirmary would lose some support.[8]

Admission procedures

At a cottage hospital:

> every medical man in the neighbourhood [was] entitled to send his patients to it, supposing them to be suitable cases; that in case of an operation being required he is to have the option of performing it; and should any fee be forthcoming, for such operation, as from the Union, he is entitled to it.[9]

Cranleigh's cottage hospital charged its patients between 3*s* and 10*s* 6*d*, with around a quarter of the hospital's funds raised from these charges. In many cases, the subscriber who issued the letter of introduction 'paid the difference between the patient's payment and the total cost'.[10]

At the Basingstoke Village Hospital, set up in the 1870s with eight beds, patients were expected to pay between 2*s* and 8*s* a week 'the amount … to be fixed by the patient's employer or person recommending with the concurrence of the medical officers'. In return, the hospital provided 'every requisite except personal clothing'.[11]

The professional status of a general practitioner working in a cottage hospital was increased and this 'enabled him to treat, under the most favourable circumstances, serious surgical cases, which before its institution, had to be transferred to the nearest county hospital'.[12]

Benefits of cottage hospitals

There were significant benefits for cottage hospital patients, in terms of the treatment they received. They were 'able to enjoy a continuous relationship with one doctor' and had the 'privilege of being able to pay something, however small, according to [their] means, for the treatment [they] receive'.[13]

Equipment for cottage hospitals was rudimentary: a list of recommended instruments in the 1870s included 'chloroform inhalers, fracture splints, an ear syringe and a stomach pump'.[14] Food, however, was plentiful in cottage hospitals and in 1870 'it was suggested that the cost of food for patients would probably work out at 11¼*d* per day; the cost of drugs at just over 1*d* a day'.[15] The bedrest and plentiful diet offered by the cottage hospitals 'were often sufficient to effect a recovery'.[16] By 1900, around 300 cottage hospitals had been established.

Chapter 9

Hospitals for Paying Patients

The voluntary hospitals, funded by charity, were established for the benefit of the industrious poor. It soon became apparent that there was a demand for hospital services from the class of people above them, who could afford to pay for their treatment.

In 1879, the Northampton Nursing Institution, which supplied domiciliary nurses from a central nurses' home, decided to rent two adjacent houses and to furnish one of them as a small pay hospital. Patients were charged one guinea for a back room and two guineas for a front room, and they were able to choose their own doctor. The first patients included 'clergymen, farmers, and tradesmen, their wives and families, governesses and tutors, schoolmasters and ladies in reduced circumstances'.[1] In the same year, the Hospital for Women in London's Soho Square provided a hospital wing for 'a superior grade of sufferers who are able to pay for their own support'.[2]

Under a scheme proposed by Henry Burdett, the first Home Hospital was opened on 27 June 1880 in Fitzroy Square 'for the benefit of a large class of the community who have no homes, or whose homes are ill-adapted for the successful treatment of serious illness'.[3] It was intended to be 'an inestimable boon' for the 'lodger class' – 'governesses and young men – clerks, students and such like … left to the tender mercies of their landlady … to the above may be added clergymen, lawyers, officers in the army, navy

Photo by]   [*Payne Jennings, Ashtead.*

The London, 1900. (*The Windsor Magazine*, December 1900)

and civil services, men who are engaged in private and public offices, persons of education with limited means'.[4] Home Hospitals 'took the place of general lodging-houses for patients without the means or the relatives to be properly looked after in their homes'.[5]

By 1902, the Home Hospital had treated 5,376 patients by a total of 1,476 doctors. In 875 cases, the patient was 'accompanied by a friend during the stay in hospital'.[6] When it originally opened, the hospital had a four-bedded ward but this was abandoned after a few months. It was found that 'When a visitor comes to a patient in a ward with more than one bed, those who have no friends quietly overhear all the visitor has to say'.[7] It seems that 'when patients were first given the choice, they insisted on privacy'.[8]

The general hospitals themselves started to offer wings for paying patients. The St Thomas' Home for Paying Patients opened on 1 March 1881, offering two single rooms at 12s a day. Patients could also be accommodated in cubicles at a cost of 8s per day. The large wards were 'divided up into compartments by means of curtains made of thick striped linen. Each compartment is furnished as a bedroom and containing every needful requirement: each has a separate window'.[9] However, these curtained compartments offered little real privacy.

In 1889, there were forty-two beds with each patient paying a minimum of three guineas. The total received in this year was £5,600, representing a net profit of £500 to £600.[10] In 1889, only £120 was generated from the pay beds in the general wards.

In 1884, Guy's Hospital decided to take charges from ward patients who could afford to pay. Although it was an endowed hospital, its finances had been 'seriously crippled by the continued agricultural depression'.[11] The hospital admitted patients 'in the common wards at one guinea a week and patients in cubicles at three guineas per week'.[12] It was also decided that if a patient in a three-guinea bed could not afford to pay a first-class surgeon, the operation was performed free of charge by the senior surgeon of the week.[13]

By 1890, payments from patients represented 5 per cent of the income of the London hospitals (including those run by the Metropolitan Asylums Board) while in the provinces, patients' payments made up as much as 15 per cent of a hospital's income. At this time, 'five out of eleven London teaching hospitals, twenty-nine out of fifty-two special hospitals, and thirty-seven out of eighty general hospitals admitted paying patients'.[14]

There was a significant development in separate nursing homes and pay hospitals in the 1880s. A pay hospital was opened at Bolingbroke House, Wandsworth Common in 1880 with a resident medical officer. Charges varied from '10s to £3 a week according to the social position of the applicant and the accommodation required'.[15] A year later, a general provident Home Hospital was opened by the provident dispensary at Hampstead.

Chapter 10

Convalescent Homes

The maximum period of time a patient could stay in a voluntary hospital was six weeks, unless his or her ticket was renewed by the medical or surgical staff. However, it was clear that a great number of patients needed more time to convalesce and recover their strength before returning home.

For this reason, many of the large city hospitals purchased or leased large houses as convalescent homes, to which they could send their discharged, but still not fit, patients. At these establishments, patients could get some much-needed rest and country or sea air. Birmingham's General Hospital had a convalescent home at Tyn-y-coed, Llanrhos in Wales while The London purchased East Lodge in Brighton, 'a mansion with two acres of land', as a convalescent home.[1] The Aberdeen Royal Infirmary sent patients to the Convalescent Hospital at Loch-Head, which was 'a very useful adjunct to the Infirmary, affording as it does to Patients, who on leaving … may be without comfortable homes, the free means of obtaining a few weeks of strengthening rest and treatment previous to recommencing labour'.[2]

Convalescent homes were also used by children's hospitals. The Hospital for Sick Children in Great Ormond Street had its own convalescent home at Cromwell House in leafy Highgate but it also sent patients to other institutions away from the city. It favoured The Royal Sea Bathing Infirmary at Margate, especially for patients with various forms of tuberculosis who were sent there 'to benefit from the supposed healing effects of sea bathing'.[3]

The Royal Sea Bathing Infirmary was opened in 1796, specifically to treat scrofula, a tuberculosis disease of the glands, joints and bones. The hospital's radical design 'facilitated the use of sea air and

Birmingham Hospital Saturday Fund's Convalescent Home, Tyn-y-coed, Llanrhos (n.d.).

sunshine as part of the treatment for tuberculosis' although these experiments were 'contrary to accepted medical opinion of the time'.[4]

The Glasgow Royal Infirmary had no convalescent home under infirmary management until the 1890s when Miss Schaw of Park Circus, Glasgow donated £40,000 for the erection and endowment of such a home 'in memory of her brother, the late Mr Archibald Schaw, Merchant, Glasgow'.[5] The new home was built at Bearsden. It had two immediate benefits: it allowed the medical staff to send to it patients who 'did not so much require active treatment as rest and a sufficiently lengthened period of residence' and, at the same time, it freed up beds for more urgent cases.[6]

Private convalescent homes

Many nursing homes and convalescent homes were founded by ladies 'with or without a nursing qualification'.[7] In 1891, there were around 9,500 beds in England and Wales in such homes. Twenty years later, this had increased to 13,000. In 1900, there were at least fifty nursing homes in London.[8]

The 'Mont Tore Establishment' at Bournemouth was a private nursing home with 120 beds. The Mont Tore treatment was said to be efficacious for 'the rheumatic, gouty, scrofulous, tuberculous and many other states, asthma, consumption, bronchitis, emphasima etc.'[9]

According to one convalescent home proprietor, it was 'essential to obtain assurances of good cases from local doctors before starting'.[10] Some of the nursing homes were 'admirably conducted and in every respect satisfactorily equipped'.[11] In others, 'no trained nurses were employed, the food was meagre and badly cooked and the accommodation was inconvenient, noisy and dirty'.[12] From 1900 onwards, the *British Medical Journal* and *The Hospital* printed numerous complaints from patients and others about 'the low standard of care received in some homes where exorbitant charges were demanded'.[13]

The Hospital argued that there was a 'not inconsiderable class of friendless people who, being in receipt of small pensions, or having invested in small annuities, drift into 'homes' of various degrees and when once there find themselves unable to get away without the assistance of outside friends whom they do not possess'.[14]

Chapter 11

Lunatic Asylums

Before the eighteenth century, the mentally ill were kept at home by their immediate family 'locked in a cellar or barn if dangerous, perhaps tended by a servant'.[1] If there was no family, responsibility would fall to the parish who might board out the lunatic to someone locally. The character of the mad Mrs Rochester, hidden in the attic in Charlotte Bronte's *Jane Eyre* of 1847 suggests that 'such informal procedures continued into the nineteenth century'.[2]

Under the Madhouses Act of 1774, all private madhouses had to be licensed by magistrates, and their annual licenses could only be renewed if admissions registers had been properly maintained. Magistrates could carry out visits to madhouses and, in London, the inspecting body was the Royal College of Physicians. However, the most important part of the Act was that which insisted on medical certification for all except paupers. This gave some protection to those who were simply an inconvenience to their families, and who might otherwise have been locked away with the genuinely insane.

Early nineteenth-century asylums

In 1800, most lunatics were kept in private asylums which operated on a profit basis within the free market economy. This was part of the so-called 'trade in lunacy'. Even as late as 1850, more than half the confined lunatics in England were in private institutions, 'some good, some bad, some indifferent'.[3]

The 1774 Act was strengthened by a series of laws passed from the 1820s, which established the Commissioners in Lunacy, first for London in 1828 and then for the rest of England and Wales in 1844.

The Royal Albert Asylum at Lancaster which opened in 1870. The asylum was exclusively for idiots and imbeciles from seven northern counties.

The Lunacy Commissioners were a permanent body of inspectors made up of doctors, lawyers, and officials whose job it was to visit and report on asylums, without prior notice. They visited all premises housing lunatics including workhouses, hospitals and private madhouses. They had the power to prosecute and withdraw licenses, and they had a remit 'to standardise and improve conditions of care and treatment'.[4] The Commissioners ensured that the worst abuses were stamped out by 'insisting on proper patient records and the recording of all cases of physical coercion'.[5]

County and borough public lunatic asylums

Although London's Bethlem Asylum was widely criticised for its barbaric treatment of its inmates, until the mid-eighteenth century it was the only public lunatic asylum in the country. In 1751, St Luke's Hospital was opened in London as a public lunatic asylum and was 'launched to an optimistic fanfare'.[6] By 1800, public lunatic asylums had been established in other cities such as Manchester, Liverpool and York with charitable support.[7]

In England and Wales, it was not until 1808 that legislation was passed allowing public money to be raised to build county lunatic asylums. These asylums were made compulsory after the passing of the Lunatic Asylum and Pauper Lunatics Act in 1845 but, by then, two thirds of county authorities had already provided asylums for the mentally ill.[8]

Under the terms of the Act, all counties and boroughs were compelled by law to erect publicly funded asylums to house pauper lunatics within three years. By 1850, there were twenty-four county and borough asylums in England and Wales, with accommodation for an average of just under 300 lunatics. This had increased to sixty-six such asylums in 1890 which could accommodate an average of more than 800 lunatics.[9]

Large towns and boroughs could fund their own asylums but smaller counties had to group together to build a joint counties asylum. This was the case in Wales in September 1846 when the counties of Monmouthshire, Herefordshire, Breconshire, Radnorshire and the City of Hereford 'entered into an agreement to form a union and erect a Joint Asylum'[10] at Abergavenny.

Private lunatic asylums

In addition to county asylums, there were also private asylums for patients who could afford to pay for their treatment, and for paupers sent there by poor law unions.

In the early 1840s, these private asylums were increasingly criticised by reformers who were concerned 'about the poor accommodation (particularly for paupers) … about the standards of care and treatment, and particularly about the excessive use of mechanical restraint'.[11] At the same time, the establishing of county asylums 'had a major impact on the various private asylums' with the number of pauper patients falling as they were transferred to the public asylums.[12]

Private asylums were marketed as being more comfortable than the county asylums. In an advertisement in *The Medical Annual* from 1896, Shaftesbury House at Formby-by-the-Sea near Liverpool was described as a 'Private Asylum Licensed for the Treatment of Ladies and Gentlemen mentally afflicted'. It boasted that 'The Rooms throughout the building are large, airy, cheerful, light, very brightly furnished, and, as the walls are tinted in various colours, there is a complete absence of anything approaching to dullness or gloom'.[13] The Holloway Sanatorium in Surrey provided 'a well-ordered environment that was considered more suitable for middle-class ladies and gentlemen'.[14]

County asylums might also have separate wards for private, paying patients which were usually furnished and decorated in a manner in which the upper and upper middle classes were accustomed.

Asylums in Scotland

Before the first inquiry into the care of the mentally ill in Scotland in 1855, there were seven large voluntary Royal Mental Asylums, in which the patients were mainly private,[15] and a network of private mental hospitals 'housing about twenty-five patients on average' and around a quarter of the total of mentally ill Scottish patients.[16]

The Royal Commission on Lunacy in Scotland was appointed in 1855 and found 'evidence of neglect and ill-treatment of the patients and profiteering by the private homes'.[17] All types of accommodation were criticised for the methods of trussing and restraint, especially during the transport of patients to mental hospitals which 'was the cause of physical injury'.[18]

The resulting 1857 Lunacy (Scotland) Act was 'more liberal than the corresponding English legislation' because it permitted the boarding out and admission of voluntary patients.[19] New asylums were built which were 'run by the state, as part of the Poor Law, and administered by the parish'.[20] The first was the asylum for Argyll and Bute which opened in 1863 and, by 1910, a further eighteen such asylums had been built.[21]

Lunatics in workhouses

Unless an insane pauper was a danger to him or herself, or to others, he or she was likely to be housed in the workhouse rather than an asylum. This was because guardians of poor law unions always had one eye on the rates, and it cost less to keep the 'harmless insane' in the workhouse than in an asylum.

Under the legislation of 1834, mentally sick paupers 'were not recognised as a separate group under the workhouse classification scheme and had no specialist accommodation assigned to them.'[22]

Inevitably, there were large numbers of lunatics and others with mental health problems such as dementia who could not be accommodated in a county or borough asylum and therefore became long-term residents of poor law infirmaries, destined to die there.[23]

The role of the asylum

At first, the asylum's main role was the segregation of dangerous lunatics, 'giving them security and maximising prospects of cure'.[24] However, from the mid-eighteenth century, it was believed that lunatics should be confined 'because intensive treatment would restore them'.[25]

Under the terms of the 1842 Lunacy Inquiry Act, a Commission was established to inspect all English and Welsh asylums and to examine the treatment and care of lunatics. The Commission's Supplemental Report of 25 August 1844 stated that the objective of county asylums 'is, or ought to be, the cure of insanity'.

In 1847, the Lunacy Commissioners defined mental illness in three categories: defectives from birth; demented and fatuous; and deranged and disordered. Mental illnesses included imbecility, idiocy, senile dementia, congenital illness and mania. Before a patient could be admitted to a lunatic asylum, a Reception Warrant had to be signed with the patient identified as a lunatic, idiot or person of unsound mind.

Increasing numbers of mentally ill

Asylum patient numbers increased relentlessly from 12,000 in 1850 to 27,000 in 1870. With the huge growth in the number of certified lunatics, by 1860 asylums housing between 500 and 800 patients were common. As so-called 'lunatic colonies', they had a 'largely custodial role, where individual treatment was impossible'.[26] In London and Lancashire, the authorities built asylums to cater for more than 2,000 patients.

The increase in patient numbers nationally put severe pressure on the asylums, with a large number needing to extend their accommodation to accept new patients. The Abergavenny Asylum was extended between 1857 and 1859 to provide beds for 466 patients. The asylum was reluctant to board out patients in neighbouring asylums as this cost 4s more per week per patient than in the home asylum.[27] Another extension built between 1873 and 1875 provided seventy more male beds but 'increased demand for female beds led to several patients being boarded out at Chester'.[28] The demand for beds continued and 250 extra beds were created in 1881.

County or borough lunatic asylums frequently let out empty beds to patients from neighbouring asylums where there was a pressure for beds. This resulted in patients being 'frequently shuttled around between asylums regardless of the wishes of relatives'.[29]

By 1900, there were over 100,000 inmates in asylums with others housed in workhouses or 'boarded out in licensed houses'.[30] In Scotland, the number of asylum patients increased from 6,000 in 1860 to 16,700 in 1914.[31]

Late nineteenth-century asylums

A consolidating Act of 1890 required two medical certificates for all lunatic patients, including paupers. This was designed to strengthen the safeguards against improper confinement of sane people.[32]

The legislation coincided with certain measures designed to 'reduce the stigma surrounding mental illness' including early out-patients clinics such as the one at Wakefield in 1890, the development of reception and observation wards in some asylums and the setting up of the first psychiatric wards in some Scottish hospitals.[33]

Chapter 12

Getting Medical Treatment

In the nineteenth century, death and disease were an ever present threat. However, when a person became ill, the medical treatment which could be received depended to a large extent on the social class he or she came from.

Attendance by a qualified general practitioner cost on average between *2s 6d* and *7s 6d* per visit, depending on the social standing of the patient.[1] Although general practitioners usually reduced their fees for the poor, such qualified advice was usually still out of their reach.

While the upper classes could afford to call out the doctor to attend to all their aches and pains, the working classes were more likely to 'leave summoning the doctor until matters were desperate and the patient often past hope of alleviation, let alone cure'.[2] This was especially true for women and children because whatever money the family had was reserved for food, rent and 'the breadwinner's needs'.[3]

An eclectic range of unqualified medical practitioners served the poorer sections of society. They included bone-setters (a person who sets broken or dislocated bones), leechmen, water casters (a person who judged diseases by their urine) and aurists (ear specialists).[4] The 'local woman' played a vital role in tight-knit working-class communities as an assistant during childbirth and as an abortionist. The Medical Act of 1858 did not outlaw such unregulated practitioners so quacks were free to dispense their services, either in person or by post.

On a more professional level, dispensing chemists and druggists were the primary providers of health-care for the working classes and the lower middle classes. For this section of society, the family receipt book (an archaic term for recipes) handed down from previous generations was still the first port of call when someone fell ill. They could take their receipts to be made up at the corner pharmacist who would also have had his own receipt book for remedies and treatments of all manner of maladies and diseases. Even into the early years of the twentieth century, most working-class medication continued to be 'self-prescribed and self-administered'.[5]

Traditional remedies and folk medicine

Traditional herbal remedies were an important form of medication for the working classes well into the twentieth century. In Ashton-under-Lyne, there were 1,400 working herbalists as late as 1913.[6] The age-old folk medicine was also a significant part of medical treatment for the Victorian poor. It was believed that if brown paper was stuck to the chest, it would ward off colds and coughs[7], eating garden snails was reputed to be a successful treatment for tuberculosis[8] and mistletoe was said to be a 'sure cure for whooping cough'.[9]

In the mid-nineteenth century, patent medicines began to replace folk medicine and herbal remedies but they were inextricably linked. Both Thomas Beecham and Jesse Boot, founders of Beechams and Boots the Chemist respectively, had backgrounds in herbalism. Patent medicines were exempt from both the 1868 Pharmacy Act, which put certain preparations in the control of professional pharmacists, and the 1875 Sale of Food and Drugs Act. They were commercially prepared medicines with a proprietary name. Customers could buy them from chemists, grocers and general stores and the number of outlets licensed to sell them increased 'from 10,000 in 1865 to 40,000 in 1905'.[10]

Evidence of the increasing popularity of patent medicines can be seen in the advertising expenditure of hugely successful companies such as that founded by Thomas Holloway. In 1842, Holloway was paying £5,000 a year for advertising, but by 1883 this had leapt to £50,000.[11]

Cod liver oil was a mainstay of both the dispensing chemist and the general practitioner. A doctor who regularly attended up to 1,000, mainly female workers employed in London shirt factories, attributed the diseases they suffered from entirely to:

... their poor living and insufficient clothing, and the bad air of their homes... They get up, dress, and take their cup of tea and a little bread and butter, all in not more than a quarter of an hour, sometimes less. They take tea again for dinner, with a potato, and perhaps a herring, and tea again in the evening. This constant living on tea weakens the digestion, and produces what I call 'languid dyspepsia'... This poor living ... lowers the vital power, and produces a great disposition to scrofula and consumptive diseases, and I am obliged to keep them up with quinine and cod-liver oil, of which great quantities are used.[12]

Opiates were used among children on a 'vast and harmful scale'.[13] Godfrey's Cordial, a mixture of opium, treacle and infusion of sassafras, was the most popular children's drug and in Coventry 'some ten gallons were sold each week', which was sufficient for 12,000 doses.[14] Opium itself was 'virtually the only analgesic available'[15] and was used especially in country areas to relieve pain. In 1867, the British Medical Association reported that 'more than half of the opium imported into the country was consumed in Norfolk and Lincolnshire alone'.[16] In such damp, marshland areas, the prevalence of rheumatism and neuralgia was particularly high. The report added there was not a labourer's house 'without its penny stick or pill of opium, and not a child that did not have it in some form'.[17]

'What Are the Wild Waves Saying? Try Beecham's Pills': an advertisement for Beecham's Pills. (*The Illustrated London News*, 25 August 1888)

Sick clubs and friendly societies

Where more skilled craftsmen were in regular, well-paid employment, it was a popular custom to contribute to a sick club or friendly society. They were a kind of insurance scheme whereby a weekly sum was paid by members. If a member fell ill, he could expect to receive benefits of around 3s 6d to 6s per week during his illness. He could also expect to be attended by a club doctor 'at a fee of 2s 6d or so per member per annum'.[18]

Working people made increasing use of medical services provided under these insurance schemes. The records of friendly societies reveal that as well as serious illnesses, 'colds, headaches and minor abrasions'[19] were frequent reasons for taking more than three days off work. Perhaps surprisingly, between 1864 and 1883 'the most common recorded diagnosis noted among the members of the Eversholt Friendly Society was a cold'.[20]

The custom of contributing to sick clubs was widespread in industrial districts such as the Black Country. In 1855, the guardians of the Dudley Union Workhouse refused to increase the number of medical officers as requested by the Poor Law Board because 'sick Clubs and Benefit Societies exist so very generally in this district, and provide medical aid for a vast amount of the population'.[21] They added that in the district of Dudley and Netherton, there were thirteen surgeons 'who are engaged either as Club or Colliery surgeons'.[22]

The Royal Infirmary, Lancaster
(no postmark).

Swansea Hospital (no postmark).

'Club' doctors were usually employed on a part-time basis, or for set fees or under a capitation system, whereby the doctor was paid an annual sum for every patient he was responsible for.[23] 'Club' practice was attractive to doctors because it guaranteed a regular salary with plenty of work, together with 'protection against a common problem of those practicing in working-class areas, the non-payment of medical bills'.[24] There was no shortage of applicants from younger doctors keen to establish themselves.[25]

By the early 1890s, there were more than 280,000 members of friendly societies in Scotland and 'cheap "six penny" doctoring was extensive'.[26] By 1900, between two thirds and a half of all friendly society members paid the ½ to 1*d* a week required for contract medical services[27] and more than 40 per cent of men aged twenty or over were members of a friendly society or 'sick club'.[28] In some clubs, benefits had also been extended to dependants, or included hospital treatment.[29]

Before 1900, employers might also make medical provision for their employees and employees' dependants. They included the Post Office, most railway, gas and canal companies as well as other 'paternalistic or progressive' companies such as Colman's and Brunner Mond & Company, producers of soda ash.[30]

The upper and upper middle classes

For the upper classes, medical treatment was easily obtained, usually from a consultant with a private practice. The same consultants worked on an unpaid, part-time basis at the voluntary hospitals, to increase the prestige of their private practices. For the upper classes, undressing was not part of the physical examination given by a doctor.[31]

The upper middle classes without a home in London who still wanted the services of the great London 'names' 'would come and take lodgings in the area where the physicians and surgeons had their consulting-rooms'.[32] In 1865 Sir Henry Thompson, Bart., who earned £6,648 plus other large fees for visits abroad 'was in the habit of having breakfast at 8am and commencing his private operations which were performed in the "lodging houses" … near his residence at 8.45 or 9am. He spent the rest of the morning seeing his private patients at Wimpole Street'.[33]

Chapter 13

Admission Procedures
to Hospital

If a person was so seriously ill that he or she required hospital treatment, admission could be sought to a voluntary general or specialist hospital, or if the patient was very poor, the poor law infirmary. The upper classes would have been treated at home or in the consulting rooms by a well-regarded general practitioner as part of his private practice. This included any necessary operations.

Getting admitted to a Victorian hospital for either in- or out-patient treatment was no easy matter. Most voluntary hospitals turned away 'pregnant women, children under six, the insane, cases of smallpox, venereal disease [and] other infectious diseases and fevers'[1] while many did not admit chronic cases. At St George's Hospital in London in 1846, the rules stated that: 'No person labouring under any infectious distemper, deemed incurable, or whose case is consumptive or asthmatic, or having old ulcerated legs, more proper for a workhouse, is to be received into the House.'[2]

No one could be admitted to a voluntary hospital who could afford to pay for their own treatment, although later in the nineteenth century some hospitals boosted their income by introducing a small number of private rooms for paying patients, or by contracting their nurses out to provide care for paying patients from the upper and middle classes. In England and Wales, the abject poor who were receiving poor relief were also excluded, and were expected to go to the poor law infirmary. In Scotland, where a different poor relief system operated, the parishes often sent their sick poor to the voluntary hospitals.

Some voluntary hospitals specified that if a prospective patient was a member of a sick club, he or she would be excluded from treatment. At the Blackburn Infirmary, no member of a benefit society with a medical officer attached could be admitted as an out-patient 'without the special permission of the Board of Management'.[3]

The medical and surgical staff kept a degree of control over the types of cases admitted to hospital, preferring to admit more 'interesting' cases as in-patients, particularly in teaching hospitals. These cases might include amputations, unusual diseases, or conditions requiring complicated surgery. It was observed that 'the beds are allotted to medicine and surgery in proportions quite different from those in which cases occur in actual practice'.[4] In urban hospitals, two thirds of all in-patients were surgical cases while in standard general practice more than two thirds of the patients were medical cases.[5]

In Scotland, it was reported that 'the honourable distinction of the hospital system is, that at the smallest as well as the largest, every disease is received…'.[6] In this way, Scottish provincial hospitals 'successfully

'Notes at a London Hospital: La Queue at the Dispensary.' (*The Graphic*, 27 December 1879)

The Infirmary,
Peterborough (n.d.).

Hospital Sunday – Re-opening of the Victoria Hospital for Sick Children, Chelsea.' (*The Graphic*, 17 June 1876)

fulfilled the duties which most of those in England decline; viz, the care of all afflictions, acute as well as chronic, and the attempt to check or mitigate the ravages of epidemics'.[7]

Subscribers' recommendations

The majority of general hospitals were 'voluntary', funded by charitable subscribers who paid an annual sum. This entitled them to recommend a specified number of people for hospital treatment per year. Unless a person had had an accident and therefore needed emergency treatment, he or she had to be recommended by a subscriber as a 'fit object' for charity.

In many hospitals, subscribers who had recommended patients for treatment were bound to remove the patient from the hospital once dismissed, and at Aberdeen patients were sent home 'at the expense of the recommender' if they had not been removed.[8]

An inquiry conducted in 1863 by John Syer Bristowe and Timothy Holmes found that 'at the great majority of London hospitals which depend entirely on private bounty, it has been found necessary, in order to conciliate the subscribers, to allow them a kind of right of nominating the recipients of this charity'.[9]

At many country hospitals, it was found that the rights of subscribers were 'more rigidly enforced' and they expected their nominees 'to be admitted for the full term of a letter which is customarily given for a period of six to eight weeks'.[10] This led to the wards of many provincial hospitals being 'filled with ambulant and infirm cases to the exclusion of the acutely sick'.[11]

Bristowe and Holmes deeply regretted that in a busy and crowded town such as Portsmouth, the Royal Portsmouth, Portsea and Gosport Hospital was 'used mainly as a refuge for a few chronic invalids who have had the good luck to recommend themselves to some subscriber'.[12]

Patients might also be able to gain hospital treatment through their employers, many of whom subscribed to hospitals specifically 'to gain the right to send any of their employees who were ill'.[13] Under this arrangement, country hospitals became sick clubs 'in which the employer pays instead of the patient'.[14] This practice was not confined to country areas. For instance, many city hospitals such as Birmingham's General Hospital had a large number of employers on its annual subscription lists.

At the three endowed hospitals of St Bartholomew's, St Thomas's and Guy's, which did not require funding by subscribers, admissions were 'subject to the regulations as to number of beds, exclusion of smallpox, and proportion of medicine and surgery'.[15] Doctors were entitled to admit acute cases as emergencies, 'a right which was increasingly used'.[16]

In the 1890s, it was found that:

> The usual practice at the general hospitals appears to be to give very slight preference to applicants bringing letters over those (and they are the vast majority) who come without them… But any person whose illness is sufficiently serious appears to be considered equally in either case a proper subject for treatment.[17]

By 1900, subscribers' letters of recommendation had been phased out by most hospitals.[18] In May 1897, the Aberdeen Royal Infirmary proudly announced that 'admission to all the Wards – MEDICAL, SURGICAL and OPHTHALMIC is now FREE, and no lines of recommendation are required'.[19]

Glasgow Royal Infirmary with the cathedral on the right, mid-nineteenth century. (NHS Greater Glasgow and Clyde Archives)

Poor law infirmaries

If a hospital could demonstrate success in terms of the number of patients cured, this was good for publicity and it increased the prestige of the medical staff. For this reason, voluntary hospitals started to take more acute cases and in England and Wales, chronic and incurable cases were routinely refused admission. As a direct result of this 'economical use of beds', a large proportion of the population's health needs 'went unmet'.[20] Those seeking out-patient treatment might get help from the local dispensary but prospective in-patients, who had been refused treatment by the voluntary hospitals, were admitted to poor law infirmaries as these institutions could not refuse admission to the sick poor. Chronic cases which had originally been accepted for treatment were also discharged directly to poor law infirmaries when beds were required for more interesting, acute cases. There was, therefore, an uneasy relationship between the two types of hospital.

Another link existed between the voluntary hospitals and the poor law infirmaries, through which poor law patients could benefit. Under poor law legislation, boards of guardians were empowered to make subscriptions to voluntary hospitals and to send pauper patients there.[21] It has been argued that few boards of guardians chose to use these new powers and 'even fewer voluntary hospitals were prepared to admit paupers'.[22]

However, some poor law unions did avail themselves of the opportunity provided under the Act, and their inmates no doubt benefited as a result. In 1876, the guardians of the Dudley Union subscribed to no less than four hospitals plus a truss society. They included the Guest Hospital, Dudley (£6 6s 0d), the General Hospital, Birmingham (£21 0s 0d), South Staffordshire General Hospital, Wolverhampton (£5 5s 0d), the Birmingham Eye Hospital (£5 5s 0d) and the Dudley Truss Society (£10 10s 0d).[23]

In July 1871, the guardians ordered that 'a further subscription of £1 1s 0d be forwarded to the Eye Hospital at Birmingham in favour of John Hobson, an inmate of the Union Workhouse.'[24] Despite this treatment, it seems that nothing could be done to improve John's eyesight as by 1875, when he was seventeen, the guardians had made the decision to send him to learn a trade at the General Institution for the Blind.[25]

Abuse of hospitals by those who could pay

All general voluntary hospitals experienced the same problem: patients using the hospitals' services who could afford to pay for their own medical treatment. General hospitals were meant for the charitable poor, and it was extremely difficult to police and monitor the class of patients applying for treatment.

Writing in 1879, J. W. F. Smith-Shand, a physician at the Aberdeen Royal Infirmary, commented on the class of people applying for free treatment at the hospital who could blatantly afford to pay: 'Gold chains and tweed suits, and the latest fashions in female attire, are not at all uncommon objects, while on one occasion last year, an old lady from the country *attended by her servant*, presented herself to me for advice with a line from her minister!'[26]

A 'line' was the term given to a recommendation by a subscriber, particularly in Scottish hospitals.

It was impossible for a busy hospital to check all the applications for treatment. A sub-committee of The London in the 1870s summed up the situation, which could be applied to the vast majority of city and provincial hospitals:

> The London Hospital is the only service of out-patient relief in the extreme East End, and has been so regarded for a very long term of years, and no fresh organisation can for a long period at least replace the great advantages it offers to the sick and needy; and any check too suddenly or too stringently applied would be detrimental to the deserving poor in the redress of their severe necessity.[27]

It was also pointed out that the medical treatment which was needed by the 'very poor ... frequently alone stands between them and the necessity for obtaining parochial relief.'[28]

According to the Charity Organisation Society, an estimated quarter of out-patients at general hospitals had a 'probable income' of over £1 10s a week. It was believed that such people 'should, as a rule, and especially when unmarried, be expected to belong to a sick club or provident dispensary'.[29] However, the medical journal *The Lancet* did not believe that abuse of out-patient departments could be taking place because 'conditions in them were so appalling'.[30]

Chapter 14

Out-Patients

The out-patient department acted like a sieve to separate the serious and interesting cases from the more mundane. In many ways, it was akin to the modern-day accident and emergency department as most cases, such as 'the cut face, the bruised arm [and] the sprained wrist' could be given immediate relief and sent home.[1] Patients with more serious injuries or complaints were admitted as in-patients.

At some hospitals like Cardiff's Royal Infirmary, out-patients could be visited in their own homes if they were not able to get to the hospital. This was a similar service to that offered by many dispensaries.[2] It has been argued that treating out-patients was less of a financial burden, allowing administrators to 'increase the work of the hospital at no great cost and, in this way, secure the public's long-term support'.[3]

Rules for out-patients

Strict rules applied to out-patients as much as to in-patients. Unless they were emergencies, out-patients were still expected to bring letters of recommendation from subscribers. At Aberdeen's Royal Infirmary, if out-patients did not return regularly on the stated day 'and if they shall twice neglect to do this without a sufficient reason', they forfeited their right to treatment and were discharged.[4]

At many hospitals, they were expected to provide 'phials or galipots for their medicines at their own expense'.[5] At the Cardiff Royal Infirmary, bottles and gallipots were provided but new out-patients had to deposit sixpence 'which shall be returned to them on their ceasing to attend, and delivering up their bottles, gallipots and cards'.[6] This undoubtedly discouraged people from missing appointments or absconding with hospital property.

'Awaiting their Turn: In the Out-Patients Department at St. Bartholomew's Hospital' drawn by Frank Craig. (*The Graphic*, 3 August 1907)

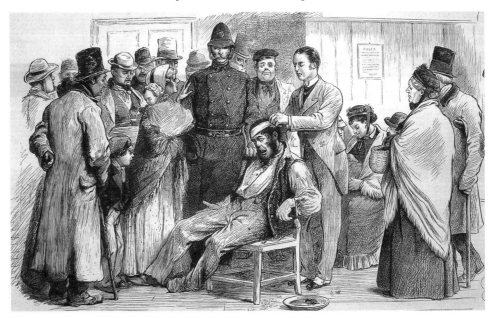

'Notes at a London Hospital: Saturday Night.' (*The Graphic*, 27 December 1879)

Typical cases

A typical scene in an out-patient department in 1867 was vividly recorded by Frederick Treves, a former surgeon at The London. He described the waiting hall for out-patients and the types of people who frequented it:

> This was a bare hall... provided with rows of deal benches, and there are nearly always people in it; a sniffing woman who has called for her dead husband's clothes; a breathless woman with a midwifery card; some minor accidents; a child who has swallowed a halfpenny; a serious casualty. On Saturday nights, when the atmosphere is heavy with alcohol, or on the occasion of a big dock accident, it is full of excited folk, policemen, reporters, busybodies and friends of the injured.[7]

Conjugal differences were a common cause of many of the cases which turned up at a hospital's out-patient department. A visitor to one city hospital was told that:

> Sometimes a good lady will come in with her face badly knocked about, and will explain that she fell over a chair, or tripped over the cat and damaged herself. A few minutes later her husband will arrive, his face bearing obvious marks of clawing, and will tell how, as he was going along the street, he lost his footing and hit himself against the gravel. They will not take it kindly if the doctor inquires too closely into the cause of their suffering; and a family fight does not strike them as being a very dreadful affair.[8]

This scene would have been repeated up and down the country, undoubtedly fuelled by the cheap and ready availability of alcohol. Saturday nights were the busiest because 'Wages have been paid and are being rapidly converted into the prime necessity of life to a large proportion of the surrounding population. The gin shops are crammed with boisterous men and women'.[9]

The doctors in the receiving room had to be on the look-out for the hospital imposter, 'fakir' or pretender, 'the man or woman who simulates serious illness in order to get the food and shelter and kindness of the sick ward'.[10] In the early 1900s in London, it was reported that one man with a glass eye who knew all about obscure nervous diseases 'simulated every symptom of the complaints he professed to suffer from in a way that took in even great experts'.[11] The man 'lived going from hospital to hospital, and remaining some time in each, but they all found him out at last'.[12]

The Out-Patient Department, London Hospital (n.d.).

Treatment for out-patients

If a patient was offered treatment as an out-patient, it was not necessarily of the highest quality. In 1869, an observer described the casualty department of St Bartholomew's Hospital in London: '120 patients were seen by the physician and dismissed in an hour and ten minutes, or at the rate of 35 seconds each… [The patients] were dismissed with a doubtful dose of physic, ordered almost at random, and poured out of a huge brown jug'.[13]

There was little improvement ten years later. An anonymous contributor to *The Lancet* wrote: 'They consist essentially of purgatives; a mixture of iron, sulphate of magnesia, and quassia [both laxatives], and cod-liver oil, fulfilling the two great indications of therapeutics – elimination, and the supply of some elements to the blood.' The writer criticised Bart's for supplying medicine 'out of jugs, and patients seen at the rate of one a minute, for sixpence or a shilling'.[14]

Surgical appliances

Treatment as an out-patient could also take the form of a prescription for a surgical appliance such as crutches, artificial limbs, spectacles or a truss for supporting a hernia. Hernias were a common complaint amongst labourers whose work involved lifting heavy loads.

When the Local Government Board queried their subscription to the Dudley Truss Society, the guardians of the Dudley Union responded that the society 'has been of great advantage to a large number of poor persons who have been enabled to procure Trusses upon receiving a Ticket on the Society from the Guardians at a reduced price, which has been a considerable saving to the ratepayers of the Union.'[15]

Scottish out-patient departments

In Scotland, the out-patient department acted more like a dispensary. In Aberdeen, there were two institutions offering out-patient advice to the poor: the General Dispensary and the Aberdeen Royal Infirmary. The General Dispensary was a separate institution but it received funds from the Royal Infirmary under an archaic bequest. In order to limit the number of out-patients at the hospital, it was decided that only 'Persons living beyond the boundaries of the GENERAL DISPENSARY requiring Advice and Medicine at the Infirmary, will be seen in the Hospital Reception Rooms every week day at HALF-PAST TWELVE o'clock p.m'. Those living within the boundary were treated at the

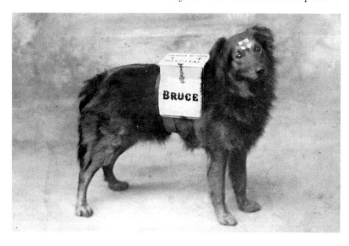

'Bruce' – The Hospital's
Friend (postmark unclear).

General Dispensary itself 'except in SERIOUS CASES, recommended by a Physician or Surgeon'.[16] Unfortunately, this was a difficult rule to police and it was frequently flouted.

The out-patient departments of Scottish hospitals differed across the country. In 1879 in Edinburgh, the out-patients were treated by the medical officers on the permanent staff of the Royal Infirmary with surgical out-patients receiving all dressings and necessary appliances 'but no medicines are supplied to either surgical or medical cases'.[17] At both the Glasgow Royal Infirmary and the city's Western Infirmary, there was a separate Dispensary Staff from those who treated in-patients.[18] The Royal gave medicine 'to the most necessitous cases' while the Western gave none.[19] The out-patient department at Dundee's Royal Infirmary was the most similar to Aberdeen's. It was run by a different staff from the ward staff and patients were visited in their own homes, receiving medicine.[20]

Increasing numbers of out-patients

A contemporary estimate puts the length of consultation time for each out-patient at 1.3 minutes, which is unsurprising given the huge numbers attending the hospitals. From 1860 onwards, the demand for out-patient services increased dramatically, putting extreme pressure on staff and resources. At The London, between 1860 and 1900 new in-patient admissions increased from 4,000 to 12,000 a year but 'the number of out-patient consultations soared from 25,000 to over 220,000'.[21]

As a result, by 1900 most large voluntary hospitals had to put in place new rules to limit the numbers of out-patients.[22] At the Cardiff Royal Infirmary, in a bid to reduce out-patient numbers, it was decided that in the case of minor accidents in patients belonging to a sick club with a doctor attached, they be referred to their club doctors.[23]

The increase in out-patient numbers could lead to a frustrating wait to be seen by a doctor, or to receive medicines prescribed. At Birmingham's General Hospital in 1879, it was found that the dispensing was not completed on Mondays, Wednesdays and Fridays by 2 o'clock 'and on Mondays often not till 4' but on the other days of the week, it was completed between 12 and 2 o'clock. There were complaints that the patients were having to wait two hours after they had seen the physician before their medicine was dispensed. According to the Dispenser, this was because of 'the rapid rate at which the patients are seen by the Medical Officer during the last part of the morning, and also to the elaborate prescriptions given – the stock medicines being now seldom used'.[24] In October, a pill machine was ordered for the dispensary, which would undoubtedly have speeded up the dispensing process.[25]

Lengthy waits for consultations or prescriptions from the dispensary could deter out-patients from attending hospital departments. This was often connected with the organisation of the treatment. In its 1871 Annual Report, the Blackburn and East Lancashire Infirmary commented:

> It has been found, with much regret, that the number of out-patients is not so great as it might be. Hitherto patients have frequently had to wait, at least for their medicines, on account of the necessary arrangements for in-patients, but the difficulty has been obviated, and if they will keep accurately to the hours prescribed, no more inconvenience will be entailed, either on the officers of the Infirmary or on the patients.[26]

Chapter 15

In-Patients

The majority of voluntary hospital patients came from the 'industrious poor'. At the time of the 1861 census, of the 10,414 patients in hospital, only 157 were classed as 'professional people' and half of these were 'local government officers, teachers and clergymen'. Only fourteen were 'persons of Rank or Property not returned under any office or occupation' while the remainder were wage-earners employed in industry, domestic service or agriculture. Around 1,630 inmates were classed as being engaged in 'Attendance (Domestic Servants) etc.'.[1]

Going into hospital

What was it like to be one of these patients in a Victorian hospital? Once in possession of an admission ticket, prospective in-patients had to present themselves at the hospital on a particular day and time, as specified on the ticket. At the Aberdeen Royal Infirmary in the 1870s, this was at 12 noon every day, except Sunday. Urgent fever cases could be admitted 'at any hour of the day' and 'accidents, requiring immediate aid, at any hour of the day or night'.[2]

The ticket also listed the personal items in-patients were expected to bring with them, which varied from hospital to hospital. At Blackburn, all in-patients were 'required to bring at least two shirts or two shifts'[3] while at Birmingham's General Hospital only a knife, fork and spoon was needed.[4] From 1870, patients at Cardiff's Royal Infirmary had to bring a change of linen, specified as 'two shirts, one night dress and a pair of stockings'.[5] By 1889, this had changed to 'two shirts, two night dresses, two pairs of stockings and a comb and brush'.[6]

At many hospitals, such as Cardiff and Derby, new patients were routinely bathed on arrival. This, however, did not apply to all hospitals and Bristowe and Holmes found in 1863 that there were no regulations regarding the bathing of patients on admission to Birmingham's General Hospital.[7]

Rules for in-patients

Every hospital was governed by a strict set of rules which applied to both staff and patients. A copy of the rules, which were set down by the Board of Governors, was prominently displayed in each of the hospital's wards. They were also periodically included in each hospital's annual report.

The stringent rules effectively controlled the life of the patient while in hospital. Patients who disobeyed the rules were considered refractory and 'disorderly' and could be punished by being discharged for 'irregularities'. In order to ensure both patients and staff adhered to the rules, the Board of Governors of every hospital appointed a visitor or team of visitors who regularly inspected the institution. The visitors were often members of the Board of Governors themselves, or subscribers to the hospital.

If a patient was dismissed for irregularities, he or she was blacklisted and could not be readmitted to the hospital, unless a member of the board allowed it. At The Royal Devon and Exeter Hospital, blacklisted patients could not return to the hospital 'on any pretence whatever'.[8]

Most hospitals had similar rules which banned smoking or chewing tobacco, cursing or swearing, gambling or drinking spirituous liquors. At the Radcliffe Infirmary, ambulant patients were forbidden to leave the hospital without permission 'in order to stop them returning drunk'.[9]

The banning of playing cards and other games of chance was a common rule, not only of hospitals, but also of workhouses and prisons. One rule constantly flouted by patients was the persistent smoking in

Left: James Hadley, who was a medical patient at the General Hospital, Birmingham in 1881, pictured with his wife Isabella, *c.*1920s (see page 59). (With thanks to Geoff Couling)

Below: 'Hospital Sunday: Convalescents Waiting on the Sick – A Scene in a London Hospital.' (*The Graphic*, 14 June 1873)

the wards, which was grounds for a discharge. Blackburn Infirmary's rules for patients also forbade using improper language or behaving themselves indecently 'on pain of expulsion'.[10]

At the Aberdeen Royal Infirmary, patients were not allowed to sit up after half-past eight at night and had to rise no later than seven in summer and eight in winter, if they were judged able by the medical officers.[11]

One of the rules at The Royal Devon and Exeter Hospital stipulated that before patients were discharged, they should 'in the presence of an officer of the hospital, offer up a prayer of thanksgiving for the help received'.[12] This rule was enforced until at least 1912.

Patients at the Glasgow Royal Infirmary had to be silent when the medical attendants, chaplain, assistants and strangers visited the wards. All patients who were able had to 'wash themselves every morning before breakfast in the basins provided' and to pay the strictest attention to cleanliness. They were expected to be particularly careful with infirmary property such as 'bed-clothes, fire utensils, spoons &c, and all bottles, phials, pots, syringes, or any drugs not used' and return them to the nurse.[13]

Convalescent patients who were able to do so were expected to assist in the work of the hospital. For female patients, this could mean cleaning the wards or doing needlework to repair bedding, and for the male patients, 'any easy work about the House'.[14]

Rules for visitors

The hospital rules were applied just as vigorously to the relatives and friends of patients. There were strict visiting hours and at many general hospitals, the number of visitors per patient was limited. Most city hospitals operated a ticket system which entitled two people at a time to visit the patient they wanted to see. At some hospitals, these tickets or cards were transferable so when the first two people had finished, they could pass the ticket on to other relatives for visiting on the same day, or another day. At others, the tickets had to be given up on arrival.

In 1884, the Aberdeen Royal Infirmary was forced to implement this system, 'much inconvenience having been caused both to the ailing inmates of the Wards, and the Nurses in the execution of their duty, by the crowds of persons who visit the Hospital on the afternoons – Tuesday, Friday, Saturday and Sunday – set apart for friends seeing patients'.[15]

At The Royal Devon and Exeter Hospital, at first there was no limit to the number of visitors allowed to visit each patient but, in 1871, the newly appointed matron and the house surgeon complained to the governors and the hospital authorities about the problems this caused. The house surgeon pointed out that 'the wards are sometimes much too crowded *to the discomfort and injury to the sick*'. The matron suggested restricting the number of visitors allowed in and ended her letter with the comment that 'frequently one patient has seven visitors in three-quarters of an hour. *It does much harm to the patient*'.[16] A ticket system was subsequently introduced by the governors, under which only two people 'were allowed to have a ticket and to visit at any one time'.[17]

This new system meant that other members of the family had to wait outside the hospital in all weathers until the ticket holder came out and handed over the ticket to them. The rule was still in force twenty years later when a local newspaper drew attention to the fact and forced the governors to allow visitors to wait in the out-patients hall in inclement weather.[18]

From 1880, at The Hospital for Sick Children in Great Ormond Street, mothers visited on Thursday afternoons while fathers could visit on Sundays. Brothers and sisters were forbidden from visiting until the 1960s.[19]

In order to deal with the distress caused by the departure of the children's parents, there was a different routine on visiting days. When the visitors had left, 'the children's tea was brought in, with extra treacle or sugar on the bread'.[20]

There were also stringent rules at many hospitals banning food and liquor from being brought in for the patients. At The Royal Devon and Exeter Hospital, the nurses' daily routine included searching the patients' lockers after visiting time to check that no banned commodities had been brought in. At an inquest in 1889, one of the surgeons reported that 'he had to act almost as a detective at times to prevent things being smuggled in'.[21]

During the nineteenth century, this rule was slightly changed so that 'it was now *expected* that tea and sugar would be supplied by the patient's relatives or friends'.[22] If a patient's relatives could not afford to provide their own tea or sugar, they had to go without. The Committee stated that they could not be provided by the hospital 'on any account'.[23]

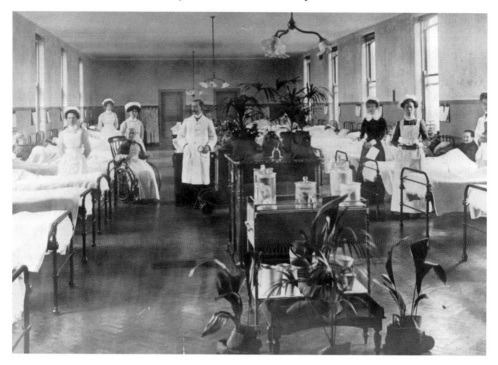

A ward scene at the Northern General Hospital, Sheffield. In the foreground is a dressing trolley with jars for sterile swabs, gauze pads, bandages and cotton wool. (Northern General Hospital History Project, Sheffield)

The duty of observing that 'no kind of food or liquor be brought into the House by any of the acquaintances of the Patients' was also expected of the nurses at the Aberdeen Royal Infirmary.[24] However, the rule banning food and liquor being brought in was not followed at all hospitals. At Guy's Hospital in London, relatives were 'positively encouraged to provide food for the patients and food sellers, including a watercress seller, visited the wards to ply their wares'.[25]

Length of stay in hospital

To modern eyes, the lengths of stay for patients in Victorian hospitals seem comparatively long, especially for medical cases. Most hospitals operated the same policy of admitting patients for a maximum of six weeks under one admission ticket. After this time, a ticket could be renewed only at the discretion of the surgeon or physician who was looking after the case. In many instances, patients were discharged to convalescent homes, the hospital clearly recognising the need for further recuperation time. In 1877 at The London, the average period of stay for in-patients was thirty-three days.[26]

Patients in voluntary hospitals could be admitted on a number of different occasions if a medical condition recurred. Researchers at Kingston University compiled this story from the records of a Great Ormond Street patient:

> Five-year-old Arthur Holland was first admitted to The Hospital for Sick Children with hip disease on 3 June 1884. After a month, he was transferred to Cromwell House, the hospital's convalescent home at Highgate, but returned to the main hospital within sixteen weeks to have an operation 'to remove some of the diseased bone in his hip'.[27]
>
> It was not until April 1885 when Arthur was sent back to Cromwell House again, his 'condition improved', to complete his recovery. Unfortunately, he suffered a setback and was transferred again to Great Ormond Street 'his hip showing no sign of improvement'. On 1 October 1885, Arthur was transferred to Cromwell House for the last time 'with the hip problem under control'. Recovery, however, was a long, slow process and he stayed at Cromwell House, moving several times between the chronic and convalescent wards, for another nine and a half months before he was finally discharged to go home. In total, Arthur had been hospitalised for just over two years of his childhood, which must have been extremely difficult for his family who were 'scraping a living in the laundry business in North

Kensington'. By 1901, although Arthur was described as a 'cripple', he was married and working as a gardener. Without the care and medical treatment he received as a child, his adulthood may not have been so independent.[28]

In 1881, James Hadley, a seventeen-year-old pattern maker in an ironworks, was suffering with pneumonia. At the time, pneumonia was one of the great killer diseases of Victorian society and one in which 'the attendance of a medical man is very necessary'.[29]

James lived with his parents and eight brothers and sisters in Smethwick, not far from where he worked. It is likely that the family had tried to treat him with their own remedies handed down from previous generations. They may also have obtained medicine for him from their local dispensary or paid for a doctor out of their meagre income. Nothing worked. It is probable that a doctor suggested to James that he should be seen at Birmingham's General Hospital where he could receive more sophisticated treatment.

As James's illness was not as a result of an accident, he needed an in-patient ticket from a subscriber to receive hospital treatment. Interestingly, the subscriber recorded as recommending him was James Gatt & Co. This was either his employer or an insurance society. It would also have been possible for James to appeal to an individual private subscriber as every community would have known who their nearest subscriber was. He might have approached him or her through his doctor or a clergyman, or possibly direct.

When James was admitted to Ward 6 of Birmingham's General Hospital on 28 February 1881, he became a medical in-patient diagnosed with 'unresolved pneumonia'. It is likely that this meant he had been experiencing recurring attacks of pneumonia. It was known that 'some people [were] liable to repeated attacks of inflammation of the lungs', a peculiarity which was 'due either to some special but unknown constitutional predisposition, or to the fact that previous attacks induce a proclivity to their return'.[30]

After diagnosis, cases were always assigned medical or surgical status and during the course of treatment, patients might be transferred between the two. James's case was assigned to Dr Willoughby Francis Wade, M.B., F.R.C.P., a physician who had been appointed to the post at Birmingham in 1865.

It is not known what treatment James received while in hospital as the records have not survived but, at the time, a combination of tartaric acid with potash and antimony, known as tartar emetic, was consid-

'The Alexandra Hospital for Children with Hip Disease: The Edinburgh Ward – Young Convalescents.'
(*The Graphic*, 11 October 1890)

ered to be a powerful remedy when treating pneumonia and in 1884 it was noted that 'since the general adoption of this mode of treatment the number of deaths from this disease has greatly decreased'.[31]

James remained in hospital for the full six weeks he was entitled to stay for under one admission ticket. He was discharged on 14 April 1881, described as 'cured'.[32] James went on to marry and to have a family of eight children, six of whom survived childhood. He became the manager of a foundry and lived into his seventies, proving his treatment at Birmingham was successful.[33]

A typical case in a poor law infirmary

The elderly poor might have numerous recurring medical complaints which made it difficult to pursue an occupation, and therefore to provide for themselves and their families. An application for poor relief was often the only option available. Sixty-five-year-old Thomas Roberts, a former Private in the 17th Lancers, moved to the Holborn area of London in late 1878 after unsuccessfully running a beer house with his family in Walworth, south of the city. The whole family consisting of Thomas, his thirty-nine-year-old wife Mary Ann and their six children had to apply for poor relief in December of that year. It is not known for how long they received payments, but by the time of the 1881 census, they were employed again. Thomas was recorded as a night watchman and two of his children were working in tailoring.

From April/May 1882 until around January 1885, the Roberts family were living at No.18 Evelyn Buildings in Holborn which was a two-room tenement. By early 1885, the family had moved to No.22 Evelyn Buildings, which was cheaper to rent as it only had one room.

In April 1885, Thomas was admitted to the City Road Workhouse Hospital for three days. By this time, he was seventy-two and described as a shoe black. Thomas had applied for poor relief a few months before his hospital admission, presumably because his illness had prevented him from working. This would have significantly affected his family as Thomas was their main breadwinner. The family continued to receive poor relief while Thomas was in hospital and for many months afterwards, as late as January 1886. This would indicate that Thomas had not recovered sufficiently from his illness to earn enough for his family.

There was an inextricable link between poverty and crime in the Victorian period. In May 1886, one of Thomas's daughters, eighteen-year-old Elizabeth, was arrested and tried at the Old Bailey for receiving £3 in stolen money.[34] It is highly likely that the alleged crime was committed by Elizabeth to help her family. At the trial, the case was dismissed due to lack of evidence.

By the autumn of 1886, the family had moved again, this time to No.25 Evelyn Buildings. They were dealt another blow in November when Thomas's wife, Mary Ann, died of bronchitis, erysipelas and pericarditis at home at No.25 Evelyn Buildings. She was forty-six. Erysipelas, also commonly known as St Anthony's Fire in England and 'the rose' in Scotland, was an infectious inflammatory disease of the skin caused by a germ. It was less common for women with children to seek medical treatment in a hospital so it is possible the only medical help Mary Ann received was through a parish doctor or a dispensing chemist if the family could have afforded to pay for drugs.

Thomas was left to care for his four children aged between ten and nineteen, his eldest two having left home before their mother died. At the time of his wife's death, Thomas was seventy-two and described as a soap boiler. It appears that he alternated between shoe-blacking and soap boiling as occupations, one or both of which may have been seasonal.

He was admitted to the City Road Workhouse Hospital again on 13 October 1887. It is not known what illness he was suffering from but he discharged himself on 5 November and returned to Evelyn Buildings. By early 1889, Thomas Roberts had bronchitis and dropsy and was admitted to the Holborn Infirmary in Holloway. He died there on 25 April 1889 aged seventy-six and was buried at the St Pancras & Islington Cemetery. Fortunately, by this time, his children had grown up and were able to provide for themselves.[35]

Effect on family of admission to hospital

When a patient was admitted to hospital, it had an immediate effect on the family he or she left at home. If the patient was the main breadwinner, it could have a catastrophic impact on how the family lived and survived. If the patient was the mother of a family of children, this would also affect the father who still had to work but had to look after his family as well. In this case, it is likely that relatives and friends would have been called upon to help out, perhaps with the family being split up for a time if there were many children to look after.

It is no surprise to find that applications for poor relief were frequently filed as soon as a patient was admitted to hospital. If out-relief was not granted, the patient's family could find themselves in the work-house for the duration of his or her stay in hospital.

John Gallacher, a forty-five-year-old ship labourer from Springburn near Glasgow, was admitted to the city's Western Infirmary on 6 November 1903. His detailed ward notes reveal just how importantly a patient's medical history was viewed compared with the early to mid-Victorian period.

Despite requiring hospital treatment, John was a hardy soul. As a child, he had survived measles, scarlet fever, diphtheria and whooping cough and when he was seven years old 'he lost full power of his legs and was confined to bed for some months but was all right again in a year'. At the age of twenty-eight, he contracted typhoid fever and had three relapses. He had colds every winter and 'usually treated them by going to bed for a day and taking a bottle of whisky and some bottles of beer.'

John was admitted to the Western Infirmary after complaining of tightness across the chest and shortness of breath which had lasted for four days. His feet and legs had also swelled up for six days. He had sent for a doctor who gave him salts and some medicine and advised him to go to the Infirmary.

On admission, urine tests were taken which revealed 'a distinct amount of albumin present' with 'tube casts, which are finely granular' and blood, but no sugar. Four days after his admission, John's urine contained 1 per cent albumin, blood and tube casts 'finely granular and Hyaline and also some coarsely granular casts'. Spermatozoa were also present.

With albumin being present in John's urine, it is likely that the physician was trying to rule out Bright's disease. By 17 November, the swelling in John's feet and ankles had entirely disappeared but he still had '½ part Esbach of Albumin in his urine plus a trace of blood'. He was 'Sent to Home' a week later. It is not clear if this was his own home or a convalescent home run by the hospital. While in hospital he was prescribed 'Ferr. of Aluminium Bisulph [an iron preparation], Glycerine , Ag Bisulph and Sig.'.[36]

At the time of his admission, John had three children living at home with his wife Matilda. Three days after he was admitted to hospital, Matilda made an application for poor relief. The documents reveal that the rent on their home at 29 Fountainwell Road, Springburn was 10s 10d per month, which was for a one-room house. She applied at 1 p.m. and was visited an hour later. Matilda was recorded as 'partially disabled' from earning as she had 'Anaemia and Ch. Bron' (chronic bronchitis). She had three daughters, Mary (born 1888) who worked as a labeller in Tennant's Brewery at 7s a week, Sophia (born 1896) and Helen (born 1899). This was her first application for poor relief and, until the Committee met, she was offered the poorhouse. Her reasons for applying were as follows: 'Applies for Outdoor Relief. Husband was on 6th inst. removed to Western Infirmary with "Bright's Disease". Has been off work 5 weeks prior worked in Beardmore's, Govan 19/ a week. No society. Wife at present in bed with "Rheumatisms". House in fair order.'

'No society' meant that John was not contributing to a sick club or friendly society so he had no form of medical insurance. The authorities recommended a donation for Matilda until her husband came home. She was granted 5s a week for four weeks from 13 November 1903.[37] This was extended for a further twelve weeks from 11 December and the payments stopped on 29 January 1904 as John had returned home.[38]

Chapter 16

Accidents and Emergencies

In the early nineteenth century, many general hospitals in the smaller cities did not have a casualty department as few emergency cases were ever admitted. For example, at The Royal Devon and Exeter Hospital, very few surgical procedures took place except for 'cutting of the stone'. By the 1830s, the situation had changed. A great deal of building work was taking place all over the city of Exeter and with this dangerous, manual labour, came the inevitable increased number of accidents. The number of surgical procedures rose significantly and the first 'operation nurse' was appointed in 1835 to help cope with the demands of the new casualty department.[1]

Some of the more serious cases brought in to The London's out-patients waiting hall included: '…a man ridden over in the street; a machine accident with strips of cotton shift, mangled flesh and trails of black grease; someone picked up in a lane with his throat cut; or a woman, dripping foul mud, who has just been dragged out of the river.'[2]

Accident and emergency cases were particularly sought after by large teaching hospitals as they provided useful material for their students. Much could be learned from observing how a surgeon or physician dealt with a gunshot wound, an accidental poisoning, a compound fracture or a severed limb.

The skill of a surgeon or physician was worthless if an accident victim was not seen promptly. In February 1885, after a complaint from the Committee of the Sick Club at Messrs Wright & Butlers, the managers of the General Hospital, Birmingham, discovered that 'a case of injury from an accident [had] remained more than an hour in the Surgery without being seen by any Resident Officer or Dresser'. The superintendent nurse was invited to resign and the Resident Surgical Officers were severely reprimanded. The managers argued that their actions were 'calculated to damage the reputation of this Institution' and reminded them that the 'primary rule of a Hospital must always be that accident cases must be inspected with the utmost promptitude'.[3]

Occupational hazards

Every Victorian occupation held hidden dangers. There were obvious risks involved in working in a mine, in the building trade, as a navvy or as a docker. Injuries caused by falling from a height could be particularly serious. At the Scarborough Hospital and Dispensary in 1873, a mason with a fractured skull was treated after he fell from a scaffold during the restoration of Christ Church. The accident proved to be fatal.[4]

The increase in the numbers working in these occupations led to a marked rise in the number of accidents treated by hospitals. In the 1840s at the Glasgow Royal Infirmary, the managers expressed concern about the growing number of accident cases, and how they affected the chronic cases:

> The urgency of accident and operation cases, renders it necessary to give to these a preference over cases of a lingering and chronic character… During the last year, a very large number of casualties of this kind have occurred, and have been attended with a proportionate increase of mortality. The most prolific sources of these have been the Public Works in and around Glasgow, the various Railroads leading in to the city, and the numerous Collieries of the mining districts.[5]

In the mills and factories, unfenced machinery posed a very real threat of loss of limb. As employers accepted no liability for such industrial injuries, the most the injured could expect 'was a token payment for a serious accident or a few charitable gestures if they were "laid up" for a longish spell'.[6] If the main breadwinner was too ill to work, his family could gain 'an extension of credit at the local grocers' and use the pawnshop before application to the poor law union became inevitable.[7]

Injuries were also prevalent in other occupations, because of their manual nature. Such injuries might include the crushed hand or fingers of a labourer after carrying (and dropping) a heavy load, or of a waggoner unloading goods from a cart. The Victorian horse-drawn society presented other dangers: being thrown by a horse or run over by a cart were commonplace accidents. Other emergencies requiring hospital treatment could include a strangulated hernia, the swallowing of a foreign object or accidental poisoning.

Burns and scalds

With open fires for both cooking and heating in Victorian homes, burns were a significant danger for both children and adults. Burns, scalds or the after effects of both were a common reason for children being admitted to hospital. Treatment might include 'surgery to relieve the contraction of skin and tissues caused by the scars'.[8] No less than 142 children under the age of ten admitted to the wards of the Manchester Royal Infirmary died from burns between 1855 and 1860.[9]

Catherine Wood, the matron of The Hospital for Sick Children in Great Ormond Street from 1878–88, wrote about the best

ONE OF THE LITTLE PATIENTS
AT THE
HOSPITAL FOR SICK CHILDREN.

Sarah Coulson, a patient at the Hospital for Sick Children in London. (Museum & Archive Service, Great Ormond Street Hospital for Children NHS Trust)

treatment for burns in her book of cottage lectures which were aimed at 'peasant women in the villages of England'. She advocated careful management of the burn in the recovery period because 'some of the most painful deformities that come into our hospitals are caused by neglect of the scar whilst the burn is healing'.[10]

In May 1850, forty-two-year-old Jane Duke was admitted to the Aberdeen Royal Infirmary with burns as a result of a gunpowder accident. It is not clear how Jane's burns were caused but the length of her stay in hospital would indicate she was badly burned, or there were complications with the healing process. Jane was admitted on 24 May and was discharged on 8 August, 'cured'.[11]

Researchers at Kingston University compiled this story from the records of a Great Ormond Street patient:

> *Six-year-old Sarah Coulson lived with her widowed mother and siblings in Derby. In March 1875, she received serious burns to her chest and was still suffering the effects six months later. She was admitted to The Hospital for Sick Children in London on 16 August 1875 and stayed there for ten days, before being transferred to the hospital's convalescent home at Cromwell House 'her condition not having improved'. Sarah's recovery was slow and on 1 May 1876, after eight months of convalescence, she returned to the main hospital 'suffering from fainting fits'. After three weeks, she was again sent to Cromwell House where she remained for a further two and a half months. Although the scar tissue on her chest was still causing problems for Sarah, on 7 August, her mother asked the doctors to release her 'on account of the great distance' from her home in Derby, and they agreed. Sarah returned home, with her condition described as 'improved, but not cured'. By the time of the 1891 census, Sarah was working as a waitress, living as a lodger in the house of a smith and his family.*[12]

Accidental poisoning

Poisons were an essential part of any Victorian home medical kit and bottles containing poisonous substances were ribbed for easy identification. Despite this, accidental poisoning was quite common and it could be particularly serious for children. Three-year-old Charles Spencer was admitted to Birmingham's General Hospital on 10 March 1862 with poisoning by opium. His notes reveal he had taken the opium at 5 p.m. and was brought into the hospital at 7 p.m. 'having been previously kept awake'. He 'was allowed to go to sleep at 2.30 a.m.'. Charles was discharged thirty-six days later, fully recovered.[13]

Childhood accidents

Two brothers, Owen and Brian Gillin, of the Gorbals, Glasgow were both treated at the Glasgow Royal Infirmary in 1864. Eight-year-old Owen, whose job was putting in rivets, was admitted on 30 June 'having had his right eye burnt by a piece of a red hot rivet falling into it'.[14] His brother Brian had let the rivet fall into it. Owen's eye was completely destroyed and a water dressing was applied.

Fourteen-year-old Brian was admitted the next day with a burn to his left eyelid. When asked why he had let the rivet fall into his brother's eye, he said he had 'put the red-hot poker onto his [own] eye'. He left the hospital on 10 July while Owen was discharged on 14 August 'with his eye out'.[15]

Large-scale accidents

General hospitals in industrial districts might find themselves overstretched if an accident took place with a considerable number of casualties. This was the situation in which the staff of Birmingham's General Hospital found themselves in December 1870 when they had to deal with the aftermath of an explosion at Messrs E. & A. Ludlow, a cartridge works at Witton. The explosion killed seventeen people outright and the scene was one of complete carnage with 'Heads and limbs and fragments of clothing scattered about, and the [horrible] appearance of many of the charred and blackened survivors'.[16]

Fifty-three women and girls were taken to the hospital, of which '51 cases were seriously burnt'. In order to cope with this huge influx of in-patients, the hospital 'issued an advertisement advising holders of In-Patient Tickets that further admission of Patients must necessarily be limited'. In addition, a notice was issued that 'all ordinary Visitors to Patients except the Explosion cases would be stopped till further notice, and under instructions from Mr Goodall the Surgeon of the week … the number of visitors to the Explosion cases [were limited] in order that the latter should be disturbed as little as

Beatrice Ward – Children's Accident and Surgical Cases, The London, 1900. (*The Windsor Magazine*, December 1900)

Mellish Ward – Men's Accident and Surgical Ward, The London, 1900. (*The Windsor Magazine*)

possible.'[17] The neighbouring Queen's Hospital offered the use of twenty beds but this offer was not taken up.

It was also reported that the lodge porter 'worked day and night' and that 'Visitors of the Hospital rendered most important assistance by directing and managing the friends of the burnt patients whose visits were consistent'. In order to supplement the nursing staff, four nurses 'were kindly sent from the nursing institution and have been very valuable…'. The nurses' duties which 'under ordinary circumstances are not light' were 'painfully increased by the extreme and constant attention that cases of serious burns always require and this care and attention was zealously and willingly rendered'.[18]

At least thirty-one of the burns victims brought to the hospital died of their injuries. One month later, E. & A. Ludlow sent the hospital £500 to 'cover the expenses entailed upon the Hospital by the late calamitous accident at our works'. The company also enclosed a donation of £50 to the Temporary Building Fund. They closed their letter by saying that 'We shall ever retain a warm appreciation of the services rendered by the officers of the Institution and those under their control the knowledge of which affords us the comforting assurance that the patients had the advantage of all that human skills and care could suggest'.[19]

Chapter 17

Conditions in Hospital

In addition to the care given by nurses and physicians or surgeons, a number of other factors affected the treatment a patient received. This included the beds and furnishings of the hospital, the food prescribed and the hygiene of the building.

Furnishings

The iron-framed beds, which John Howard had recommended in the late eighteenth century to replace the wooden ones that harboured bugs, were more common in Victorian hospitals. The fillings for the bed mattresses varied from place to place but were usually flock or horsehair. However, in cases of fever, it was more convenient to fill the mattresses with chopped straw, oat-chaff or seaweed, as at the Hull General Infirmary.[1] This was because the stuffing could easily be burnt and replaced to prevent infection of the next patient. Fracture cases were usually placed on a horsehair mattress on a bed with a firm base.

Some hospitals had curtains arranged around the beds for both privacy and warmth and this was more common by the end of the nineteenth century. In the 1880s at the Radcliffe Infirmary, there were even 'bedside rugs and Windsor chairs'.[2] In many hospitals, patients were allowed to 'bring their own clothes into the wards where they have the right to keep them until they leave'.[3] Each bed usually had a locker or box in which the patients could store their personal possessions.

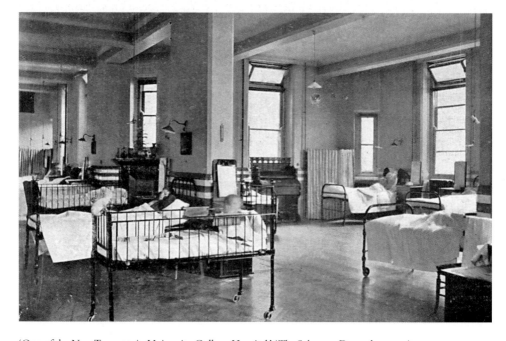

'One of the New Transepts in University College Hospital.' (*The Sphere*, 19 December 1903)

'In a Ward of the Cheyne Hospital for Children, Chelsea.' (Supplement to *The Sphere*, 16 November 1901)

Nathaniel Paine Blaker described the Sussex County Hospital in the 1850s:

> The walls of the wards were whitewashed … the floors were of deal boards with wide interspaces, and these were occasionally scrubbed… The beds were very close, with small cubic space for each. Both nurse and patients conspired to keep the windows closed, especially at night, night air being considered injurious. The smell was, consequently, sickening…[4]

There was very little other furniture for convalescent patients not confined to bed. At Birmingham's General Hospital, 'the benches in the different wards [were] found to be unfit for the use of weak patients during convalescence'. It was ordered that more suitable seats be provided, and that two or three easy chairs be put in each of the large wards.[5]

Food in hospital

The impoverished condition of a high proportion of the 'independent poor' patients meant that a liberal diet and plenty of bedrest were as valuable as the best medicine a Victorian hospital could prescribe. Groceries, food and alcohol therefore contributed greatly to the high cost of running a hospital. At the Blackburn and East Lancashire Infirmary, the Annual Report for 1871 stated that the cost of 'Butchers meat, the greatest item of regular expenditure, is exceptionally high.'[6]

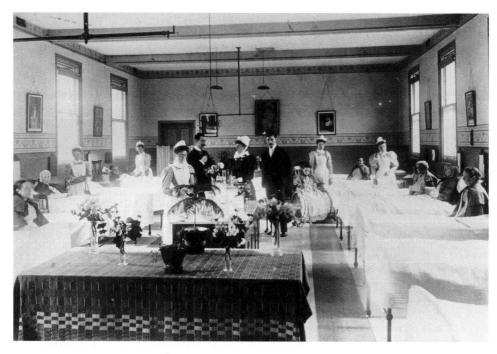

A ward scene at the Northern General Hospital, Sheffield with Matron Lawson and Dr Brander, Chief Medical Officer, in the background. (Northern General Hospital History Project, Sheffield)

On the Roof Playground at the North-Eastern Hospital for Children, Hackney Road, Bethnal Green (n.d.).

There were a number of different diets in hospital, depending on the complaint a patient was suffering from, and they differed slightly around the country.

In 1881 in Aberdeen, there was an 'ordinary diet' and a 'full diet' which was more substantial in quantity, usually with the addition of meat. Both were made up of the same ingredients: porridge with unskimmed milk, tea or milk, plus bread for both breakfast and supper. Only dinner, the midday meal, varied. On Sundays and Wednesdays, 'ordinary diet' patients were given broth, bread and cooked potatoes while those on a 'full diet' also had beef or mutton (after being boiled in the broth). On Mondays and Saturdays, Irish stew with bread was served. On Tuesdays, 'ordinary diet' patients had vegetable soup with bread and cooked potatoes while those on a 'full diet' had meat as well. Thursday was pease soup or potato soup with bread and 'full diet' patients also had stewed meat. On Fridays, milk broth or rice and milk was served with bread, plus meat for the 'full diet' patients.[7]

By contrast, in 1905 at The London, there was a bread and milk diet, diet nos 1, 2 and 3, diet no.4 for convalescents, a children's diet, a foundation diet and a milk diet. When staff from The London visited five provincial hospitals to ascertain how their cost per bed was less than their own, they discovered in particular that 'the quantities in Scotch diets are smaller than our own: fowls … are cut into five…; we cut fowls into four'. No green vegetables were given and much less milk.[8] At the Scottish hospitals, the use of large quantities of oatmeal economised the bread bill.

There was certainly a real difference in taste and customs around the country with regard to diet. One patient at a London hospital on being introduced to the Scottish diet 'cheerfully remarked that he would prefer to die on the diet to which he was accustomed than be cured on a regime of oatmeal porridge'.[9] At Birmingham's General Hospital, visitors from The London discovered that 'fish is always boiled or steamed, never fried as at The London'. They estimated that if fish was boiled at The London, they would save 36s 9d per week. However, this was not possible because 'Patients here refuse to eat boiled fish'.[10]

Patients in rural hospitals were given milk as part of their diet which was 'a rare provision in some urban hospitals'. By the same token, patients in London hospitals received more meat than elsewhere. In the 1880s, the daily diet for male patients in St Bartholomew's consisted of 'half a pound of meat, half a pound of potatoes, one ounce of butter, fourteen ounces of bread, two pints of tea and two pints of beer'.[11]

Mealtimes varied from hospital to hospital and were often set for the benefit of the staff, rather than the patients. In 1882 at Aberdeen, patients were served breakfast at 8.30 a.m., dinner at 2 p.m. (1 p.m. on Sundays) and supper at 7 p.m.[12] At around the same period in the Cardiff Royal Infirmary, breakfast for the patients was finished by 6 a.m.[13]

At the Glasgow Royal Infirmary, if a patient did not eat all of the House Allowance, the remainder had to be returned to the nurse. It was stated that any patient 'who shall give away food furnished from the Infirmary, or who shall exchange it for any article whatever, shall be expelled from the House'.[14] This must have been a difficult rule to follow if a patient knew his or her family was experiencing hunger and hardship outside the hospital.

Alcohol was generally seen to be of medicinal value and it was noted that 'the allowance of stimulants is becoming every year more liberal'.[15] In 1862, the expenses for wines and spirits at the Royal Free Hospital for 1,254 in-patients was £484 11s.[16]

Where permitted by the hospital rules, the diet could be supplemented by the patient's own supplies and with food brought in by friends and relatives. In some hospitals, patients were expected to have their own supply of tea, sugar and butter and at others, they even brought their own 'bacon, cheese, butter, bread, cakes, apples, slices of meat etc.'[17] The food and drink provided by Victorian hospitals for their patients was similar to hospitals of the eighteenth century 'except for the introduction of tea'.[18]

The liberal hospital diet did not usually extend to that provided in poor law infirmaries and the food for infirm and chronic patients there left much to be desired. The investigation by *The Lancet* into London workhouses heard 'many bitter complaints of the pea soup as causing pain and spasm in the stomach'.[19]

Hygiene in hospital

Hygiene standards in large and small hospitals differed greatly. Those smaller provincial or specialist hospitals which had been set up in unconverted private houses were far less hygienic than those in purpose-built accommodation. At one hospital it was reported that 'The beds are crowded together … the water closets are offensive and open immediately out of the wards so that in certain states of the wind the bad odour is plainly perceived in the wards'.[20] There was always a shortage of water at this hospital but the tanks were kept filled 'by the labour of prisoners on the treadmill in the adjoining jail'.[21]

Bedsores presented a huge problem to hospital staff in the 1860s and 1870s. Once a bedsore had begun, it was difficult to stop it spreading and it could quickly become infected and gangrenous. When a patient was at risk of developing bedsores, particularly if he or she was paralysed, the ideal was to be transferred to a water-bed. In the 1860s, such beds were rudimentary 'in form something like a brewer's vat'[23], nothing like the more sophisticated examples of the late nineteenth century.

Duncan Ritchie was a farm servant and underploughman at the home farm of Alexander Smollett in Bonhill, Dunbartonshire. His experience illustrates the type of case which was considered unsuitable for a voluntary hospital, and how dangerous bedsores could be to a person's health. In late August 1869, Duncan was thrown out of a cart 'in consequence of the horse having suddenly shied, and pitched on his head and shoulders, the shock apparently causing a concussion of the spine.' Following his partial paralysis, he was unable to pass urine without the aid of an instrument.[24]

He was attended by Dr Cullen of Alexandria, who strongly recommended Duncan's removal to the Glasgow Royal Infirmary to afford the best chance of his recovery and to secure regular and skilful attendance. He particularly felt that Duncan needed a water-bed which he believed would be provided at the infirmary.[25]

Although his family was reluctant that he be sent 'owing to the prejudices generally entertained by people of their class against such Institutions', Duncan was sent to the infirmary on 6 September. Following complaints from Duncan to his family that he was not being properly attended to, Alexander Smollett asked Dr Cullen to visit him at the infirmary. Before he could get there, however, Duncan had been removed to his sister's at Greenock. By this time, Duncan had a bedsore on his back described as being 'the size of a hand and in a gangrenous state'. He died a week later.[26]

The hospital denied any negligence because the House Surgeon had noted that Duncan had a bedsore on arrival in Ward 12 (Joseph Lister's ward). In fact, the hospital did not consider Duncan to be a 'fit case for a general hospital as this was not a case requiring special treatment' and requested he be removed by his family as soon as possible'.[27] Lister himself commented that the emanations from Duncan's bed were 'of a very offensive nature, calculated to be very injurious to the other patients in the ward'. He added that 'this case was one in which a cure could scarcely be looked for, and … a long lingering kind of helpless confinement to bed was really all that could be hoped for'.[28]

Both Dr Cullen and Alexander Smollett expressed their annoyance at what had happened with Smollett commenting that 'It would be quite futile for me or any other Gentleman in our neighbourhood to attempt to get any of our servants sent to the infirmary … [because] … Ritchie's case … is making a great noise in the district…'.[29]

Chapter 18

Treatment of Diseases

Before the middle of the nineteenth century, ideas about how diseases were caused were based on 'humoral' lines, attributing illness to 'imbalances of the fluids, or humours, which the Ancients believed to be the constituents of the body: black bile, yellow bile, phlegm, and blood'.[1] Treatments derived from these theories about correcting the humoral imbalances were 'almost without exception injurious to the patient'.[2]

The early medical treatments were designed to rid the body of bad humours. Popular ways of getting rid of these 'bad humours' from the body included bloodletting, sweating, vomiting, salivating, urinating and purging.

Bloodletting or bleeding

Before the 1870s, bloodletting was 'a mainstay of medical therapy' in treating fever.[3] A small folding knife called a 'lancet' was used to open a superficial vein, known medically as venesection or phlebotomy and popularly as 'breathing a vein'.[4] A more elaborate knife with multiple blades known as a 'scarificator' could also be used to cut simultaneously into the skin. Cupping was another technique used to draw blood, boils and other eruptions.[5]

Jars from a 1900s chemist. *From left to right:* Liq. Hyd. Perchl. Poison (solution of mercuric chloride), Ol. Gualther (oil of wintergreen), Inf. Gent. Co. (compound infusion of gentian), Terebenum (mixture of oil of turpentine and sulphuric acid) and Methyl. Salicyl. (oil of wintergreen). (With thanks to Gareth Edwards and Yvonne Goulding)

Bloodletting was such a common medical procedure that in 1861, Isabella Beeton in her *Book of Household Management* included instructions for undertaking one's own bleeding 'in cases of great emergency'. She also included directions on what to do if the patient fainted, for often 'the patient was supposed to be bled "until sycope", or fainting'.[6]

In the 1850s at the Sussex County Hospital, the old remedy of cupping:

> was so constantly prescribed, especially for pain in the back, that two or three out-patients were occasionally seated in chairs, in a row, and all cupped at the same time, the cupping glasses being taken off and replaced in rotation. Doctors and patients seemed to rejoice in physic, especially patients, who were not satisfied unless they had plenty, and the more uncomfortable it made them the better they were pleased.[7]

A gentler form of bleeding involved applying leeches to the skin above a supposed lesion, and 'letting the leech engorge itself with the bad blood thought to dwell below'.[8] Leeches could be placed anywhere on the body, and a protein called hirudin in their saliva prevented the body from clotting naturally and kept the blood flowing.

However, the use of leeches in hospital could prove problematic if unsupervised. On 8 February 1842, four-year-old William Kennedy was admitted to the Aberdeen Royal Infirmary for a lithotomy – the removal of a stone from his bladder. The operation was successful but the surgeon ordered 'Six leeches [to be] applied for pain in the hypogastric region, on the evening of the 6th'. However, the night nurse mistook her orders and 'persisted in the use of hot poultices over the bites until the hour of visit, 7 a.m., on the following morning, when he was blanched and almost bloodless'. William lived until the evening of the 8th but 'no means could recruit the loss'.[9]

By the 1860s, bleeding as a procedure in hospitals had started to wane and in 1862 at Birmingham's General Hospital, the cost for leeches was just 10*d* for the year.[10]

Purgatives

Physicians before the 1870s gave 'physic' or medicine, with the main aim of traditional therapeutics to open the bowels. Calomel, or mercurous chloride, was 'in every physician's bag throughout the nineteenth century' favoured for its purgative properties, and was an active ingredient in the 'blue pills' commonly used in therapeutics at the time.[11]

These traditional treatments made patients 'anaemic through bloodletting, depleting them of fluids and valuable electrolytes via the stool, and poisoning them with compounds of such heavy metals as mercury and lead'.[12]

Patients undergoing treatment for Lupus, The London (n.d.).

Traditional diagnosis

The traditional physician prescribed therapeutics based on humoral doctrines 'that totally lacked any kind of scientific basis'.[13] His physical examination of a patient was limited to feeling the pulse, looking at the tongue and observing the countenance to determine the patient's constitution. He did not usually enquire about the history of the illness the patient was suffering from and the typical consultation ended with 'the drawing up of elaborate prescriptions for laxatives'.[14]

Scientific diagnosis

By contrast, the scientifically practising physician would record a history of the present illness and perform a physical examination by pounding, listening and poking. He would then consider all the possible diseases the patient might have, based on the signs and symptoms observed. This was known as the 'differential diagnosis'. Finally, he would make a 'clinical diagnosis' by undertaking more examinations and laboratory tests to determine the disease which was most likely afflicting the patient.[15] Both the clinical investigation and the differential diagnosis were quite new and this style of scientific practice 'swept the traditional approach to primary care out the window'.[16]

'The Open-Air Galleries at Guy's.' (Supplement to *The Sphere*, 16 November 1901)

Physical examinations

Physical examinations consisted of three innovations: 'palpating the patient's abdomen, percussing his chest, and listening   at first with one's ear against the major body cavities, later using a stethoscope   to the movement of blood, gas and air within the limbs and major body cavities'.[17] These three techniques were first used by the elite physicians of the teaching hospitals in Paris during the Napoleonic years. Their use spread to other centres of medicine before 1850, finally spreading into general practice in the second half of the nineteenth century.[18]

Taking the example of a coughing patient with a blue-ish countenance who reports a history of blood-flecked sputum, it is possible to compare how traditional and scientifically practising physicians would have looked at the case. The traditional doctor might use his experience or instinct to decide the problem was 'an excess of the humour phlegm' and prescribe a laxative or purgative to rid it from the body.[19]

While at medical school, the scientifically practising physician would have studied slides of tuberculosis, pneumonia and lung cancer in a pathology class. He would therefore have known that each disease caused unique tissue changes to the lung which could be examined under a microscope.[20] From the differential diagnosis, he would identify which disease the patient was suffering from by listening to his or her chest, carrying out further tests or, after 1896, taking an X-ray. The scientific physician would then be able to give a prognosis and devise a treatment plan.[21]

The scientific doctors' better understanding of disease mechanisms and the action of drugs meant they did them no harm.[22] This strategy 'helped to prolong life' after 1860 when patients with the same diseases had died earlier in previous decades.[23] By the 1890s, even patients with chronic diseases such as tuberculosis were surviving longer.[24]

Common Victorian drugs

Illnesses treated in a medical ward of a general ward might include serious pneumonia, dyspepsia, anaemia, acute rheumatism, ague, gastric catarrh, bronchitis and laryngitis. They were treated by a range of drugs which can generally be split into the following categories: laxatives, purgatives, emetics, bitters, tonics, expectorants and narcotics or opiates.

The Infirmary, Newport
(postmarked 1907).

Laxatives to relieve the bowels included sulphur and castor oil. Purgatives, which had a more energetic effect on the bowels, included aloes, jalap, Epsom salts (sulphate of magnesia), calomel and senna.

Emetics were used to induce vomiting and were of 'inestimable value in cases of poisoning'.[25] Mustard and salt-and-water, ipecacuanha wine or white vitriol (sulphate of zinc) were useful emetics. To improve the appetite and aid digestion, bitters such as gentian, calumba, quassia and hops were given, the latter often in the form of bitter beer.

Tonics were used to 'brace up and give increased tone to the system'.[26] An example would be the prescribing of iron to treat anaemia, but preparations of bark and quinine were also frequently used. For bronchitis and coughs, expectorants were prescribed which loosened phlegm and eased the chest. Common expectorants were carbonate of ammonia, squills, ipecacuanha and tar. Narcotics or opiates induced sleep, and many could relieve pain at the same time. The most widely used was probably opium, followed by chloral hydrate.

Researchers at Kingston University have discovered a variety of drugs were used at The Hospital for Sick Children in Great Ormond Street:

> *Minute quantities of arsenic were given to patients suffering 'everything from congenital syphilis to Sydenham's chorea'. Common treatments included bleeding and purgatives, usually mercury chloride and cascara, and opiates were 'the usual recourse for patients who were required to lie still'. Castor oil and cod liver oil were regularly prescribed for most of the patients, representing a large proportion of the hospital's expenditure on drugs. In the early 1900s, the hospital helped to form a co-operative with seven other London hospitals so that all the institutions could buy castor oil and cod liver oil at cost price.[27]*
>
> *In 1887, the Medical Committee of The Hospital for Sick Children accepted an offer of £5 worth of free drugs from the pharmaceutical company Burroughs Wellcome choosing 'Fellow's Compound Syrup of Hypophosphites (a tonic), Gelsemium (a botanical product), Terebene (a multipurpose compound used as an expectorant, an antiseptic and in inhalation treatment for phthisis), Keplers Malt Extract, and Peptonizing Powders (a digestive aid)'.[28]*

One of the free drugs, Kepler's Extract of Malt and Cod Liver Oil, was described by the *Family Physician*, written by physicians and surgeons of the principal London hospitals, as 'an excellent preparation, and may be used with confidence in the treatment of consumption, scrofula, rickets, and other diseases'.[29]

The health of the nation

In the nineteenth century, epidemics of infectious diseases came and went in seemingly never-ending cycles. They were both feared and accepted as part of everyday life, and included typhus and typhoid, cholera, smallpox, measles and scarlet fever. However, by the 1880s, infectious diseases had become less significant, being replaced as the major killers of society by respiratory diseases such as tuberculosis.

Although Britain's country dwellers suffered from poverty and disease and often lived in housing better known as hovels, the population density was not as high as urban areas, making the countryside a comparatively better place in which to live. In the towns, the 'skies were black with coal smoke, their streets strewn with horse manure; in summer they were alive with flies, in winter dank with damp and fog'.[30]

Unsurprisingly, deaths from dangerous infections such as smallpox, measles, scarlet fever, whooping cough and diarrhoea were all higher in urban areas than the countryside. In 1851 half of Britain's population lived in towns but by 1901, this figure had soared to four-fifths.[31] In 1851, London was the only place in Britain with a population of more than 100,000. By 1911, there were thirty-six such places.[32]

When whole families lived together in one room, these poor living conditions were hotbeds for diseases, particularly respiratory and childhood-related. Victorian middle-class observers regularly reported 'the stench generated by unwashed people crowded together in airless rooms, in which all domestic functions – cooking, washing, sleeping, and so on – took place'.[33] Other hazards included domestic vermin behind the wallpapers and in the beds, a stifling heat from the fires used for heating and cooking, and a damp atmosphere caused by drying washing indoors.

Diarrhoea was a major killer in Victorian society, particularly in the summer months. As a horse-drawn nation, 'flies swarmed in their millions'[34] between June and October, with the inevitable contamination of food and drink. Infant diarrhoea killed thousands of babies every year.

Identification of diseases

Certified causes of death are not always an accurate indication of a why a person died. Before 1874, it was not compulsory to provide a cause of death on the death certificate in England and Wales although it had been compulsory in Scotland since the start of registration in 1855.[35] In the 1860s, around 20 per cent of recorded deaths were not certified.[36] In the 1880s, up to 7 per cent of deaths in some northern towns were certified by people who were not medically qualified.[37] By the end of the nineteenth century, it was estimated that there were still 4 per cent of certified deaths which were 'worthless for the purpose of classification'.[38]

Even for qualified doctors, many Victorian diseases proved difficult to identify. These included pulmonary tuberculosis, phthisis, bronchitis and pneumonia.[39] Many doctors were 'reluctant to admit to losing patients to puerperal fever'[40] which was the 'major single cause of maternal death'[41] in the Victorian period, so there were problems in reporting deaths in childbirth. Other internal diseases such as heart disease, cancer and 'dropsy' also proved difficult to certify. It is highly likely that deaths in elderly people attributed to 'natural causes' were actually a result of industrial or degenerative diseases.[42]

Industrial diseases

Industrial diseases have been described as 'a nineteenth-century way of life'[43] which not only affected the sufferers but also had disastrous consequences for their families. There were countless examples of diseases which only manifested themselves in specific industries. These included:

> … the notorious phossy jaw of the match industry; the grinder's lung of the Birmingham and Sheffield cutlery trades; silicosis among miners and potters; mercury poisoning in hatters, furriers and mirror-makers; anthrax among skin and fur workers; and inflated tuberculosis death rates among highly paid print workers, and among shoe and bootmakers in new, mass production factories at the turn of the century.[44]

Agricultural labourers 'whose clothes were often wet through for days on end' were frequently afflicted with bronchitis, rheumatism and general aches and pains.[45]

Lead poisoning, or plumbism, usually caused by inhaling lead dust, was a hazard of working in the white lead, pottery and enamelling industries. It could be easily identified by a pale 'bloodlessness, and the presence of a blue line along the margin of the gums, close to the teeth…'.[46] The most frequent symptom was colic. A form of acute lead poisoning could develop suddenly, and was extremely fatal. It most frequently occurred in young girls aged eighteen to twenty-four and started with a 'headache, followed, sooner or later, by convulsions and unconsciousness'.[47] Death often followed within three days, although in cases of recovery from convulsions, victims could be left completely blind.[48]

Another symptom of lead poisoning was a disturbed mind. Twenty-two-year-old enameller Emma Jones was admitted to Birmingham's General Hospital in February 1882 as an urgent case with suspected plumbism. Unfortunately for Emma, her symptoms were 'Acute Mania' which was one of the most serious side effects of lead poisoning. She was removed to the asylum a week later.[49]

Chapter 19

Surgical Cases

Before 1860, surgery was usually carried out as an emergency measure, for instance an amputation as the result of an accident or the removal of tumours when life for the patient had become unbearable.[1] This was because of the extremely high death rates caused by infections after an operation.

Hospital infections

Between the 1840s and the 1870s, patients took a considerable risk going into hospital, especially if they needed surgery. During this period, a 35 per cent post-operative death rate was usual. For an operation such as amputation at the thigh, this death rate was as high as 65 per cent. 'Hospital diseases' such as hospital gangrene, erysipelas (also known as St Anthony's Fire) and pyaemia were 'major killers'.[2] However, despite the high incidence of these diseases, shock was the main cause of death after an operation.[3]

In 1861, 42 per cent of deaths after amputations at Guy's Hospital in London were a direct result of pyaemia.[4] The name of the disease literally means 'pus in the blood', it being a form of blood poisoning caused by the spread of pus-forming bacteria in the bloodstream. The infection could spread rapidly in a hospital ward as miasmatic material could infect one patient while their emanations could infect other patients in the ward.[5] The disease had a very distinct 'sweet' smell.

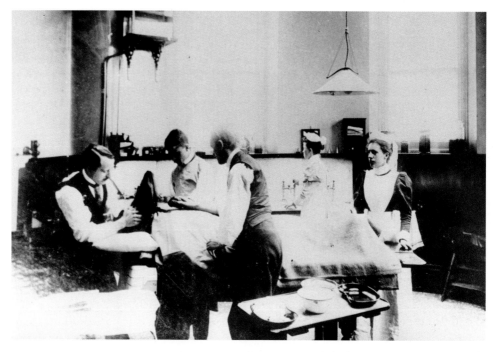

Administering an anaesthetic using an inhaler with a bag, early 1900s. (With thanks to Dr Ian Paterson, Department of Anaesthesia, Northern General Hospital, Sheffield)

Erysipelas and hospital gangrene were an ever-present threat to patients in the 1860s and 1870s. Nathaniel Paine Blaker, a surgeon at the Sussex County Hospital, recalled that in the autumn of 1864:

> … these diseases raged to such an extent that fourteen or fifteen patients, and also the head nurse, died in the male accident-ward in one week. The disease usually came on suddenly [in] …a patient with a wound…apparently going on well [who] was reported to have a rigor. This was followed by fever (there were no clinical thermo-meters in those days), restlessness, loss of appetite and perhaps vomiting. In a short time the parts round the wound became red, hot and swelled, and in a few hours gangrene commenced in a small spot and spread rapidly…[6]

A seemingly insignificant event could result in death from pyaemia. On a Saturday night in March 1864, George Milton, a fifty-two-year-old domestic servant from Glasgow, 'had his thumb seized by a drunken man who bent it back till it forced the lower end of the second phalanx through the skin & caused compound dislocation of it'. George was admitted to Glasgow's Royal Infirmary and the House Surgeon 'took off [the] lower end of bone of phalanx & replaced it'. By 14 March, erysipelas of the forearm had set in and two weeks later, the unit joint was affected with George's general health suffering. The whole of his left forearm was put up in a poultice. On 30 March, it was decided to amputate the limb below the elbow joint under the influence of chloroform. Although George 'appeared to rally a little after the operation [he] took rigor several times during the day and sank, complaining of stiffness & pain of his joints, his breath [had] a faint odour resembling that in pyaemia'. George died on 4 April, just over a month after his thumb had been injured.[7]

After a serious outbreak of erysipelas in the wards of the Cardiff Royal Infirmary, the managers temporarily reduced the number of beds from fifty-two to thirty-six, resulting in 'a considerable improvement in the sanitary condition of the wards'.[8] They also erected a detaching building in the garden containing eight beds 'constructed on the most approved plans of modern sanitary science' where infectious cases could be removed from the wards of the main hospital. The building cost upwards of £400 and, as the working men of Cardiff and the neighbourhood had already presented 'a moiety of this sum', the ward was named 'The Workmen's Ward'.[9]

Given the high death rates after operations (which through word of mouth and newspapers patients would have been aware of), it is no wonder that hospital registers record a significant number of patients refusing treatment and leaving voluntarily.

Frederick Treves, a surgeon at The London, recalled the surgical wards in the 1870s:

> The poor had a terror of it, which was not unjustified, and many an hour I spent merely trying to persuade patients to come in for treatment. Operation results were not encouraging and the general public knew it. I remember the whole of Talbot [ward] being decimated by hospital gangrene. Every man died with the exception of two who fled the building. There was only one sponge in the ward and with that deadly instrument the nurse… washed every wound in the evening using, not only the same sponge, but the same basin and the same water! … Maggots in a wound were regarded as part of the normal fauna of a hospital ward and called for no particular comment.[10]

In 1887, it was reported that a patient had escaped from the accident ward of the Cardiff Royal Infirmary through one of the lavatory windows and that this was 'the third escape of a patient in the same way'.[11] Evidently, operations were still a frightening prospect in the 1880s.

Antiseptic and aseptic techniques

It was noted that mortality rates in large city hospitals were much higher than those in small towns. Thomas Spencer Wells was a surgeon at the small specialist Samaritan Hospital in London. He reported that hospital mortality rates in the small towns of Oxford, Exeter and Cambridge were around 13 to 16 per cent while London figures for amputations were about 50 per cent.[12]

Various measures were adopted in an attempt to address the spiralling mortality rates in hospitals. They included the 'long-established practice' of white-washing walls, removing privies from wards, separating medical and surgical patients, building new wards to allow more cubic space per patient, instigating new ventilation systems, and 'attempting to prevent contaminated air entering the wards'.[13] Wards and beds were disinfected with chemicals such as carbolic acid. At this time, any substance which banished 'infection' could be termed a 'dis-infectant'.[14]

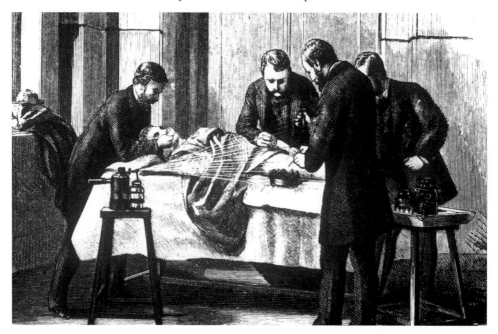

Professor Joseph Lister undertaking surgery in the 1860s with his carbolic spray in use. (NHS Greater Glasgow and Clyde Archives)

Antiseptics were not a new phenomenon. Wounds had been treated with wine and vinegar for centuries and a number of different post-operative and post-accident dressings were used to 'actively assist nature's healing powers'[15], including nitric acid, arsenic and tincture of iodine. Cleanliness was greatly emphasised in hospital management and in the treatment of wounds.[16]

While working as a surgeon at the Glasgow Royal Infirmary, Joseph Lister put forward his theory of antisepsis. He concurred with Louis Pasteur's view that germs were airborne, carried on dust particles, and that they could be removed from the air 'by filtration, heat or other means'. Lister decided to use carbolic acid as a 'filter between the air and open wounds' after hearing of its effectiveness in disinfecting sewage in Carlisle. Carbolic acid was already being used as a disinfectant in hospitals.[17]

On 12 August 1865, Lister undertook his first trial of carbolic acid on eleven-year-old James Greenlees, whose left leg had been run over by a cart. Lister 'dressed a compound fracture of the tibia with lint soaked in linseed oil and carbolic acid, and kept the dressing in place for four days. The wound healed perfectly and a healthy James walked out of the Infirmary six weeks later'.[18]

In 1867, Lister wrote about his antiseptic methods in *The Lancet*, insisting that 'germs caused infections and that infection and pus-formation were not inevitable, still less beneficial, stages in wound healing'.[19] However, most surgeons saw antisepsis as being simply 'a new type of wound dressing which involved the use of carbolic acid'.[20] Some surgeons accepted Lister's concept of antisepsis based on the germ theory, but 'most adopted only parts of it'.[21]

Lister's use of carbolic acid was not new and his method was 'difficult, cumbersome and time-consuming'.[22] The dressing of wounds was normally left to dressers or house-surgeons, but Lister's method 'seemed to demand that surgeons themselves be responsible for after-treatment'.[23] Other surgeons had already developed effective means of combating sepsis which were 'much more suited to a busy surgeon's practice'.[24]

In the 1870s, George Callender, a surgeon at St Bartholomew's Hospital, developed methods of cleanliness as an alternative to antisepsis, supplemented 'with the use of a camel hair brush to clean the wound'.[25] After an operation, the wound was 'carefully dressed, to exclude dirt, and the patient was isolated, to avoid contact with other diseased individuals'. If the operation had involved amputation, Callender implanted a rubber tube in the stump 'to collect and channel away pus'. Cotton wool bandages were used 'to protect the wound and to help it maintain warmth', small amounts of carbolic lotion were used to wash it, and carbolised oil to bathe it after operation.[26]

Out of 200 operations undertaken in August 1873 using Callender's method, there was evidence of recovery 'in all but six cases'. Callender's mortality rate was therefore 3 per cent, compared with Lister's published figures of 15 per cent.[27]

By 1871, Lister, now a surgeon at the Edinburgh Royal Infirmary, had introduced the carbolic acid spray and gauze elements of his method.[28] Nathaniel Blaker recalled his experience of using Lister's carbolic spray:

> I recollect well the ridicule and difficulty I met with when I first used this new antiseptic method at the Hospital. Although, at that time, our apparatus was very imperfect … I soon found that … wounds healed more rapidly and with less pain and constitutional disturbance than under the old treatment.[29]

The carbolic spray provided a 'partial solution' to deadly hospital infections. However, it was not widely used until the late 1870s and it did not kill air-borne micro-organisms. It also could not compensate for 'inadequate hygiene procedures, exemplified in the surgeon's operating coat'.[30]

Although Lister religiously used his antisepsis techniques, he 'did not scrub his hands, but merely rinsed them in carbolic solution [and] he operated in his street clothes'.[31] He introduced significant changes such as sutures made of catgut which could gradually be absorbed, but Lister's own surgery was 'mostly limited to bones, joints, superficial tumours, and deep abscesses'.[32]

Lister's antiseptic theories were more widely accepted after 1877 when he became Professor of Clinical Surgery at King's College, London. He continued to adapt his methods, abandoning the spray in 1887, 'publicly ruing that he had ever recommended it'.[33] By the 1890s, 'cleanliness and the germ theory were merged into the theory and practice of asepsis'[34], in a bid to exclude germs from the wards and operating theatres.

Anaesthetics

Before the introduction of anaesthetics in the 1840s, long operations or those 'demanding great precision' were impossible.[35] At this time, standard surgical work included 'dressing wounds, drawing teeth, treating syphilitic chancres and sores … lancing boils [and] trussing-up ruptures'.[36]

In 1772, nitrous oxide was first prepared by Joseph Priestley. Its suitability for use for surgery was recognised by Humphry Davy in 1800 because it was 'capable of destroying physical pain.'[37] It was discovered that if nitrous oxide and ether was inhaled, it produced 'lightheadedness and a sense of hilarity and euphoria'.[38]

Sir William Macewen (with beard to the left of the patient) in the operating theatre at the Glasgow Royal Infirmary, 1892. Mrs Rebecca Strong, matron, is on the far right. (NHS Greater Glasgow and Clyde Archives)

The first use of ether as an anaesthetic took place in New York in January 1842 when a practitioner named William E. Clarke extracted a tooth while his patient was unconscious under ether.[39]

Four years later, two public operations took place on patients anesthetised with ether. The first was at Massachusetts General Hospital on 16 October and the second at University College Hospital in London on 21 December. The latter operation was performed by Robert Liston, a top London surgeon 'renowned for his speed'. He amputated a diseased thigh while his patient was unconscious under ether, calling the anaesthetic method a 'Yankee dodge'.[40] Both these operations provided proof of the possibility of 'painless surgery'.[41]

Chloroform quickly became known as a better alternative to ether as it was considered to be a safer drug. On 19 January 1847, James Young Simpson of Edinburgh used it for the first time to 'allay labour pains' in a patient. Six years later, Queen Victoria publicly endorsed chloroform when she made use of the drug during the birth of Prince Leopold on 7 April 1853.[42]

From 1850, anaesthetics were used to provide pain relief during operations, at the same time 'extending the range and constructive aspects of surgery'.[43] Effective anaesthetics made 'otherwise unbearably traumatic internal operations feasible'.[44]

Operating procedures

By the 1880s, the bacteria which caused surgical infections were identified and were known to be 'vulnerable to antiseptic agents' like carbolic.[45] From this time onwards, hospitals strove for absolute cleanliness to prevent the occurrence of such infections. This included the medical and surgical instruments.

Louis Pasteur had suggested the benefits of placing medical instruments in boiling water and passing them through a flame as early as 1874. This became a common method of sterilisation. Robert Koch advocated the heat sterilisation of instruments in 1881[46] but this method was not widely used until the 1890s.[47]

Hugh Lett, a medical student at The London in 1896, described the procedures undertaken before surgery:

> Instruments and ligatures were boiled and placed in a tray of carbolic lotion, and before long on a sterile towel, and handed to the surgeon… Rubber gloves were still unknown, the preparation of the surgeon's hands [were] therefore formidable; prolonged scrubbing with soap and Lysol, followed by soaking in carbolic lotion, and finally immersion for some minutes in a solution of biniodide of mercury in spirit. Further, during the operation the surgeon frequently dipped his hands into a solution of carbolic.[48]

The essentials to create a sterile operating environment including rubber gloves for the surgeons, gauze face masks and the sterilising of instruments were not generally used until after 1900.[49] It was the American surgeon William S. Halsted, of the John Hopkins Hospital, who introduced the use of rubber gloves in 1890. Ironically, this innovation was not intended to protect the patient but the operating-room nurse, his fiancée, whose hands were allergic to antiseptics.[50]

By the end of the nineteenth century, The London had adopted a method of conducting serious operations with 'homeliness and humaneness and gentle courtesy':

> The patient is first taken into a little anteroom, where no knives or instruments are visible, and where three or four persons are present. Here he is given the anaesthetic, not until he is quite unconscious is he wheeled into the operating theatre. During the operation the whole of his person, except the part which comes under the knife, is kept covered. The operation over, the patient is taken away and put back in bed before he recovers consciousness. He does not even see the nerve-shaking surgical instruments.[51]

Types of surgery

Before 1860, common surgical procedures included the removal of abscesses, cutting for bladder stones, amputations as a result of compound fractures or crushed limbs, the setting of simple fractures and occasional operations to remove mammary tumours or to treat strangulated hernias. After 1860, surgery became 'increasingly constructive'[52] but it was not until the 1880s that advanced antiseptic surgery and well-equipped, sterile operating theatres helped transform the hospital 'from a refuge for the indigent into a machine for curing, the saviour of the seriously ill'.[53]

In the 1860s, ovariotomies were considered an extremely risky surgical procedure but Nathaniel Paine Blaker, a surgeon at the Sussex County Hospital, explained why patients subjected themselves to the operation:

> The position of a woman, the subject of ovarian disease, in those days was terrible. After a painful illness of a year, or, at most, two, with all the miseries of dropsy, relieved perhaps from time to time by tapping, in those days a somewhat dangerous operation, she could only look forward to a fatal termination. It is not surprising, under these circumstances, that she should take the risk of an operation that would restore her to health, though that risk might be great.[54]

By the 1880s, the procedure was considerably safer.

In 1882, excision of the gall bladder (cholecystectomy) was introduced and the removal of gallstones became a common surgical procedure. At about the same time, prostate operations and surgery on the small intestine, especially for cancer, was begun. The pneumothorax technique (the surgical collapsing of the lung to rest it) was used for a time as a form of treatment for tuberculosis. A royal endorsement for surgery was given in 1902 when Edward VII had an appendectomy after his appendix erupted just before his coronation.[55]

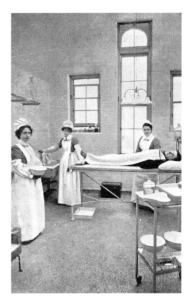

'In the Operating Room at the City Orthopaedic Hospital.' (Supplement to *The Sphere*, 16 November 1901)

Hernias were an extremely common condition among the working classes and were 'a significant cause of nineteenth-century pauperism'.[56] They were treated by the wearing of a truss which was prescribed as a surgical aid by the out-patient department of hospitals. After 1870, hernias began to be treated surgically. Between 1877 and 1893, only 2 per cent of Joseph Lister's operations were hernia repairs. Hernia operations became increasingly common and they constituted almost 12 per cent of Watson Cheyne's between 1902 and 1912.[57]

In the 1880s, an increasing number of surgical procedures were undertaken to improve the quality of life for patients, including osteotomies for children which involved the cutting of bone to correct deformities usually caused by rickets. The intense smoke pollution in British cities resulted in rickets for 'almost all urban children'.[58] This was because their bodies were not exposed to sufficient sunlight, essential as a stimulant for the skin to release calciferol, without which the body cannot synthesise its own vitamin D. In London in the 1840s, John Snow noted the presence of rickets in all social classes and in 1884, every child examined on Clydeside had the disease.[59]

Three-year-old Sarah Ellen Steer was admitted to Birmingham's General Hospital from Nuneaton for treatment for 'genu valgum' (knock-knees) which were probably caused by rickets. She was the daughter of Joseph and Emma Steer, who both worked in the cotton spinning industry. Sarah Ellen was admitted to the hospital on 29 November 1879, recommended by a private subscriber named Isaac Freer. Osteotomies were usually straightforward but there must have been complications in Sarah Ellen's case. Her admission ticket was renewed a further three times as recommended by the Loyd Haward Lodge, Tradesmens Hope and the Nelson Lodge. Her case notes have not survived to give any details but Sarah Ellen was finally discharged 'cured' on 18 May, almost six months after her admission.[60]

A similar procedure for four-year-old Alice Clarke resulted in a more usual recovery period. She was admitted to the hospital on 24 May 1881 and was dismissed on 23 July 'cured'.[61]

The invention of artery clamps to replace internal ligatures and the increased use of antiseptic and aseptic techniques 'helped to transform the range, and improve the effectiveness, of surgery' by the end of the nineteenth century.[62]

By 1900, surgery was increasingly used to improve the quality of life for patients.[63] It was no longer necessary to amputate if a patient had a compound fracture, and diseased joints 'could be excised rather than removed'.[64]

The hospital became the favoured place for surgery. According to an article in the *British Medical Journal* from 1903: 'In these days of elaborate asepsis it must be recognised that almost no ordinary dwelling-house can provide the environment that is considered necessary for the achievement of the best surgical results'.[65] The author noted a 'growing disinclination on the part of surgeons to operate in private houses'.[66]

Chapter 20

Medical Innovations

By 1860, physicians and surgeons had a 'medical view of the body as comprising identifiable structures and organs which were affected by disease'.[1] This was brought about by the invention of the microscope and developments in pathological anatomy.[2]

The microscope

Although the microscope was used in university medicine from the 1840s to examine tissue taken at autopsy, it was a valuable tool to help the typical family doctor to study specimens. He could use it to study 'blood samples taken from patients to determine if they were anaemic and to judge from the size and shape of the red blood cells the kind of anaemia'.[3] It could also be used to examine urine specimens for 'evidence of pus to see if, say, an infection of the urinary tract were causing that deep pelvic pain'.[4] Another possible use was in finding the bacteria of pneumonia, tuberculosis or bronchitis in sputum samples.[5]

The stethoscope

The stethoscope was invented by René Laennec in 1819. By 1823, he was able to distinguish between a number of different respiratory diseases, including bronchitis, pneumonia, pleurisy and emphysema.[6] Stethoscopes were not in general use until the second half of the nineteenth century, so before then physicians used their well-honed aural skills to listen to the hearts and lungs of patients.

The thermometer

The thermometer was first introduced into clinical medicine in about 1850 by the Berlin physician Ludwig Traubbe. However, it was not until 1867 that Thomas Clifford Allbutt, a distinguished Leeds physician who later became the Regius Professor of Medicine at Cambridge, 'initiated its use in England'.[7]

A year later, Carl Wunderlich's manual of thermometry was published. This valuable source instructed the physician in using the thermometer to distinguish between different febrile diseases.[8]

Identification of diseases and their causes

The early to mid-nineteenth century onwards was a time of great discovery in the field of medicine. The diagnostic differences between typhoid and typhus were demonstrated by William Gerhard in America and William Jenner in London (in 1837 and 1849 respectively).[9] The physicians Thomas Hodgkin, James Parkinson, Thomas Addison and William Bright described the diseases which were named after them.[10]

Through meticulous epidemiological observations, John Snow was able to identify the water-borne nature of cholera epidemics. William Budd used the same methods to identify typhoid epidemics as water-borne.[11] The connection between diabetes and glucose was established by Claude Bernard through physiological studies of digestion. In the 1870s, David Ferrier undertook important work on the function of the brain which led to the first successful removal of a brain tumour in 1879.[12]

In 1864 Louis Pasteur put forward his germ theory of disease, rejecting the idea that 'diseases were able to generate spontaneously given the right circumstances'.[13] By 1880, Robert Koch had discovered specific disease-causing organisms,[14] including the tuberculosis bacillus two years later. The successful

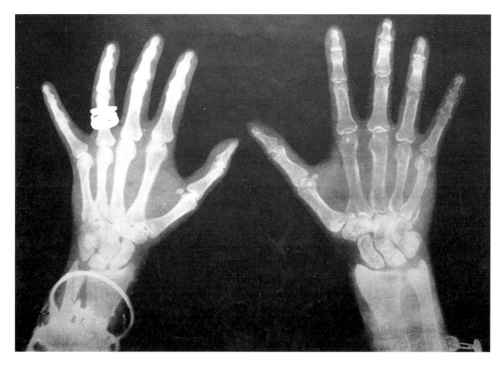

'Royal Hands by Röntgen Rays.' (Supplement to *The Illustrated London News*, 18 July 1896)

identification of specific germs or bacilli was important because it led to earlier diagnosis of diseases and to isolation procedures which helped to prevent diseases from spreading.

An antitoxin for diphtheria

One of the great Victorian child killers, diphtheria gets its name from the Greek for membrane. The bacillus or germ attacks the throat, nose or windpipe and produces a white or grey membrane 'from which poison is absorbed into the blood and carried to all parts of the body'.[15] The diphtheria bacillus preferred damp conditions so exposure to sewer gas from bad drains in the house, or to foggy or damp weather could put a person at risk of infection.

A child could become infected directly from a person already infected with the disease or indirectly through infected clothing, books, dust, milk or domestic pets such as cats. The disease was endemic in 'major towns and cities where damp and overcrowding … were held to be causes…'[16] To compound the problem, there were diagnostic difficulties in distinguishing diphtheria from throat infections like croup, thrush and quinsy, and also from scarlet fever and measles.'[17]

During an attack of diphtheria:

> … paroxysms occur in which the child springs up and fights for breath. In such attacks the colour of the child changes to a dusky blue, the eyes start nearly out of the head, the hands clutch the rails of the cot, until air is drawn into the lungs with a long hissing inspiration and the child sinks down relieved temporarily but exhausted. The frequent occurrence of such attacks rapidly exhausts a child and makes tracheotomy necessary.[18]

The bacillus which caused diphtheria was finally isolated in 1883 by Edwin Klebs and an antitoxin was developed in 1890 by Emil Behring and Shibasaburo Kitasato. This was developed further by Robert Koch in 1891 and, a year later, the first commercial vaccines against diphtheria began to be produced. Horses were used 'as experimental animals' for producing the blood serum needed for the antitoxin.[19]

This antitoxin was one of the first 'wonder drugs' of the nineteenth century. For the first time, 'medicine was truly capable of curing an infectious disease that threatened the children of every home in the nation'.[20]

Alfred Schofield, a physician with an upper-middle-class practice in London, described the first case of diphtheria he encountered after the antitoxin had arrived 'obtained from certain horses kept near Harrow for the purpose':

> I found the boy very ill, the whole back of his throat being like white velvet. I had never used the new remedy before, but determined to try it to save the boy's life. I injected a small quantity under the skin of the stomach and watched the throat. I can only compare the marvellous result to the disappearance of snow beneath a hot sun. After the second dose every trace of the membrane disappeared, and the boy soon recovered.[21]

Before the antitoxin was produced, if a child was brought to hospital with diphtheria, a tracheotomy was usually performed. In the 1890s at The London, it was reported that:

> … there has been much pressure on the Hospital owing to the number of diphtheria cases which have been brought to it… So many children are brought here who are already suffering so much that it is impossible to send them away to a fever hospital, and immediate relief has to be given in most instances by performing tracheotomy. Diphtheria antitoxin has…been used with success, and it is felt that many of these small patients may have been saved thereby…[22]

Before 1914, medicine was concerned with 'managing diseases rather than curing them'.[23] In the 1880s, effective antipyretics and analgesics became available. However, the introduction of antitoxin therapy for diphtheria in 1894–95 and Salvarsan as a treatment for syphilis in 1910, were the 'only results of any immediate clinical importance'.[24]

Analgesics

Analgesics such as opium, hashish, alcohol and ether have been used for centuries. In the nineteenth century, alkaloids of opium were introduced as alternative painkillers to raw opium, which was less concentrated. In 1855, Alexander Wood used a hypodermic needle to inject morphine into the bloodstream. This was a much safer way to administer pain relief as it bypassed the stomach. Injectable opioids were highly addictive and the old family doctors 'gave morphine at the drop of a hat…'.[25]

Chloral hydrate, made by adding water to chloral, came into medical use in 1869. It was known popularly as a 'Mickey Finn' and was a mild sedative which aided sleep. Unfortunately, it started to 'lose its efficacy after about the third night'. This powerful drug was potentially addictive and chloral addicts 'were a familiar sight in late nineteenth-century private nervous clinics'. One such addict was the poet Dante Gabriel Rossetti whose addiction to chloral led to a nervous breakdown.[26]

In 1899, at the very end of the nineteenth century, aspirin was introduced and became 'the most immensely successful domestic painkiller of all time'.[27]

X-rays

In 1895, William Röntgen, the German physicist, discovered that 'by passing a high voltage through a vacuum tube (perfected by the English scientist William Crookes), he could generate electromagnetic vibrations capable of penetrating human flesh and leaving an imprint on a photographic plate on the other side'.[28] On 22 December 1895, he made a photograph of the bones in his wife's hand using these 'Röntgen rays'. The potential for diagnostic use in medicine was instantly recognised.[29]

X-rays were invaluable in differentiating between potential diagnoses where physical examination pointed to a number of possible diseases. For instance, when percussion had indicated an area of dullness in the chest, an X-ray could determine if the problem was 'an aneurysm (or bulging) of the aorta – a typical late consequence of syphilis, a tumour or tuberculosis'. All three diseases create areas of dullness in the chest but the X-ray 'would show exactly what was at fault'.[30]

X-ray equipment was introduced to Britain from 1896 and was quickly implemented. However, updating the X-ray appliances and training the technicians was vital to gain a quick and accurate diagnosis.[31]

Soon after Röntgen's discovery, The London advertised for a medical officer to take charge of an electrical department. Dr Hedley was appointed, and was able to get his electrical power from an

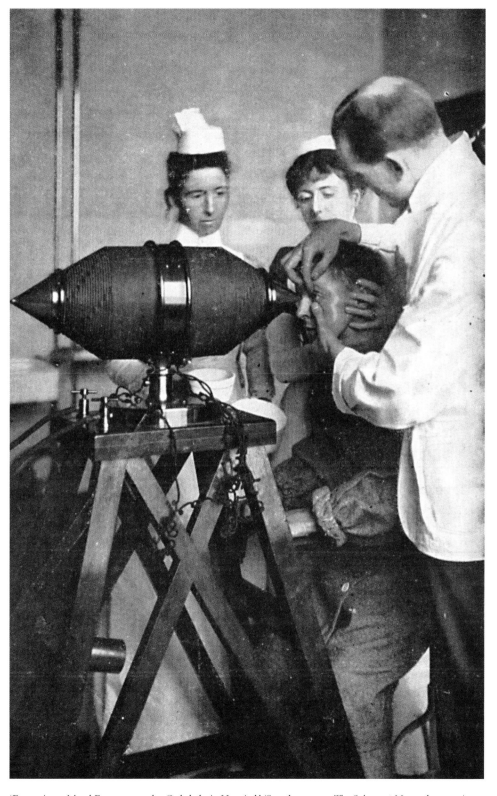

'Extracting a Metal Fragment at the Ophthalmic Hospital.' (Supplement to *The Sphere*, 16 November 1901)

The Infirmary, Cardiff (no postmark).

accumulator charged at the 'People's Palace'. This was because the hospital did not have an electrical supply as it was still lit by non-incandescent gas.[32] There was also only a small hut in the garden for X-ray work.[33]

Hugh Lett, a medical student at The London, recalled that the first X-ray technicians 'suffered seriously from X-ray burns, and both ultimately died of carcinoma', one of them 'only after both his arms had been amputated'. X-ray work was extremely dangerous and two other technicians at The London died of X-ray carcinoma before the danger was fully appreciated.[34]

The apparatus for X-rays was costly and some hospitals had to wait for a generous benefactor to provide it for them. In 1901, a 'Röntgen Ray Apparatus' was presented to the Scarborough Hospital and Dispensary by Mrs Steble, the widow of Lieutenant-Colonel Steble JP who had been president of the hospital in 1888.[35] The hospital made the apparatus available to general practitioners in the district for a fee of 10s 6d 'for a minor part, such as Hand, Foot, Forearm or Leg, for a larger Radiograph £1-1-0d.'[36]

Medical innovations meant nothing if hospitals could not afford to implement them. In the 1890s, The London, the largest hospital in Britain, had no clinical laboratory, no proper out-patient department, no adequate facilities for isolating infectious cases and no electric power anywhere in the whole building. As late as 1896, there was just one antiquated operating theatre '…in which stood a wooden table with two hinged flaps at the lower end. These could be lowered for amputations. Under it was a large tray filled with sawdust.'[37]

Chapter 21

Discharge from Hospital

If a patient was still in hospital after six weeks, he or she was either discharged or, in certain circumstances, if it was felt that hospital treatment could still be beneficial, a ticket was renewed.

Some patients were discharged 'cured' and 'relieved', others 'unrelieved' which meant that treatment had not worked or that their condition was too chronic to bring about a cure. Where a hospital had an arrangement with a convalescent home or had their own facility, patients might be discharged to convalesce at these institutions for a further period of time.

Financial effects of illness

Like the poor law infirmaries, voluntary hospitals provided a valuable form of social service to those surviving on the breadline. When a patient was admitted into hospital, he or she had usually been suffering from illness for some time and had been unable to work. This had a devastating effect on the patient's family, particularly if the patient was male and was the main breadwinner.

In many cases, clothing and the tools of the trade relating to an occupation had been pawned before going into hospital in an attempt to feed the family. Unless there were other family members willing to provide help or support, the patient's family would be forced to apply for poor relief while he or she was in hospital.

The problems did not stop once a patient was discharged from hospital. The patient could be trapped in a vicious circle, not being fully recovered from illness but needing to work as soon as possible. Many patients, especially those with respiratory diseases, had multiple stays in hospital as a result of going back to work too soon. If occupational tools had been pawned, the patient did not have the means to buy them back or to get work without them.

Charity for discharged patients

Both general and specialist voluntary hospitals began to recognise the need for some form of charity to be distributed when impoverished patients were discharged. The Samaritan Fund or Society was set up by individual hospitals to fulfil this objective. The very first Samaritan Society was set up in 1791 by William Blizard, a surgeon at The London. After being discharged from hospital, the Society aimed to send patients 'to convalesce at the sea or in the country, giving them necessary surgical appliances, or making grants of clothes or money'.[1]

In London, other hospitals followed suit, setting up their own Samaritan Societies. This happened at St Thomas's in 1852, the University College Hospital in 1867 and St Mark's Hospital in 1868.[2]

Birmingham's General Hospital also set up its own Samaritan Fund and its Annual Report for 1884 explained why:

> Domestic servants, artisans and labourers (some of whom come from a distant part of the country) through illness have been obliged to quit their places to go into the Hospital; and when discharged, perhaps only in a state of convalescence, have frequently neither a friend to receive them, nor place where to lay their head securely, till they can be re-instated in service or employment.[3]

The Samaritan Fund at Birmingham was established 'for the relief of such patients, who, on leaving the Hospital after sickness or accident, are totally without the means of paying their fare home, or of obtaining lodging, clothing or food'.[4]

Addenbrooke's Hospital, Cambridge (postmarked 1909).

The General Hospital, Birmingham (postmarked 1906).

The Report pointed out that:

> Many who, previously to their admission, have expended their last farthing, and in many instances pawned or sold their clothing, or contracted debts to support themselves and obtain medical advice, on leaving the Hospital are, under such circumstances, afforded assistance without which they would be rendered incapable of obtaining situations.[5]

It was the physicians and surgeons who 'upon being satisfied as to the real necessities of such persons' had the power to grant certificates for small sums of money. The Fund was supported by donations and small subscriptions of 5s each and upwards. Charity boxes were placed in the wards and the out-patient department 'for contributions from the patients themselves, whose feelings of gratitude towards an Institution which has rendered them such valuable benefit cannot be better evinced'.[6]

In 1882 at the Aberdeen Royal Infirmary, money from the Samaritan Fund was applied for through the superintendent and the head nurse. It was given principally to poor female patients when they left the infirmary 'to enable them to obtain articles of necessary clothing, shoes, meat, tea, &c; payment of a railway fare being occasionally made when the invalid's home is at a distance'.[7] Between £15 and £20 was distributed in this way per annum.

At the Cardiff Royal Infirmary, the relief provided by the Samaritan Fund consisted of part or whole payments for surgical appliances, spectacles etc., recommendations to convalescent homes and payment for the journey home to those who could not afford it. In 1898, twenty-eight patients were assisted by the Fund, 'of whom 16 were sent to Convalescent Homes and 12 were supplied with surgical appliances'.[8]

The Samaritan Society at St Mark's Hospital in London had a much wider remit than many hospitals. It would assist in paying the rent and '…otherwise endeavour to relieve the families of those poor men who during…their sojourn in the Hospital and subsequently, whilst recovering from their serious illness at home, are quite unable to provide for the adequate support of their wives and children.' In addition, it paid for the care of children whose mothers were in-patients, replaced occupational tools which had been pawned, sent needy patients to the seaside, provided Bibles for those without, and tea and sugar to those who could not provide it for themselves.[9]

Other hospitals operated their own form of discharge fund, often organised through a ladies' society. At the Glasgow Royal Infirmary, the ladies of the Dorcas Society attended the patients weekly to read, sing and distribute flowers. They were also responsible for 'investigating the claims of the poorer patients on leaving the Hospital, and supplying them with clothing and otherwise attending to their wants.'[10]

Comparison between hospital and home

Given the poverty-stricken backgrounds many Victorian patients came from, it is no wonder that some patients were reluctant to leave. At The London, the children's wards were 'brightest of all, with … innumerable toys, great rocking-horses and games galore [with] coloured windows and illuminated walls'. It was reported that 'many a tot cries when it is time to go back home to the miserable, overcrowded, single-room slum dwelling, away from the toys, the cleanliness and constant kindness that have made its days of pain seem like a glimpse of Paradise'.[11]

A visitor to The London was told of the case of a young newspaper seller, 'a ragged little urchin who had a strong belief in the superstition that misfortune comes on those who pass under a ladder'. He walked into the road to avoid a ladder against a house, was run over by a hansom and brought to the hospital. On leaving, one of the nurses commented on his superstition saying, 'See what happened to you by not passing under the ladder'. The boy replied:

> Yuss, miss. Blimy, wasn't it jolly lucky as I went out into the road instead of goin' under that ladder? Why, if I hadn't gone on the road, I'd never have been run over, and come to this nice place, and had enough to eat, and all of you lookin' after me as though I was the Prince o' Wales. I *am* glad I went out in the road.[12]

Chapter 22

Admission to Asylums

Anyone found unable to manage their own affairs independently could be deemed to be mentally ill, and had to be looked after in an asylum, workhouse or private madhouse. Under the terms of the 1774 Madhouses Act, a person had to be medically certified before being admitted to an asylum, although this did not include paupers. However, as paupers came under the remit of the parish before 1834, and the union afterwards, it is highly unlikely that a pauper would have been sent to an asylum without being medically certified. Part of the workhouse medical officer's role was to assess all those of unsound mind, and the high cost of asylum care meant that only very serious, dangerous cases were sent, while the remainder stayed in the workhouse. By 1890, the signatures of two doctors were required, and this included paupers.

Who was admitted?

With the increasing number of people diagnosed as insane, asylum inmates were made up of acute cases, capable of being cured, and chronic cases, for whom the prognosis was bleak. For the latter, asylums became a last resort. Chronic patients included 'the senile and the demented, along with epileptics, paralytics, sufferers from tertiary syphilis, ataxias, and neurological disorders'.[1] In addition, magistrates were encouraged to send difficult recurrent, offenders from the workhouse or jail to an asylum.

For the senile elderly, the asylum could easily become their last home. In its Annual Report of 1875, the administrators of the Somerset County Pauper Lunatic Asylum argued that 'It is cruel to send persons whose insanity is nothing but the natural decay of age, to die in the Asylum'. In that year, patients had

The Denbigh Asylum (postmarked 1909).

been admitted 'at the patriarchal ages of 83, 88 and 94 years of age, some certified even in this their day of dotage, as "dangerous to others".'[2]

Acute cases might include forms of depression (labelled as melancholia). Many such cases were linked with poverty: the worry and stress involved in struggling to feed a large family when times were hard.

Asylum patients were bathed on arrival, and a detailed record was made of their medical and physical condition. At the Duddeston Asylum, when pauper patients were admitted, they were to be 'stripped and washed, and it is to be carefully observed if there be any swelling in any part of the body, vermin, or spots on the skin; the hair is to be cut close and combed, and the patient is then to be clothed in the asylum dress.'[3]

Care for lunatics in Wales

In Wales, it was a common practice to board out idiots and lunatics with relatives, or with another person, usually a peasant or small farmer, who would look after them in return for a weekly allowance. This 'well established system of community care' was known as 'farming out'.[4]

When the Lunacy Commissioners produced their Report in 1844, there was no asylum in South Wales. The Commissioners suggested that 'some parents in Wales were unwilling to educate their children' and presented them as imbeciles to claim parish allowance for them. At the time, there were 'no less than 1177 pauper lunatics' in Wales.[5]

It is believed that Llewelyn Bevan was being 'farmed out' with his maternal uncle at Nantmoel Uchaf farm on the Baran mountain at the time of the 1861 census. Llewelyn was described as being an unmarried, thirty-seven-year-old land proprietor. As the eldest son, it is likely he inherited the proceeds from the sale of Nant-y-gaseg farm when his father died in 1857.

This 'farming out' arrangement did not last long as he became a patient at the Vernon House Asylum at Briton Ferry near Swansea in around February 1862. This private lunatic asylum was licensed to take both pauper and private patients, but in 1858 there were 183 pauper patients and only twenty-six private patients. Vernon House was one of the licensed asylums in the area to which the local poor law unions could send their pauper lunatics, as there was no county lunatic asylum at that time. It is not known whether Llewelyn was classed as a pauper at this stage, given his inheritance. Even if he was a private patient, it is likely that his funds would have rapidly dwindled to pay for his fees at the asylum.

When the Glamorgan County Lunatic Asylum at Angelton near Bridgend finally opened on 4 November 1864, Llewelyn was the third patient to be admitted that day. He had been transferred there from the Vernon House Asylum, which would indicate that Llewelyn was now a pauper and chargeable to the union. He had been deemed to be insane for seven years prior to his admission to Vernon House.

On arrival at the Angelton Asylum, Llewelyn was described as having '…a listless and apathetic manner and a confused and vacant look: answers questions with difficulty or not at all.' However, when he was focused, Llewelyn appeared 'intelligent and rational', leading to speculation that 'his more usual listless state was a form of perversion – under his control.' No possible cause was attributed to his condition, but he was not epileptic or suicidal and was in good bodily health. Although he had been occasionally violent at home, at the asylum he was 'quiet and sullen'. He often had to be reminded to eat his food. Llewelyn was generally considered to be lazy, although he enjoyed his daily work in the garden.

Over the years there was little change in Llewelyn's condition, but on 2 April 1866, after striking another patient with a chamber pot, he was moved to a separate room to sleep alone. In 1882, he struck a Mr Davies, which was noted in his report as being his 'first outburst for years'. On 12 October 1903, it was noted that 'He has been failing for some time, refusing his food and gradually becoming weaker. He slowly sank and at 8.40 p.m. today he died.'

Llewelyn had spent forty-one years in the care of asylums. A post-mortem revealed that he had died of senile decay, an unsurprising conclusion given the fact he was eighty years old. Unlike other pauper lunatics, he was not destined to be buried in a pauper cemetery. His body was returned to Nantmoel, his place of residence before entering the asylum, where he was buried in the Baran Chapel cemetery with his parents and brother.[6]

Admission to Scottish asylums

The rules in Scotland regarding the mentally ill were more liberal than those in England and Wales, because they allowed for voluntary admission to asylums and for the boarding out of lunatics.[7] On the first three occasions that Christian Watt, a fishwife, was admitted to the Aberdeen Asylum, she went as a voluntary patient for a 'rest', as recommended by her doctor. She was not certified as insane until she had had a complete mental breakdown.[8]

Lunatics in workhouses

In 1884, after an attack by a supposedly harmless patient on a female attendant, the medical superintendent of the Prestwich Asylum argued that 'all insane persons are dangerous to themselves and others, and that the phrase "a harmless lunatic" is simply a contraction in terms'.[9]

What, then, of the thousands of 'harmless lunatics' kept in workhouses? Unless certified by the medical officer as dangerous to others or suicidal, such people would stay in the workhouse indefinitely, simply because it was cheaper for the unions. This was despite the fact that the majority of epileptics, paralysed and senile dements needed constant care and attention and 'few, if any, workhouses are capable of doing justice to the wants and requirements of these helpless lunatics'.[10] There were simply insufficient staff in union workhouses to provide the care that such epileptics and imbeciles needed on a daily, and nightly, basis.

The physician-superintendent at Aberdeen had a more positive point of view about the mentally ill in poor law care: 'All patients who are demented, or are labouring under harmless delusions, and who are cleanly and quiet, and not specially requiring Asylum treatment, are regarded as best suited for the Poorhouse or to be "boarded out".'[11]

Classification of lunatics

The patients in lunatic asylums were classified according to a complex system and 'males had to be separated from females, incurables from curables, the violent from the docile, [and] the clean from the dirty'.[12] This not only aided their recovery, it also made it easier for the staff to manage them. As was usual asylum practice, at Lancaster, convalescent and quiet patients were separated from those who were 'refractory, noisy or dangerous' and 'the clean [were] at all times separated from the dirty patients'.[13]

Asylum keepers had to establish so-called pathways of progress so that 'improving lunatics could move, stage by stage, nearer the exit' while chronic cases occupied the back wards. The challenge faced by the asylum keepers was to achieve all this 'without prejudice to order, economy, efficiency and discipline'.[14]

At Aberdeen, there were many different detached buildings which enabled the staff to enforce the classification of patients into distinct groups. The patients were 'distributed in sitting rooms and parlours of moderate size, having constant access at pleasure to the open air, and not in large halls and galleries with only periodic egress'. As the patients had a liberal diet and warm clothing, they were able to 'combat the insidious effects of the east winds while still enjoying the benefit of fresh air'. The 'most disagreeable cases' were isolated at night in single bedrooms to avoid disrupting the other patients.[15]

Chapter 23

Pauper and Private Patients

In the 1830s and 1840s, the increasing numbers of lunatic patients put considerable pressure on the poor law unions. The demand for asylum accommodation for those pauper lunatics who were too dangerous or too difficult to manage in workhouses was not met by the county asylums, of which there were an insufficient number at the time.

Private asylums for pauper and private patients

As a result, a number of new licensed private asylums were established to meet this demand, including the Duddeston Hall Lunatic Asylum which opened in 1835. Once the home of a banker, this mansion near Birmingham was 'licensed to accept ninety patients, sixty of whom would be paupers'.[1] It was run by Thomas Lewis, a surgeon, 'largely on the basis of an arrangement with the Birmingham and Aston Boards of Guardians to admit the unmanageable pauper lunatics from their workhouses'.[2] The asylum was also used by other unions in the region including Solihull, Warwick, Nuneaton, Rugby and Kidderminster.

In addition to the paupers, Duddeston Hall also accommodated private patients, and the division between the two was clearly marked. The private patients 'were housed inside the mansion, with its spacious rooms' and were 'allowed access to the gardens and grounds for recreation and exercise'. The paupers and the poorer private patients were accommodated in outbuildings 'which were of a much inferior standard'. These outbuildings contained beds which were 'hard and knotty' with insufficient bedding.[3] In 1844, recreation for these patients consisted 'only of "one dull yard" each for the male and female paupers'.[4]

During the night, the lunatic patients at Duddeston were locked in their rooms and 'the more disturbed would be strapped into their beds'. The wealthy private patients who were 'convalescent' were first to be let out of their rooms in the mornings and on Sunday evenings 'they would be allowed the privilege of eating with the superintendent … and his family'.[5]

Some private madhouses offered very superior accommodation and living conditions for those who could afford it. Founded in 1792, Ticehurst House in Sussex had separate houses in the grounds for the rich who were allowed to install their own cooks, and ride to hounds. However, most early madhouses provided 'at best Spartan and at worst brutal conditions for their inmates, especially the poor'.[6]

Although Aberdeen was a public asylum, it also took private patients. In 1861, a separate property adjoining the asylum's grounds was built 'in a style resembling a large mansion'. This was known as Elmhill House, which was 'devoted to the treatment and care of patients of the middle and upper classes paying higher rates of board'. Surrounded by an extensive park and pleasure grounds, it was designed to accommodate sixty-five ladies and gentlemen in 'the maximum of comfort'. The house was not suitable for acute or troublesome cases, and these would be transferred, often temporarily, to the main asylum.[7]

Public asylums for paupers

An extensive programme of asylum building was put in place after the passing of the Lunatic Asylum and Pauper Lunatics Act in 1845. The Abergavenny Asylum was one such new asylum, built to a corridor design and capable of housing 'two hundred and ten patients in twelve wards on the ground or first floor, with attic windows and loft space available for expansion'.[8] Dr John Stewart Allen of the St Marylebone Lunatic Infirmary in London was appointed as superintendent on 1 September 1851 at a salary of £350 per annum, and the first patients were admitted on 3 December. Later, a chapel was built in the grounds and in 1853, 'a site within the grounds was consecrated as a cemetery'.[9]

A medical certificate for Mary Ann Royle, stating that she was of unsound mind. (With thanks to John Royle, reproduced with the permission of Gloucestershire NHS Trust and Gloucestershire Archives)

Although some harmless lunatics were accommodated in workhouses, difficult or dangerous cases could not be managed in such places, and they were sent to an asylum for specialist care. This was the fate of Mary Ann Royle, a forty-three-year-old married woman of no occupation, who was admitted to the County & City of Gloucester Lunatic Asylum at Wotton, near Gloucester on 8 September 1883. She had been an inmate at the Gloucester Union Workhouse for twelve months and her attacks of insanity had started four months earlier. Richard Mount Cole, the workhouse surgeon, certified that she was a 'person of unsound mind'. The medical certificate he signed describes the facts he observed indicating her insanity:

Throws herself about the bed, tears up her clothes and bedclothes; passes urine and faeces under her and smears herself with them. She says her bowels have not been open since she had an infection some months ago … Hannah Letts the Nurse says that if Mary Ann Royle is left for a minute she will get out of bed and lie naked on the floor. She picks the plaster from the wall and passes it up the rectum.[10]

As Mary Ann was a pauper, an Order for the Reception of a Pauper Patient had to be completed before she could be admitted to the asylum. The Order had to be jointly signed by a Justice of the Peace and the Relieving Officer. Joseph Smith, the Relieving Officer for the Gloucester Union completed the statement about Mary Ann.

At the time, Mary Ann's husband, a hotel porter, was living at the Mechanics' Home in Liverpool. Mary Ann had returned to Gloucester alone to live with her mother, Ann Goddard, and it is possible that her marriage had broken down. In 1881, Mary Ann had spent time as an in-patient at the Gloucester Royal Infirmary in Southgate Street while her only son was being looked after by her sister. It is not known what condition she was suffering from but it was not connected with her mental health. Her asylum records from 1883 state that this was her first attack of insanity and she had never received mental care or treatment before. According to her admission records, Mary Ann was not deemed to be epileptic, suicidal or dangerous to others but her insanity was attributed to 'domestic trouble' and 'poverty'.

The Notice of Admission to the asylum has another statement about Mary Ann's mental state, written by J. Hurst Craddock, the medical officer of the asylum. He states that she 'is suffering from Dementia; she has been in bed ever since her admission, where she lies with her eyes shut, moaning & groaning. Says she also has no use of her eyes, but looks straight enough when told to, is wet and dirty in her habits & very restless'. With respect to Mary Ann's bodily health and condition, she 'is thin and delicate, she is paralysed in her lower extremities, her internal organs are normal; there were a few small bruises on her legs when admitted.'

On arrival, Mary Ann was described as an 'anaemic, emaciated woman'. On 10 September, the medical officer wrote:

> Since her admission this patient has been in bed with her knees curled up nearly to her chin and affirms that she cannot get them down. But however she can do when made to. She constantly complains of the treatments she has received from a nurse in the workhouse, who she says hurt her in giving her an enema… She is wet and dirty in her habits. Quiet sleep at night but whines & complains night and day. She takes her food well.

Ten days later, it was noted that Mary Ann had 'a delusion that she has a tumour in her abdomen. The patient appears to be blind.' By 29 December, she became 'more and more demented. Lies or sits always with her legs doubled up, is constantly crying & whining & complaining of being "treated brutish in that Workhouse".'

In March 1884, it was reported that Mary Ann 'Grows more demented & feeble – is disgusting in her habits & full of complaints'. By the end of the year, there was no change in her condition, or during the first half of 1885. By 29 September 1885 more than two years after she had been admitted, she was described as 'Very abusive. Uses very foul language. Is very dirty in her habits. Still has the same delusions. In poor bodily health.'

Again, there was no change in the first half of 1886 but on 29 June it was reported that during the last month, Mary Ann had been 'suffering from large carbuncles on her back'. An opium mixture was prescribed but she was 'in a very exhausted condition.'

On 4 July the medical officer wrote: 'Medicine has been stopped. Is failing fast. Takes her nourishment fairly well. Her lungs are becoming somewhat congested.' Finally, on 6 July, Mary Ann 'Gradually sank & died today'.[11] The cause of death was oedema of the lungs and long-standing heart disease.[12]

Chapter 24

Mental Illnesses and Their Causes

In the Victorian period, there were a number of different diagnosable mental illnesses, which could be caused by a wide variety of circumstances. All lunatic asylums had to produce annual reports including statistics compiled by the medical officer listing the forms of insanity admitted during the year, and their attributed causes.

In 1881 at the Aberdeen Asylum, there were five different forms of insanity which would have been similar in other asylums. In ascending order of the number of patients with the condition, they were listed as amentia (a severe congenital mental deficiency), monomania (the obsession of the mind by one idea or interest), melancholia (a form of depression, often with ill-founded fears), dementia and mania.[1]

The medical officer also had to assign a cause to each case of mental illness admitted. In 1881, in seventy-nine of the cases at Aberdeen, no cause could be attributed. Fifty-two of the cases were caused by 'Hereditary Predisposition' while seventeen (the majority of which were male patients) were attributed to intemperance. The remaining forty-nine cases were attributed to a wide variety of causes including childbirth (puerperal mania), death of friends, epilepsy, disappointment in love, over-anxiety, lactation and 'climacteric change' (the menopause).[2]

Mania

One of the most difficult mental illnesses to treat was mania. Such cases could be a danger to themselves or others as their illness was marked by periods of great excitement and violence. Alfred Woodhurst, a forty-nine-year-old former bonnet maker of Bethnal Green, was admitted to Middlesex County Lunatic Asylum at Hanwell in July 1877. He had already spent sixteen months in Hoxton House Asylum following his release from Nottingham Prison. His case notes reveal that he was both epileptic and dangerous, but not suicidal. His mental illness was 'mania' which manifested itself in delusions of grandeur and paranoia about being persecuted and murdered. Alfred's overall health was good and he was well nourished although he only weighed 8 stone 9lb.

As a pauper lunatic, Alfred's time at the asylum was paid for by the Bethnal Green Union Workhouse. Whilst there were countless harmless epileptics maintained in workhouses, Alfred was considered dangerous to others. The asylum records describe his mental state on admission to Hanwell:

> He is truculent & overbearing in manner and is incessantly grumbling about the quality of the food, clothing, bedding, etc. He says the attendants put chloroform in his tea & throw chloroform over his clothes: is under the impression that he is Lord Woodhurst, & rebukes those about him for not addressing him as 'My Lord'. Appetite good.[3]

Alfred's delusions of grandeur continued throughout his confinement at the asylum and, in September 1878, it was noted that he was 'continuing haughty, overbearing & very abusive to the officers. He believes he is a nobleman & is most irritable if argued with on the subject, & no persuasion in the world will induce him to wear one of the asylum caps, he rather goes bareheaded'.[4]

Throughout Alfred's asylum records, regular notes are made that he worked well with the airing-court party, the pumping party or in the grounds and that he was a 'hard worker'. However, in March 1895 it was reported that he 'Struck recently the gardener with whom he had been working for so long. Under the impression that he was slowly poisoning him.'

Alfred's general health remained good, but his delusions continued which developed into thoughts that he was being persecuted and murdered by others. Alfred was transferred to Leavesden Asylum in October 1910 and died there on 5 March 1915.[5]

Hereditary predisposition

In many cases, the causes for mental illness were attributed to a 'hereditary disposition' if, on investigation, a member of the patient's family had also been mentally ill.

Alfred Woodhurst's brother, James, was also destined to end his days in a lunatic asylum. It is not known if the two brothers were suffering from a hereditary disease or whether the fact they were both afflicted with a mental illness was simply coincidental. Born in 1818, James was a police constable who resigned in 1849 and rejoined in 1851. He was dismissed from the police force in 1857. The reason for his dismissal is unknown but it is possible that it may be connected with his later illness. After leaving the police force, he followed various occupations including railway porter, labourer and warehouseman.

In February 1875, James was admitted to the Hackney Union Workhouse, recorded as 'ill'. He discharged himself in mid-March and was re-admitted in April, again leaving at his own request in May. On 20 July, he was admitted to the workhouse again, this time described as being 'of unsound mind'. Three days later, Dr John Bradshaw White of the Hackney Union Workhouse Infirmary certified that James was experiencing various delusions and that his wife claimed he had tried to commit suicide on two occasions.

On 24 July, James was transferred to Bethnal House, one of the Metropolitan Licensed Houses which accommodated paupers when there was insufficient accommodation at the county asylums. His transfer was ordered by John Charrington, a Justice of the Peace, who had examined James himself and had seen Dr White's certificate. James remained at Bethnal House for more than two years, and was finally transferred to Banstead Asylum, Middlesex's third county lunatic asylum, in September 1877.

James's admission record to Banstead describes his mental state as deluded, incoherent and suicidal. He died at the asylum on 10 January 1882, aged sixty-two, of chronic brain disease.[6]

Dementia

Patients with dementia might have memory disorders, personality changes and impaired reasoning as a result of brain disease or injury. This category would have included elderly patients with senile dementia.

Bereavement and the breakdown of a relationship or a marriage were often cited as possible causes of a mental illness like dementia. Arthur Brown, a twenty-five-year-old labourer/donkey driver, suffered both in 1878, the year he was admitted as a pauper patient to the Brookwood Asylum (the Surrey County Lunatic Asylum). It is not known if this was Arthur's first attack of mental illness but, in the same year, his mother died and his wife Louisa left him, so it is likely his condition was caused by the stress of these two events. Arthur was admitted to the asylum by his brother who found him to be behaving irrationally. His case notes reveal he was 'utterly demented, very destructive, tearing at clothes, & pounding feet grotesquely'. The diagnosis was dementia and, sadly, Arthur's condition did not improve. He was a patient at the Brookwood Asylum for six years until his death there in 1884 at the age of thirty-one. He died of 'Exhaustion from Organic Brain Disease and Diarrhoea'.[7]

Melancholia

The Victorian term for depression was 'melancholia', an acute mental illness with a good prospect of recovery in many sufferers. Richard Morgan, a forty-six-year-old married labourer from Canton in Cardiff, had been employed on the tramways for ten years. He was admitted to Bridgend Asylum on 29 December 1899 suffering from acute melancholia. Richard had been depressed for three to four months and, at the same time, had lost about a stone in weight. This was his first attack of mental illness. Richard had 'No phthisis' and 'No drink', he was not epileptic but he was suicidal and not 'under proper care and control'.[8]

His detailed case notes describe him as 'poorly nourished' and 'very low and miserable crying with-out obvious cause. Is under a delusion that his son is going to South Africa. Beating his head & is afraid something is going to happen to him and he wants to die. Says he would finish himself.' It was noted that he had 'been strange in his manner for the past three months. Miserable and fretting without obvious

Richard Morgan, a patient at the Bridgend Asylum between December 1899 and July 1901. (With thanks to John Royle DHGL 10/75 Case No.7447, reproduced with the permission of the Glamorgan Record Office)

cause, threatening to do away with himself & recently wanted to get his wife out of the way saying "I won't be here long".'

By 5 January 1900, Richard was 'still depressed, nervous & apprehensive sits apart & takes little interest in anything.' A week later, it was reported that '…the deluded ideas are still present but he strongly asserts he had no intention to injure himself…'

On 19 January, there was little change. 'Though more energetic, he soon subsides into a corner & looks worried and very suspicious. It is difficult to engage him in conversation.' By 13 March, the medical officer wrote 'He is not progressing. He is much concerned about his past sins which he says are many & great. He sleeps well.'

Throughout 1900 he gave 'little trouble' and 'worked industriously'. On 5 January 1901, it was reported that Richard 'is more miserable & moans & groans a good deal & he has been stubborn about the taking of sufficient food & not sleeping quite so well. There has been slight oedema of ankles but no albumen has been found in the urine.'

By June 1901, Richard had diarrhoea, a headache and a temperature of over 100. He was 'very weak, has all the appearance of general tuberculosis; …the breathing is harsh over both lungs'.[9] He died on 10 July 1901.[10]

Poverty and mental illness

There was an inextricable link between poverty and mental illness, and it was often temporary. Christian Watt, a forty-six-year-old widowed fishwife, was admitted to the Aberdeen Asylum for the first time in 1878. The stress of having to feed and look after her seven children by herself caused her to have a breakdown, and she went voluntarily to the asylum on the advice of her doctor 'for a rest'.[11] It is not clear how long she stayed at the asylum, but she recovered and returned home in the spring.

The stigma of being an asylum patient meant that work was harder to find so Christian found it even more difficult to make ends meet. After a 'terrible winter of hard work and near starvation', she fainted and nearly fell in the fire. Her doctor again suggested going to the asylum for a rest, to which she readily agreed. To her, the asylum was 'a blessed haven of peace'.[12]

Christian returned home again in the spring/summer of 1879 but with the oncoming winter approaching, her illness returned. In December of that year, she received news that her application to emigrate to America with her children had been turned down because of her medical examination. Christian plunged into a deep depression.

Of this time, she wrote: 'I knew the exact moment my reasoning broke. I struggled to hang onto it, it was as distinct as a butter plate breaking on the floor. A bottle of paraffin lay near the hen-house, I remember pouring it over the small shed and my son George struggling with me.'[13]

There was to be no voluntary admission to the asylum this time. Two doctors and a policeman visited Christian and certified her as insane. Her estates were taken over by the Crown to be administered by Chancery, and her children were split up to live with various friends and family. Amidst all this worry and upset, 'Nobody would take the dog Ranger, so he had to be done away with.'[14]

Christian recalled the moment she was taken away:

> A cab drew up at the door. I was dressed and ready. My young children were screaming murder and clinging to my skirts as I was hustled out … but I was too ill to care whether I lived or died. It was lack of food and sleep, for I had gone hungry to give it all to the children. I reached Aberdeen and never was the Asylum more welcome. I cannot have enough praise for these doctors and nurses who give so much of their life to heal the sick. With nourishing food and rest, I quickly recovered.[15]

At the Somerset County Pauper Lunatic Asylum, patients admitted with 'stress of poverty' as the cause of their insanity only received dietetical treatment in the infirmary wards. The administrators found that 'better living and more cheerful surroundings' were all these patients needed. They argued that this evidence pointed to 'the necessity of more being done by parochial officers to meet the requirements primarily affecting the *bodily* health of patients prior to admission'.[16]

Epileptics

Epileptics, or anyone suffering with fits from another cause, were placed with the imbeciles and lunatics in asylums and workhouses. In many cases, apart from their fits, these patients had no symptoms of mental illness and would have been sound and lucid.

Although, in a workhouse, epileptics were more likely to be surrounded by sane inmates, they received better care when looked after in an asylum. This was because there was a lack of paid attendants in the workhouse, especially at night and 'countless lives were needlessly put at risk'.[17] As one Visiting Commissioner in Lunacy pointed out in 1891, 'epileptic patients are especially liable to death from suffocation caused by their turning on their faces in a fit, not necessarily severe, without making sufficient noise to attract the notice of any but a trained attendant specially watching the patients'.[18] At the Leicester Asylum, the chapel was built with 'four wide porches, so a patient could be treated if they had a fit during a service'.[19]

Idiots and imbeciles

An idiot was defined in some of the early legislation as 'any individual with a mental age of under three years'. An imbecile was defined as 'someone with low to moderate mental deficiency and a mental age of between two and seven years'.[20] Colloquial terms for idiots included fools and naturals.[21] In 1885, there were at least 30,000 imbecile and idiot persons in England and Wales alone, the majority of whom would have been accommodated in workhouses.

William John Brannon.

Above left: Edward Farrington, born 1876. Abandoned at birth as a cretin, he was a patient at the Abergavenny Asylum between 1886 and 1907. (Reproduced with the permission of the Gwent NHS Trust and the Gwent Record Office)

Above right: William John Brannan, born 1875. He was a patient at the Royal Albert Asylum for idiots and imbeciles between 1885 and 1893. (Reproduced with the permission of the North Lancashire Primary Care Trust, the Lancashire Care NHS Foundation Trust and the County Archivist, Lancashire Record Office – HRRA 52/14)

People suffering from congenital conditions, who could not be cared for by their relatives or adequately by the poor law unions, might be sent to an asylum. One such person was fourteen-year-old Edward Farrington, admitted to the Abergavenny Asylum in February 1886 from the Caerleon Industrial School where he had been abandoned at birth. He was a 'cretin, with a disproportionably large head but the body of a five year old'.[22] Edward was described as being 'in a feeble bodily condition, constantly wet and dirty, an idiot with little intelligence who required constant care.'[23] In July 1907, he was transferred to Caerleon Asylum.[24] Many cretins in asylums were treated with thyroid extract but this would have been ineffective as a cure for cretinism unless administered from birth. The condition is now tested for, and treated, at birth.[25]

Young children were admitted to some lunatic asylums. On 1 July 1876, a six-year-old boy from Wellingborough was admitted to the Northampton Berry Wood Asylum. He had been subject to fits since a child and had suffered congestion of the brain for the last five and a half years. He had been moved to the asylum because he had become 'noisy and excitable, and required watching day and night'. His admission records state: 'This is a case of idiocy. The child is unable to speak distinctly, is restless and constantly moving from one position to another'. The boy died in the asylum on 4 September 1888 aged eighteen from epilepsy and a meningeal haemorrhage (brain haemorrhage).[26]

In the mid- to late nineteenth century, there was increasing concern about the housing of idiots in county lunatic asylums. One medical superintendent pointed out that 'The habits and ways of adult lunatics make it most desirable that children of such tender years should not be forced into close companionship with them…'.[27]

The authorities at the Somerset County Lunatic Asylum argued that:

> Idiots are teachable and imitative, and either acquire bad habits and lessen their small intelligence if they are neglected, or, on the other hand, if properly cared for, improve, and will, many of them, be able to maintain themselves, and it is believed that if detained in a separate Asylum the costs of their maintenance would be considerably reduced.[28]

Gradually, asylums exclusively for idiots were opened, including the Earlswood Asylum at Redhill, Surrey in 1847 and the Royal Albert Asylum at Lancaster in 1870, which catered for idiots and imbeciles from seven northern counties. Epileptic or paralytic children could not be admitted because of 'the dismay occasioned to children of weak intellect by the sight of one falling into a fit'.[29] Originally, the Royal Albert took children aged from six to fifteen for a period of seven years 'in which time it is hoped (from the experience of Earlswood and elsewhere) that some of the patients will become self-supporting and may be able to contribute towards their own maintenance.'[30] By 1886, the asylum admitted patients from the age of five and upwards. In 1881, it housed 2,422 idiots although, according to the census, there were 8,764 idiots and imbeciles in the seven northern counties at that time.

Children were sent to the Royal Albert Asylum 'either by election or by the payment of charges varying with the requirements and the circumstances of the friends who sent them'. In the list of candidates for fifty places in June 1884, the parents of the idiots included 'the widow of a National schoolmaster left with three children, one a cripple besides her idiot boy, lets lodgings for their living; a labourer with four motherless children to keep and care for; and a charwoman, with three children, whose husband has deserted her'. In each case, their difficulties were magnified by the burden of an imbecile child. For those fifty places, there were 107 candidates, leaving fifty-seven to be bitterly disappointed. Where payment was possible, parents were encouraged to contribute something to their child's support to keep up 'a sense of responsibility and interest in their hearts'.[31]

The aim of everyone employed at the Royal Albert Asylum was 'to discover, to draw out, and to develop any faculty possessed by their defective intelligences'.[32] Music was such a great part of the children's training that 'almost all the attendants are required to play on some instrument; and concerts are got up weekly, often by the resident staff alone, with the aid of their imbecile patients'.[33]

Most of the older inmates were employed in industrial occupations. In 1885, 172 boys were employed in this way, and of these fifteen were gardeners, twenty-five were weeding-boys and eleven worked on the farm. Ninety-six of the girls were more or less trained to industrial work including bed-making, general house-work, laundry-work and sewing.[34]

The Royal Albert also took the hopeless cases, 'the poor creatures who in private houses would be hidden away from sight, and doomed to utter wretchedness'.[35] At the asylum, they were warmly clad and fed, kept clean and comfortable in light, airy rooms and were taught 'at least to sit upright, or leaning against the table'.[36] This category included cretins and others with stunted limbs.

General paralysis of the insane

'General paralysis of the insane' was a mental condition which, in the majority of cases, was caused by tertiary syphilis. In the 1890s, the medical profession were divided in their opinion about whether general paralysis of the insane was only caused by syphilis, or whether it was a separate mental illness.[37] The connection was not fully proved until the twentieth century.

In any case, this debilitating illness was almost always fatal. There was no effective treatment for syphilis until 1909 when Salvarsan, a compound of toxic arsenic, was discovered. Until then, mercurial compounds such as iodide of potassium and mercury were used to treat the symptoms of the disease.

John McGregor, born in Gorbals in 1846, was the son of a confectioner. He was destined to be struck down by syphilis. He started his working life as an umbrella maker and later set up a successful wholesale and export umbrella manufacturing company in Glasgow. He was married with three children, although only one survived childhood.

The first documentary evidence of John's poor health can be seen in the fact that he wrote his will at the Glenburn Hydropathic Hotel in Rothesay on 13 August 1894. As a wealthy man, he could afford to stay at such an establishment and it is possible that he was seeking treatment for the first symptoms of tertiary syphilis such as numbness or loss of coordination. It is not known how long he stayed at the hotel. This hydropathic establishment was the first to be set up north of the border in 1843 by Dr Paterson. Hydropathy was based on a series of water treatments which treated a wide range of diseases, but the high cost meant that hydropathic hotels were only frequented by the rich.

It is possible that the practitioners at the hotel were trying to treat John for mental overexertion. In the 1880s, hydropathy became known as an effective way to treat this disorder, popularised by Alexander Stewart, the medical superintendent at the Heathcot hydro near Aberdeen.

When John died on 27 December 1895, the cause of death was 'General Paralysis of 3 years standing'.[38] The place of death was 1055 Great Western Road, Glasgow which was the address of the Glasgow Royal Asylum (later the Gartnavel Royal Hospital). It was common for death certificates to record the addresses of institutions, rather than their names, to avoid the inevitable stigma in Victorian society. The Glasgow Royal Asylum had been established in 1814 and moved to the Gartnavel site in 1843. It ceased to accept pauper patients in 1889 and started to develop as 'one of Britain's leading fee-paying psychiatric hospitals'.[39]

Metal poisoning

Many cases of mental illness were caused by exposure to toxic metals which were a hazard of a large number of Victorian occupations. This could include mercury poisoning in hatters, furriers and mirror-makers, lead poisoning in white lead and pottery workers, and copper poisoning in the tin industry.

John Davies was an engineer at the Margam Tin Works in Neath, near Port Talbot in Wales. On 20 January 1877, when he was fifty-four years old, John was admitted to the Bridgend Lunatic Asylum from the Neath Poor Law district. It is believed that he was suffering from copper poisoning. His medical certificate stated that 'he believes his wife is in collusion with persons unknown to pain his body and soul and that they torment him at night'. It was said that he was at times violent and destructive but the cause of his mental illness was unknown. Although John was not epileptic or suicidal, he was considered dangerous, hence his admission to the asylum. He was in fair bodily health but he complained of 'pain in his head and a burning sensation in his stomach'.[40]

John's mental condition remained unchanged although his physical health started to deteriorate. By mid-March, there was a 'marked dullness' over the base of his right lung and he was complaining of pain in his side. The doctor ordered that poultices should be applied over his right side. A month later, the dullness over the right side of his chest was 'still very marked' with increased dullness in his liver and a slight oedema in both ankles. On 24 April, John was recorded as coughing up 'a deal of rusty-coloured sputas'.

By 14 May, John was 'sinking fast' and two days later, he died. George Snell, the Assistant Medical Officer, certified that his apparent cause of death was chronic pneumonia which had lasted three months.[41] It is not known if John's wife Mary ever visited him at the asylum. One can only imagine her torment because, to the very end, John believed 'that his illness is due to his wife and enemies'.[42]

Chapter 25

Living Conditions in Asylums

The design of asylums had to facilitate 'maximum security, ample ventilation, efficient drainage … total surveillance and, not least, differential classification and housing of distinct grades of lunatics'.[1] The earliest asylums were usually designed with rows of single cells leading off from long, wide galleries which doubled as day-rooms.[2] Later asylums included dormitories and separate recreation rooms so that the complex classification system could be put into place.

'Suggestions and Instructions' were issued by the Lunacy Commission for local authorities, offering advice on asylum architecture and the layout of grounds. A 'modified traditional country house estate' in a rural setting was the preferred option. The Commission specified that airing courts be built next to the asylum and within the boundary walls, to be used by patients and staff for therapeutic purposes.[3]

The diet in asylums

Victorian lunatic asylums were self-sufficient estates with extensive grounds cultivated to grow fruit and vegetables for the patients to eat. A liberal, nutritious diet was an essential part of the treatment for the mentally ill, many of whom were in poor physical condition on arrival.

At the Somerset County Pauper Lunatic Asylum, breakfast for male patients consisted of 8oz bread, ½oz butter and 1 pint of coffee or broth. Females had the same but 1oz less bread. Supper for male patients was 8oz of bread, ½oz butter and 1 pint of tea with 7oz of bread for females. Dinner was the only meal which varied. On Mondays, Wednesdays and Fridays, it was uncooked meat, including bone with vegetables and beer or cider. On Tuesdays, meat pie was served while Thursdays were soup and bread days. The soup consisted of peas, onions, carrots, turnips, parsnips, celery, salt, pepper, parsley, thyme and marjoram plus shins of beef or other pieces of meat stewed down. On Saturdays, the patients ate Irish stew prepared with meat, potatoes, onions, suet, flour, salt and pepper. On Sundays, dinner was fruit pie.[4]

The lunatic patients at Somerset who were sick were 'dieted at the discretion of the resident Physicians'. Extra diet for the sick included arrowroot, bacon, beef steak, beef tea, calf's foot jelly, eggs, essence of beef, milk, mutton chop, rice pudding, sago, soup, ale, porter, stout, brandy, gin, port and sherry.[5]

Working patients also had extras in their daily diet. At 11 a.m., they were given 2oz of bread, ¾oz cheese and half a pint of cider, with an extra half pint of cider at 4 p.m. The laundry patients were given half a pint of tea. Tobacco and snuff were also given to the working patients.[6]

At the Duddeston Hall Lunatic Asylum, the pauper patients had thickened milk for breakfast. For dinner, they had 'meat and vegetables three days per week, broth twice a week and pease soup once a week'. Supper alternated between 'bread and cheese on the days when they had broth or soup for dinner, and thickened milk when they had meat for dinner'.[7] Working patients were rewarded with 'an extra meal of bread and cheese, and tobacco once a week'.[8]

Entertainments and amusements

Recreational activities were an important part of the daily routine in Victorian lunatic asylums as they occupied both the mind and body. In the early years of the Abergavenny Asylum, there were 'walking parties in the grounds and surrounding hills, cricket, bagatelle, skittles, rounders, bowls, football, croquet [and] games.'[9] At the Aberdeen Asylum during 1881, 'twenty cricket matches were played against various clubs of the town'. There were also frequent assemblies for dancing and performances were given by the Aberdeen Amateur Opera Company and the Kean Dramatic Society.[10]

DIET SCALE.

BREAKFAST.

Days of the Week.	Males: Bread.	Males: Butter.	Males: Coffee or Broth.	Females: Bread.	Females: Butter.	Females: Coffee or Broth.
	Oz.	Oz.	Pt.	Oz.	Oz.	Pt.
Sunday.......	8	½	1	7	½	1
Monday......	8	½	1	7	½	1
Tuesday......	8	½	1	7	½	1
Wednesday..	8	½	1	7	½	1
Thursday.....	8	½	1	7	½	1
Friday.......	8	½	1	7	½	1
Saturday.....	8	½	1	7	½	1
Weekly Totl.	56	3½	7	49	3½	7

DINNER.

Days of the Week.	Males: Uncooked Meat, including bone.	Males: Meat Pie.	Males: Fruit Pie.	Males: Irish Stew.	Males: Soup.	Males: Bread.	Males: Vegetables.	Males: Beer or Cider.	Females: Uncooked Meat, including bone.	Females: Meat Pie.	Females: Fruit Pie.	Females: Irish Stew.	Females: Soup.	Females: Bread.	Females: Vegetables.	Females: Beer or Cider.
	Oz.	lb.	lb.	Pt.	Pt.	Oz.	lb.	Pt.	Oz.	lb.	lb.	Pt.	Pt.	Oz.	lb.	Pt.
Sunday.......	0	0	1	0	0	0	0	½	0	0	1	0	0	0	0	½
Monday......	8	0	0	0	0	0	1½	½	8	0	0	0	0	0	1	½
Tuesday......	0	1	0	0	0	0	0	½	0	1	0	0	0	0	0	½
Wednesday..	8	0	0	0	0	0	1½	½	8	0	0	0	0	0	1	½
Thursday.....	0	0	0	0	1½	4	0	½	0	0	0	0	1	4	0	½
Friday.......	8	0	0	0	0	0	1½	½	8	0	0	0	0	0	1	½
Saturday.....	0	0	0	1½	0	0	0	½	0	0	0	1	0	0	0	½
Weekly Totl.	24	1	1	1½	1½	4	4½	3½	24	1	1	1	1	4	3	3½

SUPPER.

Days of the Week.	Males: Bread.	Males: Butter.	Males: Tea.	Females: Bread.	Females: Butter.	Females: Tea.
	Oz.	Oz.	Pt.	Oz.	Oz.	Pt.
Sunday.......	8	½	1	7	½	1
Monday......	8	½	1	7	½	1
Tuesday......	8	½	1	7	½	1
Wednesday..	8	½	1	7	½	1
Thursday.....	8	½	1	7	½	1
Friday.......	8	½	1	7	½	1
Saturday.....	8	½	1	7	½	1
Weekly Totl.	56	3½	7	49	3½	7

The Sick throughout the Establishment are dieted at the discretion of the resident Physicians. Extra diet for the Sick:—Arrowroot, Bacon, Beef Steak, Beef Tea, Calf's Foot Jelly, Eggs, Essence of Beef, Milk, Mutton Chop, Rice Pudding, Sago, Soup, Ale, Porter, Stout, Brandy, Gin, Port, Sherry. At 11 a.m. the Working Patients have each 2 ozs. of Bread, ¾ oz. Cheese, and Half-pint Cider; at 4 p.m. Half-pint Cider. The Laundry Patients have Half-pint of Tea. Tobacco and Snuff given to the Working Patients. The Coffee is made by boiling 4 lbs. of Coffee with 8 lbs. of Sugar in 40 Gallons of Water, to which is added 3 or 4 Gallons of Milk. The Tea:—3¾ lbs. Tea, 11 lbs. Sugar, to 60 Gallons of Water and 4 Gallons of Milk. The Broth is made from the Liquor of the Meat the day previous, with 30 lbs. of Flour, 1 peck of Onions, Milk, Pepper, and Salt, to 37 Gallons of Water. The Meat Pie is made with 135 lbs. of Meat, 2 Sacks of Potatoes, 2 Pecks of Onions, Pepper 1 lb., Salt 3 lbs., Flour 130 lbs., Suet or Dripping 60 lbs., Water from 6 to 7 Gallons: Herbs when insea son. For the Soup on Thursdays:—Peas 5 Pecks, Onions 2 Pecks, Carrots 1 Bushel, Turnips, ½ Bushel, Parsnips ½ Bushel, Celery about 2 dozen Heads, Parsley, Thyme, and Marjoram, in proportion, Flour 60 to 70 lbs., Shins of Beef, or other pieces of Meat are stewed down and added to the Soup with Salt, Pepper, &c. The Irish Stew is prepared with Meat 135 lbs., 2½ Sacks Potatoes, 2 Pecks Onions, Suet 30 to 40 lbs., Flour about 60 lbs., Salt and Pepper.

The diet scale at the Somerset County Pauper Lunatic Asylum, dated 1875. (Reproduced with the permission of the North Lancashire Primary Care Trust, the Lancashire Care NHS Foundation Trust and the County Archivist, Lancashire Record Office – HRRA 31/1/6, p31)

At the Somerset County Pauper Lunatic Asylum, the patients participated in cricket in the summer and football in the winter, as well as 'numerous dramatic representations'. Along with a variety of daily papers and periodicals, there were a number of games available for evening amusement such as draughts, dominoes and cards.[11] Asylums seem to have been one of the few Victorian institutions to allow cards; in workhouses, prisons and hospitals they were banned because they were associated with gambling.

The patients at the Lancaster County Lunatic Asylum had a packed schedule of entertainments for every day of the week. In 1884, on Sundays there was a sacred concert and on Mondays, a social meeting with songs. There was a small dance on Tuesdays and on Wednesdays, the weekly ball was held 'in the recreation-hall in winter, and on the green in summer'. On Thursdays, music was played in the Annexe and on Fridays and Saturdays, 'the patients themselves give entertainments, either unaided or with assistance from attendants and nurses'.[12] Lancaster asylum patients also had access to 'an ample supply of books and cheap publications of a cheerful nature' in addition to Bibles and prayer books.[13]

Exercise

Exercise was another important part of an asylum patient's daily routine. Airing-courts were part of the design of the first lunatic asylums, later it became more important to have larger open spaces for exercise. At Lancaster, the wards opened out onto airing grounds, which were accessible to the patients for at least three hours in the morning and three hours in the afternoon when the weather was favourable.[14] Almost all the patients who were able 'go regularly beyond the airing-courts for exercise', some went beyond the Asylum grounds and a select few walked 'on parole where they please unattended'.[15]

Accommodation in workhouses

Facilities for lunatics, imbeciles and epileptics in workhouses varied considerably across the country. At the small Lampeter Union Workhouse in 1900 where there were five inmates classed as imbeciles, the

Visiting Commissioner in Lunacy was 'glad to find that the imbeciles all have flock beds above the straw mattresses' and that 'the patients are kindly treated and properly cared for'.[16]

However, such excellent care was not evident everywhere. The main problem faced by lunatic paupers in workhouses was a severe lack of personal space. Overcrowding in the imbecile and lunatic wards was common in most medium to large workhouses, mainly because the county asylums themselves were overstretched and had insufficient beds to meet the demand.

The Colney Hatch Asylum was opened in 1851 solely to cater for pauper patients from the London unions. By 1867, it had 'turned down 3,800 applications, due to lack of vacant beds'.[17] The Medical Officer of the Poplar Union commented that 'it has become a perfectly hopeless matter to obtain admission for a pauper … in any lunatic asylum in Middlesex'.[18]

Overcrowding in the imbecile wards was a serious problem at the Dudley Union Workhouse. It was observed that:

> … the beds are so close that they touch each other at the sides and the patients have to climb into and out of their beds over the bottom. Apart from the insufficient space it can easily be imagined how objectionable it must be for insane patients, many of whom are of dirty habit … to sleep in beds actually touching each other at the sides.[19]

The problem was eventually resolved by converting the old schools into accommodation for the imbeciles.

The quality of life for mentally ill paupers depended to a large extent on how they were viewed by the workhouse medical officer. If they were considered to be non-medical cases, they were likely to be left in the 'dubious care of pauper nurses'.[20] In the Leicester Union Workhouse, the medical officer visited the insane only once a quarter, and elsewhere 'the doctors attended the insane only if they became physically ill'.[21] At the Cardiff Workhouse Infirmary, the imbeciles led a life 'which would be like that of a vegetable were it not that they preserve the doubtful privilege of sensibility to pain and mental misery'.[22]

Generally, the lunatics and imbeciles had separate male and female day rooms and dormitories from the other inmates, but at smaller workhouses this segregation was not possible. Even in workhouses where the lunatics and imbeciles were properly segregated, there was little to occupy the mind. The boredom and monotony felt by imbeciles in the workhouse was highlighted by a Commissioner in Lunacy to one union in 1889. He commented '…in the men's yards I noticed some pigeons, which are much petted by the imbeciles and clearly afforded them some pleasure and these afflicted men, especially those who cannot be walked out, sadly need something to enliven the dull monotony of their lives'.[23]

The airing shelters at the Abergavenny Asylum. (With thanks to Louise Williams)

Chapter 26

Treatment in Asylums

The treatment for mental illness in the Victorian period relied largely on keeping the mind and body occupied, hence the widespread use of work therapy. A nutritious diet and plenty of exercise were also prescribed, as were drugs when necessary to calm patients.

Work therapy

Most Victorian asylums were built in the countryside, which meant they could become self-sufficient, running their own farms, laundries and workshops, 'partly for economy's sake, partly to achieve cure through labour.'[1] Work therapy in horticulture and agriculture was widely used in asylums.

The site chosen for the Abergavenny Asylum was the thirty-six-acre Lower Farm, north of Abergavenny. It was selected 'for its southern aspect, cheerful view, close proximity to the town, and a spring which produced six to eight gallons of water per minute'.[2] In order for the asylum site to be as compact and secure as possible, land around the farm was bought from different landowners. At Abergavenny, the 'men worked on the farm and garden and the women worked in the laundry or sewing room and at a wide variety of domestic chores'.[3]

For patients at the Somerset County Pauper Lunatic Asylum, work therapy was part of their 'Moral treatment'. The administrators commented that an occupation 'by judicious means can relieve the monotony of life even among the suffering and comparatively helpless'. Even the so-called incurable patients were employed in domestic duties.[4]

At Lancaster, workshops and tools were provided for the male patients and 'artisans and others [were] encouraged to follow their particular calling and to learn shoe-making, tailoring and other common useful trades'. The female patients undertook needlework and straw work.[5]

The medical superintendent at the Prestwich Asylum argued that 'Success in the treatment of the insane, apart from the medical treatment, largely depends upon the perfection of the appliances in an Asylum for fully engaging all patients who are physically capable of employment, in one sort of occupation'. As well as restoring 'hundreds of curable patients to perfect health', work therapy prevented others from sinking into a lower state of mental illness.[6]

As asylums became more and more overcrowded, it became more difficult to provide work for all those who were able, especially for the male patients. Wherever possible, extra land was purchased by asylums, on which patients could labour.

In 1888, when it was found necessary to find extra accommodation for the inmates of the over-crowded Aberdeen Royal Asylum, the managers were able to buy a large estate consisting of new and old mansion houses and 283 acres. This became a branch of the institution at Daviot where male and female pauper patients were accommodated, accustomed as they were to agricultural and other outdoor labour. At Daviot, it was thought that the 'conditions under which the inmates live and work are ideal'. The estate was self-supporting and was able to provide butcher meat, vegetables and flowers for the main Royal Asylum.[7]

Medical treatment

In the nineteenth century, the 'humoral' theory of disease was also applied to mental illness. It was believed that an 'excess of yellow bile (choler) would overheat the system, causing mania or raving madness: by contrast, surplus black bile (melancholia) would induce dejection.'[8] This theory led to the frequent use of purgatives and laxatives to open the bowels of lunatic patients, which it was believed would rid the body of harmful excess toxins.

Drugs were prescribed for patients, particularly to calm them or to help them to sleep. This could include opium, chloral hydrate, morphine or potassium bromide. In some cases, electric shock treatment might be used to curb compulsive behaviour. If lunatic patients were physically ill, they would be treated in the infirmary section of the asylum with similar drugs to those used in hospitals.

Restraint

At times, it was necessary to restrain mentally ill inmates who were a danger to both themselves and others. However, in England from the 1830s, a new philosophy of non-restraint was introduced, largely due to the initiatives of Robert Gardiner Hill at the Lincoln Asylum and John Conolly at the Middlesex Asylum at Hanwell. Gardiner Hill and Conolly abolished 'all forms of mechanical coercion, not just manacles but even straitjackets'.[9] They claimed that security could be maintained through 'surveillance by vigilant attendants and a regime of disciplined work and exercise designed to stimulate the mind, tire the body, and foster self-control'. At the Lincoln Asylum in 1834, 647 incidents had occurred which had required some form of manual restraint but four years later, there were none at all. What's more, this dramatic result had been achieved without any deaths or suicides.[10]

Although the Aberdeen Asylum operated a policy of minimal restraint, in 1841 the medical officers pointed out that there were cases in which 'mild restraint is both judicious and humane'. This might include 'a case of furious nymphomania or the unbridled violence of an outrageous maniac'. The medical officers stated 'We have no more hesitation in such cases, when other means have been useless, in applying the waist-belt, or the muff, than we would have in applying leeches or a blister against the will of the individual…'.[11] The waist-belt had leather bracelets attached to it 'allowing the hands a modified degree of liberty…'.[12]

Every instance of restraint had to be recorded in a Register of Restraint and Seclusion. In 1900 at Aberdeen, there were 182 entries in this register. While this might appear a high number, the majority of the entries related to just two patients. One hundred and nineteen entries referred to the use of 'a waist-belt with straps to secure the arms above the elbows in the case of a female patient who makes sudden and dangerous attacks on her fellow patients and the attendants'. Forty-three of the entries referred to 'the use of the camisole in the case of a female patient in order to prevent her injuring herself and others'. Eighteen of the entries were for cases regarding surgery where restraint was required and the remaining two cases referred to seclusion in the treatment of two patients.[13]

In poor law unions, restraint could only be used when sanctioned by the medical officer and a record of each occasion had to be made in the Register of Mechanical Restraint. At the Dudley Union in 1896, a Visiting Commissioner disapproved of the restraint jacket as 'being of a type that we do not permit fastened by numerous leather bands and buckles. Proper light canvass [sic] jackets with closed sleeves ends and tapes will have to be provided according with the recently published Commissoners' Rules'.[14] By their very nature, workhouses were not designed to accommodate the special needs of lunatics or imbeciles. In 1892, a Visiting Commissioner in Lunacy to one union workhouse complained that 'there is no padded room for noisy turbulent cases dangerous to themselves'.[15] Despite the criticism, very few workhouses would have had padded rooms fitted out especially for lunatics at this time.

Treatment of a typical patient

Excessive worry or being of an extremely nervous disposition could lead to mental illness. John Oatley, a sixty-six-year-old weaver turned labourer from Melksham in Wiltshire, was admitted to Wiltshire County Lunatic Asylum in Devizes on 20 May 1862 because he was melancholic with a suicidal propensity. Grief may also have played a part in John's mental illness as his daughter Sarah had died a few months earlier.

His wife stated that he had always been of a nervous, anxious temperament and was apprehensive of all kinds of evil misfortune which had never happened to him. On the day before his admission, John had gone to a nearby river with the intention of drowning himself and 'regretted very much being prevented'. Then he 'accused himself of imaginary crimes – declared that he had been telling his wife falsehoods & had been a deceiver ever since they were married for he had never been in the army'.[16] He had always claimed to have been in the army for six years and to have fought at the Battle of Waterloo but, interestingly, no army record has been found for him, so it is possible John was telling the truth when he said he was a 'deceiver'.

METHOD OF APPLYING GALVANISM.

'The West-End Hospital for Paralysis and Epilepsy, Welbeck-Street: Method of Applying Galvinism.' (*The Illustrated London News*, 20 January 1883)

At the asylum, John complained frequently of a pain in his stomach, 'declaring there were evil spirits in it constantly prompting him to destroy his family'. He was noisy and restless by night, shouting and groaning constantly. By 26 June, it was reported that he had gradually improved in his state of mind. As a result of the 'horrible noises' he made in the night, he had been moved from a dormitory to a single room where he was timid and subdued. He was moved back to the dormitory and 'began making a noise one night but since being told he would have to go to a single room again has controlled himself & kept quiet'. John started working on the farm every day and was 'all the better mentally & bodily & allows that it is so'.[17]

At this time, John was being prescribed morphine by day and night which would have sedated him and made him more manageable. However, by October, he had relapsed into his previous restless state, probably because he had become habituated to the morphine. On 23 December, it was decided to change his medication to a tincture of opium which, it was noted, he benefited from. In 1863, it was noted that he 'has continued the Tinct: Opii & has been very well all the summer… Has taken all his meals or great portion of them with great regularity: has been less restless though his state of mind has been as peculiar as formerly'. John was invariably quiet at night but as soon as his room door was opened in the morning, he would start to moan and groan.[18]

On 30 September 1863, despite hot water bottles to his feet and a mustard poultice applied to his neck, John became unconscious in his sleep and died. A post-mortem revealed 'adhesions between dura mater and archnoid' [the outer and middle membranes around the brain] and blood between the arachnoid and pia mater [the middle and inner membranes]. Today, this is known as a sub-arachnoid haemorrhage which would account for John's coma, his fixed pinpoint pupils and his irregular respirations. There were also adhesions in John's colon which would have caused his constipation and a possible stricture which could account for his colicky pain.[19]

Treatment of long-standing mental illness

John Henderson, a painter, glazier and auctioneer born in 1832, had a long-standing mental illness which was treated in a number of different asylums including Malling Place for private patients, Dr Harmer's Hawkhurst Asylum, Dr Stocker's Peckham House Asylum plus Barming Heath, the Kent County Lunatic Asylum.

He was admitted to Barming Heath on 5 October 1874 aged forty-two, with his illness attributed to anxieties about his business. He was not epileptic but was deemed to be suicidal and dangerous. John 'believed himself to have been poisoned … by having his nostrils plugged with creosote, and in consequence his head is filled with endless strands of flannel and coils of wire'. He had cut his throat on 11 June 1873 and 'desired when he left the last asylum … to place his head on the railway for the Engine to cut it off, having first got away from his friends for that purpose'.[20]

While at Barming Heath, John worked for Reverend Hornbrook in the library but it was 'not considered safe taking into account his suicidal dispositions that he should be so long left alone'. John's wife Charlotte and his sister Elizabeth pleaded for his release on trial, although the doctor believed he was 'so suicidal and melancholy that he cannot sanction his release even upon trial'. After appealing to the committee, John was released 'not improved'.[21]

When he was admitted to Malling Place on 8 April 1884, he was 'brought about midnight by a police sergeant and several constables in a fly from town Malling: he is very violent and excited. Manacled and his ankles bound by a rope…' He was suffering from acute mania and was said to have had a previous attack nine years earlier which had lasted for three years. John was believed to be 'dangerous more or less at all times'. By 11 April, he was refusing solid food and was not taking the volume of nourishment he needed. To solve the problem 'under the threat of the use of the stomach pump he drank from a feeding cup 2 eggs B:tea [beef tea] & menthol spirit.'[22]

While at Malling Place, John was regularly given chloral hydrate and potassium bromide to calm him and to help him sleep. He frequently tore his blankets and clothes to pieces and talked wildly about dynamite, murder, poison and being a devil. He also believed that electricity and clockwork were acting upon him – perhaps the nineteenth-century equivalent of getting messages through the television.

Around ten days after John's admission, he was permitted an interview with his wife as he was concerned about his business affairs. Unfortunately, 'he was with difficulty parted from his wife when it was found the interview was increasing his excitement'.[23] One can only imagine the anguish of both John and his wife.

John suffered with chronic bronchitis and exhaustion which was incurable. His condition was treated by keeping him warm with rugs and blankets, nursing him while he was sitting up in a chair and maintaining the temperature and humidity of his room by means of steam from a kettle.[24] In the absence of modern drugs and techniques, this was the right medical treatment for his condition. John 'lapsed into a sinking state' and died on 24 April 1884.[25]

Chapter 27

Recovery

Mental illness was not always permanent. Many of those afflicted enjoyed periods of good health. A good proportion of those who were sent to an asylum were deemed treatable and were expected to make a recovery.

Discharge from the asylum

William Battie, the physician of the St Luke's Hospital, a public lunatic asylum in London, argued that, if handled humanely, lunacy was 'no less curable than any other disease'.[1] If a patient was believed to have recovered from mental illness, he or she would be released into the care of family or friends on a trial basis. This was sometimes referred to as being 'on license' or 'on parole'. In some cases, especially for those whose health had improved but who had no family or friends to look after them, they might live permanently 'on parole' in the asylum. These patients had extra privileges such as being able to go to the nearest town by themselves.

Pauper lunatics were not discharged until the guardians of the relevant poor law union had agreed to it. Every union appointed a visiting committee to regularly visit the asylums which housed their lunatic poor. This enabled them to check on how many lunatics were chargeable to their union and to discuss each individual case with the asylum superintendent. If a pauper was deemed well enough to leave the asylum, he or she did not necessarily return to the workhouse. In many cases, such paupers were discharged to live with their family or friends, who were subsidised to look after them.[2]

Relapse of mental illness

Sadly, a relapse of mental illness was all too common for many patients. In their medical report for 1841, the physician and resident medical officer of the Aberdeen Asylum explained the most common cause of relapses or 'secondary attacks' of mental illness. Those who were discharged from the asylum, particularly those of the labouring classes, found it difficult to procure employment. This was mainly because 'Patients liberated from such an institution generally find the public prejudiced against them, and doubtful of the validity of their recovery…' When coupled with 'the evils of idleness, poverty, and scanty diet', it was believed that 'no combination of circumstances could be contrived more likely to prove fruitful of secondary attacks'.[3]

After leaving the Aberdeen Asylum for the first time, Christian Watt quickly realised how much of a stigma was attached to being an asylum patient: 'When I came home I found folk constantly trying to shun me as if I had leprosy. The usual pattern was to smile and be pleasant for a moment, then make some kind of excuse they were in an awful hurry to do something.'[4]

Unable to cope with the stresses of the outside world, Christian spent the last forty-five years of her life in the asylum, effectively living on parole. She worked in the laundry and as a fishwife, 'buying fish at Aberdeen Market, cleaning them and delivering them' to the asylum.[5]

Repeat admissions to the asylum were common. Benjamin Games was a patient at the Abergavenny Asylum on eight separate occasions, 'and apart from the last admission of almost eight years, he was usually a patient for less than a year'. Between 1887 and 1895, his case notes reveal he had had 'at least ten previous attacks of mainly recurrent religious mania'. He was described as 'very mischievous, noisy and excited, shouts and sings and is destructive and quarrelsome'. He was prescribed drugs but died on 6 June 1895 from vacuolar disease.[6]

The chapel at the Abergavenny Asylum. (With thanks to Louise Williams)

In many cases, patients preferred to stay in the safety of the asylum. In 1900, it was reported that six former patients of the Aberdeen Asylum had voluntarily applied for admission at the door. The patients were either 'labouring under morbid depression with the usual accompanying delusions, or were seeking the protection of the Asylum from imaginary tormentors'. The physician-superintendent argued that this proved that former patients appreciated the value of the treatment at the asylum and would go to 'disprove the erroneous ideas and prejudices entertained by many of the general public' about the way asylums worked and how patients were treated.[7]

Chapter 28

Physicians and Surgeons

At the beginning of Queen Victoria's reign, medical men were not usually drawn from the upper classes. They were the sons of 'men of the secondary professional classes or of tradesmen, of intelligent artisans and sometimes tradesmen and domestic servants' families'.[1] In fact, during the period 1800–89 only 3 per cent of the Fellows of the Royal College of Surgeons were classified as 'gentlemen' compared with 45 per cent of naval officers between 1814 and 1849.[2]

The link with tradesmen can be explained by the fact that medical practitioners were competing for business with apothecaries, druggists and pharmacists (and quacks). For the sons of pharmacists, becoming a bone fide medical practitioner was 'a greater source of esteem than remaining in the parallel trading occupation'.[3]

Twenty-five-year-old Bennett May, the house surgeon at Birmingham's General Hospital in 1871, spent part of his childhood in Edinburgh. At the age of fourteen, he was working there as a chemist's assistant. It is possible that he studied medicine at the University of Edinburgh before moving south to obtain his first post. By 1881, Bennett May was living with his French wife Emilie in Ilkeley, boarding at a lodging house, but ten years later he was back in Birmingham. The couple were living in Edmund Street where their neighbours were also surgeons.

Whichever social class the medical student came from, his family would have needed significant funds to put him through the course, unless he won a scholarship or prize. It has been argued that the 'expense, duration and nature of medical education' restricted the social class from which medical men were drawn from.[4]

The development of medical schools

Scotland had a 'virtual monopoly of university medical education' until the first of the new London medical schools opened in 1821.[5] The universities at Edinburgh, Glasgow, Aberdeen and St Andrews all had established medical schools, and, as a result, in the first half of the nineteenth century 'almost 95 per cent of doctors in Britain with a medical degree had been educated in Scotland'.[6]

In 1800, most medical teaching was provided by private profit-making schools. Only three London hospitals had medical schools attached (St Bartholomew's, the United Hospitals (St Thomas' and Guy's) and the London).[7]

The medical schools expanded as a result of the increase in demand. By 1841, there were 200 pupils at St George's and 300 at St Bartholomew's Hospital plus hundreds of students in other London hospital schools. London also had a teaching university with two colleges, King's and University. Both of these had 'medical faculties and purpose-built hospitals to provide clinical instruction'.[8] By 1858, twelve of London's hospitals had medical schools, accounting for 80 per cent of the general hospital beds in the capital.[9]

Doctors needed hospitals for teaching and research and in the first half of the nineteenth century many hospitals were founded for this specific purpose, such as St Mary's and Charing Cross.[10]

Students at the provincial hospital-based medical schools were entitled to sit the examinations for the University of London. If they passed, they qualified for the university degrees of M.B. (Bachelor of Medicine), or Ch.B (Bachelor of Surgery), C.M. (Master of Surgery) and M.D. (Doctor of Medicine). From the 1840s, medical students at the Universities of Oxford and Cambridge went to London or elsewhere to undertake their two or three years of clinical work because 'neither city was populous enough to possess a hospital sufficiently large to provide comprehensive clinical training'.[11] They then returned to their universities to be examined and qualify for the Cambridge or Oxford medical degrees. Cambridge

Right: 'Notes at a London Hospital: Medical Students Old Style.' (*The Graphic,* 27 December 1879)

Below: 'Notes at a London Hospital: The Medical Student New Style.' (*The Graphic,* 27 December 1879)

had just half a dozen medical students in the middle of the nineteenth century, but by 1900 there were about a hundred.[12]

In Birmingham, the Queen's Hospital was opened in 1841 and it became the first hospital in the city dedicated to the medical instruction of students at the Queen's College Medical School. It originally had seventy beds but an additional twenty-eight-bed fever ward was added in 1845.[13] The hospital's location near the centre of the city meant it received 'a disproportionate number of accident cases'.[14] Run like a private business, by 1852 the number of beds had more than doubled to 150, 'approximately 100 less than were found at the General'.[15] This apparent success was not matched by student numbers and tuition fees declined considerably over this period. A rival medical school called Sydenham College was set up by staff at the General Hospital in 1851. By 1868, the two medical schools had merged.[16]

After the 1860s, medical students had the option of studying at provincial centres such as Bristol and Manchester, which were in addition to Oxbridge and the cities in Scotland.[17] The training of students was vital to specialist institutions such as maternity hospitals. For instance, London's New General Lying-In Hospital admitted students as pupils to the attending male midwives (or accoucheurs).[18]

Qualifications and training

Under the terms of the 1815 Apothecaries Act, all apothecaries had to be licensed by the Society of Apothecaries. They had to pass examinations and 'needed to present certificates proving attendance of lectures on anatomy, chemistry, botany, materia medica, and the theory and practice of physic' to become Licentiates of the Society.[19] Apothecaries also had to spend six months working in a hospital, infirmary or dispensary. This six-month placement did not have to be full-time so students, who were usually still apprentices, spent a year or more of their apprenticeship in London attending lectures and undertaking clinical training.[20]

At the Cardiff Royal Infirmary, the House Surgeon, Thomas Jacob, was given leave of absence in 1838 and 1839 'to complete his professional Education, by attendance upon Lectures, &c. in London'.[21] He was allowed to go because he had procured the services of James Lewis, Junior to carry out his duties on a locum basis while he was away.

In the 1840s, almost 95 per cent of newly qualified doctors were members of the Royal College of Surgeons and holders of the Licence of the Society of Apothecaries.[22] At first, surgeons had a lower social status than physicians, and could operate and treat externally but were not allowed to give medicines internally. By 1854, there were approximately 200 fellows and 8,000 members of the College of Surgeons. They performed most of their operations at their patients' homes.[23]

By 1860, the old system of medical qualification by apprenticeship had largely been replaced by a formal medical education which included lectures, a syllabus and written examinations.[24] Through the hospital wards and the new medical textbooks, students could learn about recently identified diseases such as diabetes, poliomyelitis, muscular dystrophy and multiple sclerosis, and the most up-to-date ways of treating them.[25]

It was common for the more advanced medical students to take on a clerking role for several months, which 'could be a prelude to a house appointment and gradual advancement through the ranks to a consultancy'.[26] It was vital for students to make a good impression because consultants at teaching hospitals were usually chosen from their ranks.[27]

Ambitious medical students needed to get on the staff of a London teaching hospital and to obtain a fellowship of one of the Royal Colleges, a goal only the very wealthy could achieve. Medical fees varied dramatically. At the London School, they were between '£71 8s 0d at the Westminster and £100 16s 0d at King's for all the classes and hospital practice required for a diploma'. In the provinces, fees were not as high with Queen's College, Birmingham charging £52 10s 0d for the same provision.[28] Election (without examination) to a fellowship of the College of Physicians cost more than £110 while the College of Surgeons charged £31 for the same distinction but no examination was required.[29]

New legislation

The 1858 Medical Act marked 'a new era for medical practice in Britain'.[30] Although it did not outlaw unqualified practitioners such as homeopathists, herbalists, naturopaths and quacks, the Act established the Medical Register which ensured that no one who was unqualified could pass themselves off as a 'proper' doctor. This annual register listed all qualified practitioners with their qualifications which members of the public could check.

Above left: John Taylor Porter 1819–74, a Sheffield surgeon (see page 122). (With thanks to Prue Stokes)

Above right: William Smith Porter, a Sheffield physician, 1895 (see page 122-123). (With thanks to Prue Stokes)

Britain's medical corporations included the Royal College of Physicians, the Royal College of Surgeons, the Society of Apothecaries and the Royal Colleges or Faculties in Edinburgh, Glasgow and Dublin. Under the new Medical Act, candidates could be examined and certified to practice medicine by the medical corporations, the universities or hospital medical schools. The Licentiate of the Royal College of Physicians (the L.R.C.P.) and a university degree of M.B. (Bachelor of Medicine) were roughly equivalent, although the latter was a 'tougher qualification to achieve'.[31]

The Act also defined the qualifications required from recognised medical schools and set up the General Medical Council, which was responsible for keeping the Medical Register and 'policing the doctors' professional and ethical behaviour'.[32] This included 'sexual misconduct with patients, blatant advertising … and misrepresentation.'[33]

Most official medical posts were now restricted to properly qualified men who were listed in the Medical Register. This included hospital consultancies, public vaccinator posts and medical officerships in insane asylums, prisons, the colonies, the Poor Law and the public health service.[34]

Getting established

Once a doctor was qualified, his struggle for recognition and financial success began. A private practice was usually run from a doctor's own house, and in most towns, there was a 'medical district' in which the most successful doctors lived.

Even after years of dedication and training, a young physician or surgeon had to establish himself in an area before he could be considered a success. Sir James Paget, the eminent physician, surgeon and lecturer at St Bartholomew's Hospital, London traced the careers of 1,000 of his pupils over fifteen years, dating from when they entered the hospital. Of these 1,000 pupils, more than half (507) achieved fair success, defined as 'those who acquired a moderate practice – enough to live with – or ordinary public appointments'. Sixty-six who achieved considerable success were 'those who gained good practices, or more than ordinary esteem and influence in society' while only twenty-three achieved distinguished success, gaining and maintaining 'leading practices in counties or large towns, or held important public offices'. One hundred and twenty-four achieved only very limited success and 'were not in moderately good practice nor likely to obtain it'.[35]

Newly qualified doctors, or those with 'unfashionable practices in poor areas', struggled financially.[36] In 1886, more than two thirds of GPs were members of the Royal College of Surgeons, meaning that they could offer surgery and midwifery as part of their general practice. Even established general practitioners with a good reputation and paying patients could feel threatened by hospitals. Their wealthier patients could be tempted to visit hospital specialists acting as consultants, who might then offer them more general services.[37] GPs with a less wealthy clientele particularly feared losing their working-class patients to the out-patient department of the local hospital. It has been argued that it was particularly difficult to become established in Glasgow or Edinburgh because of the 'output of large numbers of graduates from the Scottish medical schools'.[38]

By 1914, the number of registered practitioners had increased to almost 45,000. However, the number of patients per qualified practitioner 'fluctuated at around 1,500'.[39] Doctors tended to prefer practices in urban areas rather than less lucrative, rural ones. In England, they also preferred the south to the north.

Duties of a hospital doctor

The number and type of medical officers in a hospital depended on the size of the institution. However, as a minimum, a hospital had several honorary part-time consultants, employed on an unpaid basis, plus a resident house surgeon who was paid.

In 1882 at the Aberdeen Royal Infirmary, there were three honorary physicians and four surgeons, one of whom was a junior surgeon. The physicians and the three senior surgeons were unpaid but they were all expected to give clinical lectures 'sharing equally in the fees'.[40]

There were also two assistants, one for the medical and one for the surgical department who were required to be medically qualified and of 'good moral character'. These assistants were similar in status to a house surgeon or house physician, resident in the hospital. Each assistant had free board and lodging in the hospital with a separate sitting room and bedroom. They were to give 'the whole of their time and attention to the professional duties of the department assigned to them' and neither could be absent without permission and 'on no account' could both assistants be absent at the same time. All members of staff who lived in the hospital were bound by the strict rules of the institution, and the assistants were not allowed to be out of the hospital after ten o'clock at night without permission.[41]

The assistants' main duties were to accompany the visiting physicians and surgeons on their rounds of the wards 'and take direction from them as to the treatment of Patients'.[42] They also had to provide a weekly record listing the patients in the infirmary and visit the wards 'without previous notice – especially between Eight and Ten in the morning, Two and Four in the afternoon, and Seven and Nine at Night'. This was specifically to check that prescriptions had been attended to and that the wards were in good order 'particularly whether any smoking has taken place in the Wards'. They were also required to visit the convalescent hospital at Loch-head once a week.[43]

In cases of emergency, the assistants were allowed to 'prescribe for any Patients whose diseases may have become aggravated, or who may have been admitted after the Medical Officers have left the House…' In addition, the Surgeon's Assistant was expected to perform minor surgical procedures, when required by the medical officers or in an emergency, but he could 'permit the Clerks & Dressers to perform them occasionally in his presence'.[44] In all serious accident cases arriving at the hospital, he had to send for the visiting surgeons.

Junior hospital posts

In 1860, there were approximately 15,000 registered medical practitioners. Less than 1,200 were working in 117 of the larger voluntary hospitals.[45] Of these, only 579 were classified as being 'physicians and surgeons who have charge of in-patients'.[46]

The remainder were working as assistants and junior housemen. These junior doctors chose the most interesting cases for their seniors from the out-patients. On a day-to-day basis, they supervised their seniors' in-patients when they were absent from the hospital. For instance, at the Westminster, Sir Anthony Carlisle was the senior surgeon responsible for between thirty and forty beds in 1838, 'but frequently left his patients in the care of former housemen'.[47] In some larger hospitals like The London, there was a house surgeon and a surgical registrar, while at other smaller institutions the role was combined.

Junior doctors gradually took over the work which had previously been done by apothecaries. The title of apothecary for the resident medical officer started to disappear and was dispensed with by The London in 1854, in St Thomas' Hospital in 1871 and in the Middlesex Hospital in 1886.[48] Most of the teaching in hospitals fell to the resident medical officers, who were followed on their daily rounds by the medical students.[49]

At first, junior doctors were not paid for their work. Small salaries started to be introduced for resident medical officers, varying between £50 and £100 per annum with full board.[50] In some hospitals, 'diligent students' might be appointed to a very junior post 'for which payment was demanded'.[51] Many provincial hospitals forbade even their most experienced 'registrars' from engaging in 'private practice lest they take business away from their seniors.'[52]

Vacancies for hospital surgeons at the Birmingham General Hospital were advertised nationally in the *Times*, *The Lancet*, the *British Medical Journal* and the *Medical Times and Gazette* as well as locally in *Aris's Gazette*, the *Birmingham Journal* and the *Midland Counties Herald*.[53]

Applications for resident medical officers at general hospitals came from a wide geographical area. In 1870, when Dr Welch resigned as the medical officer at Birmingham General Hospital, there were seven applications for the post including: Dr Arbuckle of Glasgow University; Dr Harrison of Liverpool Workhouse Infirmary and of King and Queen College Ireland; Dr Lough, House Surgeon to the Infirmary for Children in Liverpool and of Dublin University; Dr Marshall of Birmingham and of London University; and Dr Jefferies of Edinburgh University.[54]

Every hospital had a number of 'dressers' who were appointed by the surgical officers. These men were usually still students, and the role was an excellent form of apprenticeship. They had to attend every day when the surgeon visited the hospital and could assist in the operating theatre if required. The dressers could perform minor operations 'under the authority of the Medical Officers and in their presence, or in that of the Physicians' or Surgeons' Assistants'.[55] Despite their specialist role, they were not allowed to put on or remove any dressings 'unless in the presence of one of the Medical Officers or by his direction'.

Hugh Lett was a medical student who trained at The London. In 1896, he entered the wards as a dresser to McCarthy. He described McCarthy's rounds:

> He did not often operate in the theatre but, on his ward rounds, was accompanied by an attendant wearing a white coat who carried, suspended from his neck by a broad leather strap, a wooden tray covered with a white cloth on which lay one or two scalpels, a trocar and cannula for tapping hydroceles, catheters and steel dilators for treating strictures. For McCarthy did minor surgery, ranging from opening abscesses to tapping hydroceles, while taking his dressers round.[56]

According to Lett, at the time:

> There was only one surgical registrar, who was non-resident and not allowed to operate, his principal duty being to check and supplement the notes made by the house surgeon and the dresser…So, although his office afforded opportunity for *seeing* a great deal of surgery, lack of actual operating was a considerable omission in his training at a time when it was advancing rapidly…[57]

By contrast, Lett considered the great responsibilities of a house surgeon to be 'a magnificent training'.[58] This was largely because 'there was no registrar available at night to whom a house surgeon could turn for advice, [so] he had to decide for himself, in the case of emergencies, whether he should ask his chief to travel down to the Hospital to see and perhaps operate on a patient.'[59]

Senior hospital consultants

On a less frequent but more formal basis, both medical and surgical consultants 'walked the wards' with their medical students, providing knowledge and expertise in physical diagnoses and in interpreting post-mortem results.[60] These consultants usually worked part-time in the hospitals on an unpaid basis as they also retained lucrative private practices. As teachers, they generally kept a portion of students' fees'.[61] This part-time system continued well into the twentieth century. Professors of medicine, surgery, obstetrics and other subjects at the university-based schools in Edinburgh, Glasgow and University College London and others in the provinces 'would regularly retain varying amounts of private practice.'[62] It has been argued that 'both teaching and hospital patient care were sources of prestige but not much direct income'.[63]

Frederick Treves, former surgeon of The London,
1900. The 'Elephant Man' was one of his patients.
(*The Windsor Magazine*, December 1900)

By 1900, consultants with private practices had established themselves as 'the elite of the profession'.[64] In London, they often operated from premises in Harley Street and in other provinces and cities, in areas which rapidly became known as medical districts.

Physicians with private practices treated 'elite patients: those belonging to the aristocracy, the gentry and the well-to-do middle classes'.[65] This amounted to no more than a tenth of the population.[66] When these consultants worked in hospitals, the less affluent in- and out-patients had access to the best medical care available.

Surgeons also had private practices but increasingly, their operations were carried out in hospitals for convenience and safety reasons. This was because of the 'development of the anaesthesia and hygienic operating rituals, the requirement for a sterile operating environment and the need for numerous assistants'.[67] By 1900, the specialised operating theatre was the surgeon's 'normal place of work'.[68]

Poor law medical officers

In England and Wales, it was not until 1842 that the Poor Law Board decreed medical officers should be appointed on a salaried basis.[69] Before then, appointments were made on a contract basis, just like the tradesmen who supplied goods for the workhouse. Many penny-pinching boards of guardians were keen to secure 'the services of local doctors willing to make the lowest bid'.[70]

Applicants for the post of both workhouse medical officer and district medical officer had to possess a diploma or degree as a surgeon from a Royal College or University in England, Scotland or Ireland. In addition, he needed a degree in medicine *or* a diploma or licence of the Royal Physicians of London *or* a certificate to practice as an apothecary from the Society of Apothecaries of London. He was also qualified to apply if he had 'been in actual practice as an apothecary on the first day of August one thousand eight hundred and fifteen' or if he had a warrant or commission as surgeon or assistant-surgeon in Her Majesty's Navy, Her Majesty's Army or the Honourable East India Company prior to 1 August 1826.[71]

When a qualified doctor had not been able to establish himself in a hospital as a house surgeon or physician, he might apply for a post within a poor law institution. In 1844, one in six doctors held such posts. The guardians of the poor law unions often used competition as a lever to lower conditions of service and pay.

The appointment of doctors for the poor law service in Scotland was a thorny issue. Reforms in 1845 had legislated for doctors joining the staff of poor law institutions, but as late as the 1890s almost 10 per cent of parishes still paid general practitioners for individual visits and services for the poor.[72]

The duties of the workhouse medical officer were many and varied. It was his responsibility to examine the paupers in the receiving ward on admittance to the workhouse, and if any pauper was 'labouring under any disease of body or mind', the medical officer had to direct the master to place him or her in the sick ward.[73] With regard to the paupers of unsound mind, the medical officer had to decide whether they were fit to stay in the workhouse. If he deemed them to be too dangerous, he had to give the order to send them to a lunatic asylum, and report to the guardians accordingly.[74]

The workhouse medical officer had to supply drugs from his own salary, a requirement which was a contentious issue throughout the nineteenth century. To compensate, medical officers often recommended extras like food and beer to provide nourishment for the sick paupers under their care. In an attempt to ensure that inmates received the best possible medicines, a circular letter of 1865 issued by the Poor Law Board recommended that 'Cod Liver Oil, Quinine, and other expensive medicines, shall be provided at the expense of the Guardians'.[75] However, this reliance on the medical officer to supply drugs at his own expense continued into the early twentieth century.

By 1888, every London workhouse infirmary was run by a superintendent with one full-time assistant medical officer. These superintendents were often former resident housemen from voluntary hospitals 'who had failed to establish themselves as consultants'.[76] By 1905, the salaries of the superintendents working in London workhouse poor law unions were between £350 and £500 a year, plus 'spacious accommodation, coal, gas and laundry' and extra fees for 'vaccinations and the certification of lunatics'.[77]

The assistant medical officers working in poor law infirmaries were usually young practitioners 'who found the work a useful introduction to general practice'.[78] Junior medical assistants were paid £100 per annum while the starting annual salary of senior assistants was £120, which could rise to a maximum of £160. Most assistant medical officers resigned after two or three years while some poor law unions appointed them for one year only.[79]

Working in the poor law service

Born in 1869 in Gainsborough, Lincolnshire, Frederick Henry Waddy came from a family of ministers. His father, grandfather and brother were all Wesleyan ministers but Frederick chose the medical profession, the first in his family to do so. He studied medicine at the University of Glasgow, graduating with an M.D., C.M. in 1893 followed by an M.B. in 1896.

After several house appointments, Frederick was appointed as the senior resident medical officer at the Fir Vale Union Workhouse Infirmary in Sheffield, a post he held for three years. Frederick was highly regarded at Fir Vale and on leaving in 1899, the medical staff presented him with a glass-topped coffee table, under which was a signed painted picture featuring all their signatures, together with a souvenir album of photographs.

Frederick had decided to set up as a general practitioner in the city and at the time of the 1901 census, he was living with his wife Ellen and a servant in another part of Sheffield, described as 'physician and surgeon'. They had been married for just a year. It would have taken Frederick some time to establish his general practice and the financial implications of this would have been great. An initially low income could explain why Frederick and Ellen were not living in an area associated with medical men.

Although he later obtained the Diploma of Public Health, Frederick chose to remain in general practice and retained his association with the guardians of the Fir Vale Union as a parish doctor and public vaccinator. His family remembers that he would not send a bill to a patient if he thought he or she was suffering from genuine hardship. Sadly, Frederick was diagnosed with encephalitis lethargica in 1924 and his ill-health forced him to retire from general practice three years later. He died in 1948. Frederick's obituary records that 'he followed his profession for nearly thirty years with a degree of integrity and philanthropy that led to his being profoundly respected'.[80]

Women in the medical profession

By the end of the nineteenth century, the status of the medical profession had risen to such an extent that middle-class women clamoured for admittance.[81] The first registered female doctor in Britain was Elizabeth Blackwell, who qualified in the USA in 1849.

The first woman to qualify as a doctor in Britain was Elizabeth Garrett. She cleverly exploited legal loopholes to gain the diploma of the Society of Apothecaries in 1865, and so secured her place on the Medical Register. By 1870, she had 'developed an extensive private practice, established St Mary's Dispensary for Women, received a medical degree from Paris and married the wealthy James Anderson'.[82] She helped to establish the London School of Medicine for Women in 1874 'and by her very respectability proved a persuasive diplomat for the claims of women to be doctors'.[83]

However, between 1856 and 1881, women were prevented from accessing 'medical schools, clinical instruction, examinations and medical licensing'.[84] By 1891, there were 101 registered female doctors in Britain and this number rose to 477 twenty years later. Despite this apparent victory, once qualified, most female doctors worked in local authority services or in women's or children's hospitals which were 'professionally less contested areas of work'.[85]

In 1892, the managers of the Glasgow Royal Infirmary resolved that 'the female students should be afforded facilities for education in the Wards, and also for pathological instruction, separate from male students'. A surgical and medical ward was allocated for this purpose.[86] The female students came from St Mungo's College, Edinburgh, London, Bombay, Canada and the United States. Their number also included missionary students who only attended the dispensary.[87]

Working as a surgeon

Nathaniel Paine Blaker was born in Sussex in 1835, the son of a farmer. His great-uncle, Harry Blaker, was one of the 300 original surgeons in the Royal College of Surgeons so it is likely Nathaniel's medical ambitions were influenced by his relative. He was sent away to school, and on returning home at the age of sixteen, he started to learn farming with his father. This was the time of the agricultural depression and he stayed at home for a year before deciding that he wanted to enter the medical profession. His father secured for him a pupilage at the Sussex County Hospital, the advertisement for which appeared in the *Sussex Express*. On 21 June 1852, Nathaniel started his professional education as a resident pupil on probation for a month; and was afterwards regularly apprenticed to the House Surgeon for the time being, for five years, 'with implied permission to spend the last two years at a London School of Medicine'.

The fee which Nathaniel's father had to pay was £300, a not insubstantial sum, so it is likely that he was a 'gentleman farmer'. At first, Nathaniel spent his mornings working in the dispensary while afternoons were used for studying for a new examination.

At the time, the resident staff at the hospital consisted of the house surgeon, the matron, three or four pupils and the dispenser. The House Surgeon, 'besides having the care of the patients and the supervision of the Wards, was answerable for a good deal of the executive work, and, being by statute resident master of the establishment, all cases of difficulty were referred to him'. Although the dispenser was responsible for the making up of medicines, this was mostly done by the resident pupils. There were also a number of non-resident pupils, 'who in those days were apprenticed to various medical men in the town, and were allowed to see the practice at the Hospital on payment of £10 per annum'.

Nathaniel left the Sussex County Hospital for Guy's in 1855, and completed two winter sessions before having to return home after contracting phthisis. Eighteen months later, he returned to the medical profession. It was the last year of the 'old regime which required only three winter and two summer sessions at a recognised Hospital' and a one hour viva voce examination divided into four quarters, a quarter of an hour being spent at each of four tables. Nathaniel had spent almost five years at the Sussex County Hospital which was a recognised institution, so he was allowed to take both the Apothecaries Hall Diploma and the College Examination, which he passed.

After qualifying, he spent three months covering for a house surgeon at the Sussex County Hospital and then several months at Guy's working in the wards. In the autumn of 1859, he was appointed as the assistant surgeon at the Convict Hospital, first at Lewes, then at the newly built model prison at Knapp Hill, close to Woking. The surgeons were responsible for about 300 invalid convicts, 'of whom about 20 or 30 were mental cases, some bordering on insanity; a considerable number were convalescents after accidents or acute disease, sent from able-bodied prisons, and some were chronic invalids'. In 1860, Nathaniel was appointed as the house surgeon to the Brighton and Hove Dispensary. He left the Dispensary after two years and in the mid-summer of 1864, he was elected as house surgeon to the Sussex County Hospital, 'a post which had been my aim since the time I was pupil there'. Nathaniel was appointed Assistant Surgeon to the hospital in 1869.[88]

Medical staff at Sheffield with William Smith Porter fourth from the right, 1880s (see page 122–123). (With thanks to Prue Stokes)

A group of women doctors, 1910. (NHS Greater Glasgow and Clyde Archives)

Staff at the FirVale Infirmary with Frederick Waddy on the left, 1899 (see page 119). (With permission of the Waddy family)

Born in Sheffield in 1819, John Taylor Porter was the eldest of six children, the son of a respected tea merchant. It is not known what prompted John to choose the medical profession but there were several medical men in his mother's family. His great-grandfather was a surgeon and mayor of Chesterfield, and two other relatives were also surgeons.

John studied at the Sheffield Medical School and at University College London. In 1840, he became a member of the Royal College of Surgeons for England and a year later, he spent some time studying in Paris. He became a pupil and later a partner of Mr Henry Thomas, a Sheffield surgeon.

In 1848, he applied for the position of surgeon to the Sheffield General Infirmary but was defeated as a candidate by thirteen votes, with Mr Samuel Gregory getting the post. This was also the year he married Sarah Smith, the eldest daughter of William Smith, barrister-at-law and JP. John was later elected as surgeon to the Sheffield Public Hospital & Dispensary which became the Royal Hospital.

For several years, John Taylor Porter was a lecturer at the Sheffield School of Medicine. He was also a district surgeon for the Midland Railway Company, which was probably a form of 'club' work. In 1871, he became a Fellow of the Royal College of Surgeons and was still a consulting surgeon at the time of his death in 1874.[89]

Working as a physician

Once a man was established in the medical profession, it was common for sons to follow in the footsteps of their fathers. Family connections would certainly have been helpful in obtaining a first post in a hospital, making the career path for sons slightly easier than it had been for their fathers.

William Smith Porter, born in 1855, was the only surviving son of John Taylor Porter. He was born in Surrey Street, the doctors' and dentists' quarter in Sheffield. A number of other medical men lived nearby in houses with stables for their horses and carriages, including Dr Walker who did his rounds on horseback and charged an extra fee for an examination with a stethoscope.

It was only natural that William should follow in his father's footsteps into the medical profession. He studied at Leeds (1873–77), King's College, London (1877–79) and Durham University at Newcastle

(1879–1880). William became a member of the Royal College of Surgeons in 1878 but after this, he must have decided to keep his options open by undertaking further medical qualifications. He became a Licentiate of the Royal College of Physicians in 1879, a Bachelor of Medicine in 1880 and a Doctor of Medicine in 1882.

Although William's first post was as house surgeon at the Sheffield Infirmary from 1881 until 1883, his later positions were all as physicians. This would indicate that he made a conscious decision to specialise in medicine, rather than surgery. Between 1883 and 1887, he was the Honorary Physician at the Sheffield Public Hospital. From there, he moved back to the Sheffield Infirmary as an Honorary Physician, a post he held until his retirement in 1920. In the same year, he was elected Consulting Physician at the Royal Infirmary.

As an Honorary Physician, William would have had time to undertake other fee-paying medical activities. This included lecturing to medical students. Between 1885 and 1888, he lectured at the medical school on physiology and on medicine between 1888 and 1899.

William was one of the first to draw attention to the prevalence of lead poisoning in Sheffield which was traced to the water supply flowing through lead piping. He gave evidence to the commission of inquiry in 1890. In the same year, William and Dr Duncan Burgess represented the Sheffield Medico-Chirurgical Society in Berlin at the investigation by Dr Robert Koch into a new treatment for tubercular diseases. Their report was presented to the society on 11 December 1890. William was also President of the Society between 1911 and 1912.

William was well established in his career by the time he married in 1893. His bride was his second cousin, Jessie Lockwood, and they had three daughters who were all born in Glossop Road, Sheffield. Their house had consulting rooms indicating that William was also gaining an income from private practice. By 1904, the family moved to Hope in Derbyshire where William had a house built for them. He continued to work in Sheffield, travelling into the city each day by train.

Dr William Smith Porter diagnosed his own terminal illness and died in October 1927 at the age of seventy-one. The obituaries describe him as one of Sheffield's oldest and most respected members of the medical profession. The *British Medical Journal* noted he was 'A man of wide general culture, the soul of honour, a model of courtesy and kindly consideration for patients and colleagues alike… Help and advice he gave would be based upon wide experience, sound judgement and, above all, a disinterested love of truth and right'. *The Lancet* added that 'Porter will be remembered first not as a physician … but as a gentle, courteous, kindly companion, who never said an unkind word or thought an unkind thought of any man'.[90]

Chapter 29

Matrons

The Victorian period saw a great change in the role of the hospital matron, and in the qualities, qualifications and class of person who undertook the role. Until the last quarter of the nineteenth century, her duties revolved around the housekeeping and economy of the hospital; afterwards, she was charged with the training and selecting of nurses, and was expected to be a trained nurse herself.

The first matrons

Until the 1870s, hospital matrons were efficient housekeepers whose main role was to supervise the domestic arrangements of the institution, such as managing the laundry, cooking and cleaning. They were not trained nurses, and although they appointed the nursing staff who worked in the hospitals, often in consultation with the medical staff, they did not instruct them in their work. It was not the matron's duty 'to tell the sisters what they ought to be doing for the doctors'.[1]

Jane Eliza Bigwood, the matron of Birmingham's General Hospital in 1871, was born in St Catherine's, Bath, Somerset. She gained experience of running an institution as matron of the Martley Union Workhouse before being appointed as matron at Birmingham. Later, she became the Lady Superintendent at the Blackwell Road Sanatorium in Bromsgrove, a much smaller institution.

Matrons (and nurses) were expected to be unmarried or widowed without 'encumbrances'. If a prospective matron had dependant children, she would only be appointed if she could demonstrate that they were being looked after by someone else in her family.

Responsibilities

Even before the role changed, the value of an efficient matron to a hospital was immeasurable. In 1847, a complaint about the matron, Mrs Hill, was entered in the Visitors' Book of the Cardiff Royal Infirmary. She had been matron for five years, and it was alleged she had quarrelled with a patient and 'scolded her to such a degree that she had left the Institution in consequence'.[2] On investigation by the managers, it was found that 'much irregularity' had taken place regarding the diet table. The matron's explanations 'were not satisfactory' and she was given notice to leave.[3]

The Committee at Cardiff decided it was vital to have 'a superintendent of superior character and position' as Mrs Hill's replacement. To this end, they offered £30 a year instead of £20 a year, 'with the hope of securing the services of a more competent and highly qualified person…'.[4] Mrs Ann Jacob was appointed and remained as matron until 1865. It is believed she was the mother of Thomas Jacob, who had previously been house surgeon at the hospital. Ann Jacob was described on the census as the widow of a surgeon so she may have had previous experience of hospital life.

Anna Morrice, the matron at the Royal South Hants Infirmary, was especially talented when it came to economical management. Between the years 1855 and 1861, her salary ranged from £41 5s 0d to £48 15s 0d. In every year except the first, she was able to raise funds for the hospital in excess of her annual salary, simply by selling the kitchen waste or 'refuse'.[5] In 1861, £59 4s 10d was raised for the hospital in this innovative way. In effect, the matron was more than paying for her own salary, making her a very valuable employee.

New matrons

The new matrons, sometimes termed 'Lady Superintendents', were educated women and fully trained nurses. They were no longer simply housekeepers, in fact many were permitted to appoint a housekeeper to relieve them of 'the general drudgery of housekeeping'.[6] They had complete control over the nurses and also the female servants, in terms of selecting and training them, as well as their day-to-day routine and living conditions. They were answerable only to the superintendent of the hospital. Arguably, the most important aspect of their role was to put into place a system of training for the nurses. Many of them were Nightingale-trained nurses, who brought the ideals and methods of that pioneering training system to their new posts.

As had been the case prior to the change of role, the new matrons were expected to be without 'encumbrances', and this could sometimes mean making sacrifices. In July 1879, Mrs Rebecca Strong was appointed Matron of the Glasgow Royal Infirmary, as a replacement for Anne Tait who had held the post for fifteen years.[7] Rebecca Strong was a

Miss Eva Lückes, matron of The London Hospital, 1900. (*The Windsor Magazine*, December 1900)

Nightingale-trained nurse who had gained staffing experience at Winchester, the Royal Victoria Military Hospital at Netley, and at the Dundee Infirmary where she was matron.

The daughter of an innkeeper, Rebecca had been widowed at the early age of twenty-two and was left with a one-year-old daughter, Annie Ellen, to provide for.[8] Rebecca remained 'anxious to make her life of some use'[9] and when Annie was three, she decided to try nursing and entered the Nightingale Training School in 1867. Annie was looked after by members of Rebecca's family in London. It is not known how frequently Rebecca saw her daughter but she was dedicated to her role as matron at Glasgow, a post she held until 1885 when she set up her own private nursing home. In 1891, she was reappointed as matron at Glasgow, staying until she retired from the post in 1907.

Changing of the guard

In 1865, when Ann Jacob, the matron of the Cardiff Royal Infirmary, retired after eighteen years in the post, the managers promoted Emily Markham, the head nurse, as her successor. Emily Markham had been appointed as an efficient, trained nurse from 'one of the metropolitan hospitals' two years earlier to take sole charge of the nursing department. She was, in fact, one of the first trained 'Nightingale' nurses and came from a typical working-class background.[10] Emily was born in Louth, Lincolnshire in 1839 and was the daughter of a coachbuilder. Her promotion at Cardiff could be seen as a real changing of the guard. However, it appears that she did not last long in the role. By 1869, the managers were singing the praises of Caroline Barnard, their new, highly efficient matron.[11] Emily Markham went on to be matron at the Royal Portsmouth Portsea & Gosport Hospital, but by 1891 she had moved to Islington to be the superintendent of a Girls' Training Home, where her younger sister Jane (who was also Nightingale-trained) was the matron.

Matron Rebecca Strong and nurses of the Glasgow Royal Infirmary, 1890s. (NHS Greater Glasgow and Clyde Archives)

Matronships as a career

Working as a hospital matron represented a real career path to Victorian trained nurses. Ambitious women sought matronships across Britain, and were extremely mobile in their pursuit of the ideal post where they could make their mark. Some chose to stay at one hospital for twenty years or more, while others chose to move regularly between hospitals.

In 1882, when Birmingham's General Hospital needed to appoint a new matron, there were more than forty applications. Five women were selected for interview and Anna Aeton Gwyn, a trained nurse and the daughter of a land proprietor, was appointed.[12] In June, the matron objected to her present sitting room and asked for another, but the Committee informed her 'there was no other room'.[13] By 1 September, the Committee were receiving applications for the post of matron again[14] so it seems that Anna Gwyn could not cope with the accommodation provided. She continued her career as a matron at the Royal Bath Hospital, Harrogate and The Royal Hants County Hospital.

As the matron of Blackburn Infirmary, Mary Whitton was praised in the hospital's annual report of 1871 for her 'unremitting, judicious and faithful attention to her most anxious duties' which had 'the highest testimony of the Board.'[15] Mary trained at the Nightingale School at St Thomas's Hospital between 1866 and 1867. Described in her training record as 'a person of moderate capacity', while training she had to undergo an operation for a tumour.[16] Before becoming matron at Blackburn, she had worked at St Thomas's and Lincoln County Hospital.

Aberdeen's Royal Infirmary had its first Nightingale-trained nurse when Margaret Bothwell was appointed as head nurse in 1875. She had been one of a party of thirteen nurses sent to the Edinburgh Royal Infirmary from the Nightingale Training School as soon as she had finished her training in November 1872. At Aberdeen, she was 'appointed unseen' and stayed in the post of head nurse for ten years. In effect, she was carrying out many of the duties of the new matrons in other city hospitals because she was responsible for the selection and training of new nurses. When Margaret joined the staff, the nurses 'were still carrying coals from the cellars to the wards and were cleaning and scrubbing the ward floors'. Afterwards, the porter carried the coals and two 'respectable women' were engaged as scrubbers 'to scrub and clean between 6 and 9 o'clock every week day'.[17] At the time, in addition to Margaret Bothwell, there was another member of staff in place who took on housekeeping duties. Margaret appears to have become a 'victim of the disintegrating management structure', in particular, the fact that the medical superintendent could not cope with his colleagues or the 'dual responsibility' of the head nurse and housekeeper.[18]

By 1885, the hospital had decided to appoint a Lady Superintendent who was to be an educated, trained nurse with the ability to train the nurses under her, and Margaret Bothwell was asked to leave. The salary was to be £100 with residence and board in the hospital, and the post was to be advertised.[19] However, it does not appear that an advertisement was ever placed as the post was offered to Miss Rachel Lumsden, who was the Honorary Lady Superintendent of the Sick Children's Hospital. Rachel was the daughter of a gentlemen of Glenbogie, and had trained at the Hospital for Sick Children in Great Ormond Street before transferring to King's College Hospital 'to train under the Sisters of St John'.[20]

A minute dated 29 October in the Aberdeen Royal Infirmary records state that 'her emoluments shall be £150 per annum with rooms and board in the House'. However, a letter from Rachel Lumsden dated 6 November stated 'I prefer to give my work without remuneration.' She was therefore appointed on an honorary basis.[21]

In 1879, Miss Swift, who had been matron of The London for twelve years, resigned and in the following year, Miss Eva Lückes was appointed as her successor. The new matron was the daughter of a country gentleman who had been given the advantages of a good education, 'first as a "parlour boarder" at a school in Malvern, then at Cheltenham College and finally on the Continent'. She returned home to Gloucestershire after the death of her father, spending her time helping to run the house and visiting the sick in her parish. At this stage, Eva Lückes became interested in nursing as career and joined the Middlesex as a lady probationer. Ill-health forced her to give up this post after a few months, but later she re-started and completed her training at the Westminster under Miss Merryweather.[22]

After qualifying, she became a night sister at The London for a few months, before being appointed as Lady Superintendent at the Pendlebury Children's Hospital in Manchester. It was said that she had differences of opinion with the governors there because she 'tried to establish a "nursing despotism" over the medical staff'.[23] At the tender age of twenty-four, Eva Lückes applied for the matronship of The London when it fell vacant. When interviewed by the Committee, many of the members believed she was 'much too young and pretty' to be a hospital matron. Her nursing experience was not extensive either but 'something in her personality must have appealed because she was elected by a small majority'.[24]

Within twenty-four hours of taking up her duties at The London, Eva Lückes tackled the House Committee, 'a collection of timid, middle-aged and elderly gentlemen, heavily handicapped by lack of funds'. She told them that The London's nursing staff 'was grossly inadequate both in quality and numbers'.[25] Her first recommendation was that 'lockers should be installed in the children's ward so that each one might have a separate towel and flannel instead of the same towel being used for all at the risk of spreading contagion'.[26]

Conflict with medical staff

The matrons' new role often brought them into conflict with the medical staff. In 1880, at Guy's Hospital in London, the matron, Margaret Burt, had established a nursing staff 'responsible through her directly to the hospital governors rather than the medical staff'. The medical staff complained that 'the regimented rhythm of patient life in hospital – washing, eating, visiting, and so forth – was arranged around the structure of the nurses' day rather than the good of the patient (or the convenience of the medical staff)'.[27]

It has been argued that if the matron was to undertake her duties efficiently, she 'had to carve out an empire of her own'.[28] She had to take over some of the responsibilities of the medical staff and the lay administration.[29] If the hospital governors supported the matron, resistance from the lay administrators could be easily overcome. However, any conflict between the unpaid doctors and the new matrons became 'a battle of the sexes'. The matrons had to 'win a position of power for their sex in an institution which was exclusively controlled by men'.[30]

By 1880, the matrons had assumed control in the majority of London's leading voluntary hospitals. It has been argued that the change was achieved quickly because 'the ladies who sought power in the hospitals moved in the same social circle as the committees that ran them'.[31]

Chapter 30

Nurses

The comfort and welfare of patients in hospitals … depends in no small degree upon the amount and kind of nursing which they receive. The good which a good nurse is capable of affecting, and the evils which result from the employment of careless and incompetent nurses … are very considerable.[1]

So wrote Bristowe and Holmes in 1863 of nursing in hospitals across Britain. This observation was undoubtedly true because, of all the hospital staff, it was the nurses with whom patients had the most contact.

Before nursing reforms

Before the 1860s and 1870s, voluntary hospitals were staffed with untrained nurses, usually drawn from a class similar to that of the patients. While Bristowe and Holmes insisted that 'A fish-fag, a hawker, or any person habituated to a coarse or debasing kind of life, is evidently neither by education nor habit fitted to become a nurse'[2], there were benefits to what became known as the 'old-style' nurses.

A consultant at The Royal Devon and Exeter Hospital commented that the old-style nurses '…had a homeliness about them that made the patients, especially the old folk, feel at home in the hospital … they could enter into the troubles of their patients and act as an intermediary'.[3] The ability of these nurses to put their patients at ease was undoubtedly because they were drawn from the same social class.

Frederick Treves, a former surgeon at The London, described one of the old school untrained nurses from the 1860s as 'one of the most remarkable women in the Hospital'. He added:

> She was completely without education. Yet her experience of casualties of every kind, and death, was vast and indeed unique. Further, she was entirely self-taught… [she] was coarse in her language, abrupt yet not unkindly in her manner… The dressers regarded her with respect, and from her they learnt the elements of minor surgery and first aid. The house surgeons admired and were a little frightened of her. Her diagnosis of an injury was usually correct, so sound was her observation and so wide her experience…[4]

Despite this natural affinity with patients, in the early nineteenth century, the nurse's role was quite limited. She could help the doctor with dressings but only 'by fetching tins of warm water'. She was allowed to 'apply bread or linseed poultices but the rule was that "as soon as dressings of lotion and lint were ordered, the pupil will take charge"'. The pupils were men employed as assistants to the trained doctors or apothecaries.[5] The pupil system died out in the nineteenth century and it fell to the nurses to carry out what they had previously done.[6]

Florence Nightingale's training school for nurses

In the 1860s, the usual route into nursing was for potential recruits 'to enter hospitals as scrubbers, and work their way up'.[7] There was no system of training in place and little incentive towards career progression in terms of salary, accommodation or working conditions.

Nursing reform started very slowly with Florence Nightingale establishing her training school at St Thomas's Hospital in 1860. Miss Nightingale knew exactly what kind of women would be most suitable for the rigours of nursing. She wanted 'the morality and spiritual devotion of religious orders, the education of the middle-classes, combined with the hardiness of working-class girls'.[8] However, this combination of qualities was difficult to find and the first trainees or 'probationers' were from the working-classes.

The first Nightingale probationers were chosen by Mrs Wardroper, the matron of St Thomas's Hospital. The training was free and probationers were given rations of tea and sugar, washing, some outer clothing and £10 for the one year's course. They were also given a gratuity of £3 or £5 'according to their class of award on evidence of their serving in a hospital for the poor sick following their training year'.[9]

Like the matrons, nurses had to be unmarried or widowed without dependant children. Florence Nightingale expected her probationers to work hard and insisted that each probationer's time 'ought to be fully taken up with her ward work, her necessary sleep and exercise and what making and mending she has to do for herself…'[10] She was adamant that a common day room for the probationers was unnecessary because it encouraged 'dawdling and gossiping'.[11] A secure nurses' home was, however, considered essential. Once trained, the Nightingale nurses were known as 'sisters'.

The first Nightingales were expected to sign on for six years, and after the first year, they could be sent wherever they were needed. According to Rebecca Strong, a Nightingale-trained nurse who became matron at Glasgow Royal Infirmary, by the end of the first year of training, 'you were supposed to have picked up enough knowledge and wisdom to fit you for pioneer work in other hospitals [and] you went wherever you were sent'.[12] At the end of the six-year period, the Nightingale nurses were free to apply for posts of their choice.

There were fourteen sub-divisions under which the Nightingale probationers were assessed:

  1. Dressings
  2. Applying Leeches
  3. Enemas
  4. Management of Trusses and Uterine Appliances
  5. Rubbing
  6. Helpless Patients
  7. Bandaging
  8. Making Beds
  9. Waiting on Operations
  10. Sick Cooking
  11. Keeping Wards Fresh
  12. Cleanliness of Utensils
  13. Management of Convalescents
  14. Observation of the Sick[13]

Probationers were graded 'excellent', 'good', 'moderate', 'imperfect' or '0' in all fourteen sub-divisions. They were also assessed on 'Punctuality, Quietness, Trustworthiness and Personal Neatness'.[14] Finally, the probationer's moral character was commented upon.

The quality of the training at the Nightingale School was by no means perfect. Emma Rappe, who came to St Thomas's by special arrangement from Sweden, declared 'We did not learn this or that at St Thomas's and there was not held a single lecture in anatomy or physiology while I was there'.[15] Rebecca Strong agreed, recalling that 'Theoretical instruction was almost *nil*, which was a great disadvantage, the more enterprising had recourse to medical books'.[16]

Nevertheless, the Nightingale training system had far-reaching influences as the superintendent nurses took the system throughout Britain and overseas to Australia, Canada, New Zealand and the United States.[17] In Britain, Nightingale-trained nurses were seen as a real asset and it was something of a coup to have such a nurse working on the staff.

Lady probationers

After 1867, Florence Nightingale decided that the Nightingale Fund should 'aim at better educated recruits in order to supply training sisters'. These new lady recruits were termed 'special probationers' who paid for their board and lodging and who were to be 'groomed for superintendence'.[18] The new 'specials', also known as lady probationers, demanded better training and Mr John Croft was appointed to give lectures to them. He saw 'his brighter pupils as ancillary doctors able to take on the measuring and treatments previously done by doctors'.[19]

An unknown nurse, *c*.1900. (Northern General Hospital History Project, Sheffield)

A matronship was the goal of every ambitious lady probationer. By the 1880s, almost all teaching hospitals had lady probationers 'who went forth to pioneer nurse training … as acceptable assistants to doctors in hospitals now catering for the middle class.'[20] A probationer was a real asset to a hospital, especially if she paid for her own training.

Those who became sisters were drawn from a very different class of society to ordinary nurses. They were people who had been 'head servants in gentleman's families', 'widows in reduced circumstances' or 'persons who have lived in a respectable rank of life'.[21] They were paid between £20 and £40 per year.

The class difference meant that the new lady probationers expected a better standard of living accommodation. This was deemed especially important because, as they were paying for their training, they were not under contract and could leave whenever they wanted.

The training of nurses in Britain

In the 1870s and 1880s, most large voluntary hospitals had put into place a variation of the probationer system of nurse training, albeit imperfect and evolving. Probationers were a mixture of ordinary nurses who were usually paid by the hospital during their training period, and lady probationers who paid for the privilege of receiving the training.

There was a nurses' training school at The London as early as 1873, instigated by the matron, Miss Swift, who 'was not Nightingale trained, but had imbibed many Nightingale ideas'.[22]

At the Aberdeen Royal Infirmary in 1875, the trustees of the late Robert Donaldson 'offered to grant a sum of money yearly to approved applicants who might … desire and agree to qualify themselves as Nurses'. This became known as the Donaldson Scheme, under which women undertook twelve months of training on the wards. Preference was given to applicants 'willing to receive a portion of their time in the Fever Wards'. At the end of the twelve-month period, eligible nurses received a Certificate of Efficiency and a monetary payment, 'the whole amount, including Dress, Lodging and Gratuity, not to exceed Fifteen Pounds to each Person'. The hospital's administrators reported that the services of the trained nurses 'are much valued and eagerly sought by professional men and private families'.[23]

With the introduction of antiseptic techniques, the effective training of nurses, in both practical and theory, became more important. The problem was addressed by Eva Lückes, the new matron at The London, through lectures given to the probationers by herself. She gave her first lecture on 30 June 1881 and three years later, the lectures were published in her book *General Nursing*.[24] She also started giving lectures to the sisters twice a year and 'Hospital Sisters and their Duties' was included in the second edition of her book published in 1886.[25]

Eva Lückes persuaded the medical staff to help her with the nurses' training, and lectures on elementary anatomy and surgery, as well as physiology and medicine, were given. Specialists were also asked to lecture on their own subjects.[26] Examinations for the probationers were introduced in 1882, with certificates awarded to those reaching the required standard.[27] Of the first thirty candidates to take the examination, sixteen passed, eleven failed and three were absent.

By December 1886 at the Aberdeen Royal Infirmary, the matron Rachel Lumsden had initiated a similar system of nurse training which included three courses of lectures: general nursing, elementary anatomy and surgical nursing, and elementary physiology and medical nursing. Five years later, a three year training programme was introduced.[28]

In Cardiff in 1888, the nurses were receiving three lectures a week from the surgical and medical staff. In October of that year, the House Surgeon applied for a number of requisitions for the nurses in connection with his classes, including:

I – Diagrams and Illustrations similar to those used by the St John's Ambulance Association (required for the lectures)
II – Lucker's Lectures on Nursing (a copy for each nurse) [this was probably Eva Lückes' manual]
III – Berkeley Hills 'Essentials of Bandaging' for circulation amongst the nurses
IV – Two copies of Blackie's Physiology
V – A copy of Hoblyns Dictionary of Medical Terms[29]

A large supply of probationers were needed because the nursing profession was made up of young women who could not continue their careers if they chose to marry. However, finding the right applicants was a difficult task and at Birmingham's General Hospital in the 1890s a minimum height of 5ft 2in and a minimum weight of 8 stone was specified for probationers, presumably to ensure they were strong enough for the work.[30] By 1900, because of the lack of applicants which matched this criteria, the minimum weight of 8 stone had to be withdrawn.[31] It was also thought that women between twenty-three and thirty-five were the most suitable age for nursing.

The nursing arrangements at the Glasgow Royal Infirmary were typical of most large voluntary hospitals in the 1880s. There were sixty-two nurses for the thirty-one wards divided into day nurses and night nurses, with one of each devoted to each ward. In addition, there were twenty-nine probationers which the Royal used as a kind of 'floating staff'. There was usually one probationer assigned to each ward as an assistant, but the most experienced were 'selected to do duty for the regular nurses when on leave of absence or disabled by sickness'.[32] The nurses were assisted by twenty scrubbers and cleaners, and sixteen washerwomen and laundrymaids.[33]

Preliminary nurse training schools

While theoretical instruction was undoubtedly a good thing for the nurses' training, it was extremely difficult for them to get the most from the lectures because they had very little time off the wards. Rebecca Strong, the matron at Glasgow's Royal Infirmary, recalled that 'it was weary work; sleepy, tired nurses trying to take an interest in what they knew would be useful to them, and we unable to give them leisure'.[34] This realisation led to the establishment of the first Preliminary Training School for Nurses in Britain at Glasgow in 1892, instigated by Rebecca Strong and the medical staff at the infirmary.

It was some time before the idea was copied elsewhere in Britain, but by June 1895 The London had its own preliminary training school at Tredegar House.[35]

The role of trained nurses

Much was expected of Victorian nurses and Eva Lückes, matron of The London, did not believe a nurse was an ordinary woman or 'she would not have chosen work which taxes her feelings and energies, mental and physical, so much'.[36] Writing of the qualities of an ideal nurse, Florence Nightingale stressed the need for 'hygiene, fresh air, stern discipline, *esprit de corps*, and devotion to nursing as a vocation'.[37]

By 1898, Burdett's Official Nursing Directory described the nurse's position as 'subservient … there to carry out orders … not to decide what method of treatment is proper'.[38] This new model nurse was 'single, conscientious [and] diligent on aspects of cleanliness and hospital economy'.[39]

Working hours

Nursing was an extremely strenuous occupation and hours were long. At first, they were expected to do the scrubbing and cleaning of the wards, as well as the nursing. In 1870, at Birmingham's General Hospital, it was reported that 'one of the most valuable of the nurses on the Surgical side had given notice to leave in consequence of having to do the hard work of cleaning and scrubbing the Wards'. The nurses objected to 'the laborious menial work that they had to perform, which in all other large Hospitals is done by a separate class of female scrubbers and [to] … the inadequate remuneration which [is] … the lowest of any large Hospital in England.'[40] This disquiet amongst the nurses at Birmingham prompted an extensive review of the nursing arrangements.

In the late 1880s at The London, the hours of duty for day nurses was fourteen hours with two hours off, while for the night nurses it was twelve. Days off 'were few and far between' and the nurses had a fortnight's annual holiday.[41]

In 1892 at the Glasgow Royal Infirmary, all nurses (sisters, staff nurses, assistant night nurses, assistant day nurses and probationers) had at least two hours off duty every day. Of the day nurses, the probationers started earliest, rising at 4 a.m., taking an early breakfast and being in the wards by 4.45 a.m. All the nurses were on duty for at least eleven hours a day, except the probationers who worked for ten hours.[42] Lights out in the public rooms at the nurses' home was at 10 p.m. and 10.35 in the bedrooms, while the doors were locked at 10.30 p.m.[43]

At first there was a mistaken belief that 'a night nurse is a person of lower status' to a day nurse, so the practice was adopted of alternating day and night nurses.[44] However, this arrangement had the disadvantage that no one person was responsible for the ward inventory, attending the visiting staff and seeing to the general discipline during the working day. This led to the appointment of 'sisters' or 'head nurses'. In the

'Notes at a London Hospital: Good Night Sister.' (*The Graphic*, 27 December 1879)

'Notes at a London Hospital: The Nurse New Style.' (*The Graphic*, 27 December 1879)

1880s at the Western Infirmary in Glasgow, each ward was attended by two nurses of equal status plus one cleaner. In addition, for every two wards there was one sister and one probationer.[45]

Diet

Despite the physical nature of the occupation, at first, nurses were not adequately fed and no regular meals were provided for them. In the 1860s at Glasgow's Royal Infirmary, the food consisted of 'such articles as herrings, chops, eggs or cheese, which they cooked in their respective wards'. As this diet was so insufficient, the nurses 'were under great temptation … of adding to their own scanty fare from the diet supplied for the patients'.[46] By 1892, there was a separate nurses home with a dining hall in which all the nurses took their meals. Breakfast, dinner and supper was provided.[47]

Before 1880 at The London, meals provided for the nurses were few and far between. No breakfast was served to the day or night staff before going on duty and although they were all issued with rations, there were no set break times so they had to eat them 'when and where they could'. Within a year of Eva Lückes' appointment as matron, breakfast, dinner and supper was available for everyone in the dining-room.[48]

Accommodation

It has been argued that 'the major obstacle to the generalised introduction of the new nurses, particularly whilst they were in training, was the cost of the provision of board and lodgings'.[49] In order to reduce the expense of providing a nurses' home, some hospitals used 'special donations to purchase or adapt existing property and then [named] the nurses' home after the donor'.[50] In less successful cases, 'totally unsuitable accommodation which might have been left to the hospital in a bequest could be used as a nurses' home'.[51]

'Notes at a London Hospital: The Nurse Old Style.' (*The Graphic*, 27 December 1879)

In 1883, although nineteen sleeping apartments had been provided for nurses at the Glasgow Royal Infirmary, there were still thirty day nurses, twelve night nurses and ten probationers scattered throughout the hospital. They were 'sleeping in small rooms off the wards where they are exposed, day and night, to the atmosphere of the ward, and to the noise and bustle which the carrying out of the work necessarily entails'.[52] A year later, a sitting room for the nurses was fitted up 'and found to be a great comfort to them'. The room included curtains, a piano and a valuable library of books.[53] A new nurses' home was finally opened in August 1888 with eighty-eight separate sleeping apartments.[54]

The accommodation for nurses at The London 'remained the barrier to any real improvement in the standard of nursing'.[55] According to the matron Eva Lückes, the bedrooms of her sisters and nurses were 'scattered in five directions, not including the apartments allotted to the erysipelas and isolation wards which are of necessity separate.' The sisters still slept in rooms between the wards while 'some of the night and day staff "Boxed and Coxed" in Grocers' wing'. In May 1887, the new Nurses' Home was opened which could accommodate more than a hundred nurses.[56]

Pay

The pay of nurses varied across the country. They were paid 2s 6d per week in Oxford but their salary was two to three times higher in London.[57] The first probationers at The London received £10 in their first year and £20 in their second. The pay for the second year was increased to £30 and the staff nurses were paid £40 per annum. In 1880, a probationer at the Glasgow Royal Infirmary was paid £12 a year while training. After qualifying, this rose to £20 a year which was increased by £2 a year up to a maximum of £30 a year.[58] At Birmingham's General Hospital, no salary was paid to probationers in the first year. In the second year, the salary was £16 and in the third, £18 increasing by £2 per annum thereafter to a maximum of £24.[59] Although these rates of pay were low, probationers were the equivalent of 'apprentices, paying in work done for their training'.[60]

'Notes at a London Hospital: A Probationer.' (*The Graphic*, 27 December 1879)

By 1901, the average hospital nurse 'received £17 annually plus maintenance for a seventy-hour week … and could be hired out for private nursing by her hospital to boost fee income'.[61]

Health

As nursing was such a physically demanding occupation, good health was essential on commencement of training. In the first seven years of the Nightingale Training School's operation, among the probationers there were '14 diagnosed cases of typhoid, typhus, scarlet fever, and diphtheria, with another 16 off with fever'.[62] More frequent ailments which prevented the probationers from being on duty included sore throats, septic fingers and diarrhoea. Dismissed for poor health, Elizabeth Pratt was a probationer who contracted scarlet fever and diphtheria. Her training record states she 'would have made a good nurse'.[63]

It was vital that the would-be probationer was in good health at the start of her training, given the physically demanding work she was expected to undertake. No new probationers were accepted at The London unless they had been interviewed and had passed a medical examination. Under this system, new probationers had to complete a month's trial before a contract with the hospital could be signed.[64]

Nursing in a hospital which admitted infectious cases held significant dangers. In 1850, twenty-one-year-old Margaret Beattie, a nurse at the Aberdeen Royal Infirmary, was unlucky enough to contract two infectious diseases in one year: a case of fever in May and then erysipelas in December. Both cases forced her off the wards for two weeks but Margaret survived her illnesses.[65]

Dismissals and resignations

Of the 180 women trained by Florence Nightingale at St Thomas's in the first ten years, sixty-six did not complete their contract, with four dying in training and seven resigning for unspecified reasons. Of the remaining fifty-five, 'half were dismissed for misconduct with at least five for insobriety while the remainder were dismissed for poor health with some remark like "not strong enough for our work".'[66] Resignations in nursing usually fell into three categories: not being suited to the work and leaving nursing altogether, leaving a hospital for a better paid post, or leaving to get married.

Nurses were governed by strict rules set out by the hospital authorities. At St George's Hospital in London, the rules stated that nurses could be dismissed if they were to 'receive any money, treat, present, or gratuity, either from a Patient, or any relation or friend of such Patient, or from any other person, in respect for the services of such Nurse … in the Hospital…'[67]

This was a common rule of most hospitals, as was the banning of nurses and medical students from meeting and associating outside the hospital. In April 1895 at Birmingham's General Hospital, Nurse Mason (who had come from the Stoke-on-Trent Institution for training), was dismissed 'for repeatedly walking out with a Student'.[68]

Nursing as a profession

For Victorian women, nursing offered a rare opportunity: a career structure.[69] Along with teaching, nursing was 'one of the few occupations a middle-class girl could contemplate'.[70]

In 1881, there were 35,216 female nurses in Britain.[71] This had risen to 53,003 by 1891 and 64,209 by 1901. Of the latter figure, only 12,500 were trained or registered. This meant a very high proportion were either probationers in training, acting as 'wet' nurses or nursing in a more informal capacity. In 1901, less than a third of nurses worked in hospitals and most of the rest 'nursed the wealthy'.[72]

In 1887 the British Nurses' Association was established by Mrs Bedford Fenwick. Before her marriage to Dr Bedford Fenwick, she was Ethel Gordon Manson. Like Eva Lückes, she had been appointed matron of a large hospital at the early age of twenty-four. She was made matron of St Bartholomew's in 1881. Unlike Eva Lückes, Ethel Manson left her post six years later to marry and there was a distinct rivalry between the two women.[73]

The British Nurses' Association sought to give nursing full professional status through registering qualified nurses, with an emphasis on uniforms and adequate training. Florence Nightingale, Eva Lückes and some sections of the medical profession bitterly opposed the registration of nurses fearing it 'would limit numbers'.[74] However, registration was supported by London general practitioners and hospital doctors because 'relationships between doctors and nurses were already clearly delineated'.[75]

By the 1880s, nursing represented a respectable profession for middle- and working-class girls and women. Mary and Charlotte Lightfoot were the daughters of a labourer, born in York in 1856 and 1858 respectively. Both girls went on to become certificated nurses, after first gaining experience in the more lowly roles of domestic servants or 'scrubbers' in hospital wards.

After leaving school, Mary became a general domestic servant with a family in York but by the time of the 1881 census, she was working as a domestic servant in a ward at the Leeds Fever Hospital. As a 'scrubber', this would have been extremely hard work. Ten years later, at the age of thirty-four, Mary was listed as a certificated nurse at the Prince of Wales Hotel in Scarborough. To become 'certificated', she would have undergone and passed a year's formal training as a probationer. It is possible that the hospital she was employed by had contracted her out to provide private paid nursing care for someone at the hotel. This was an important source of extra income for hospitals as trained nurses were much in demand by the upper and middle classes.

Mary's sister Charlotte followed her into the nursing profession although it took longer for her to achieve trained nurse status. She worked as a domestic servant in York for various families until at least 1891 when she was thirty-three. By 1901, Charlotte had left York and became a hospital nurse in Kintbury Holt, Berkshire.

Both sisters remained unmarried and, in their later years, they both became shopkeepers. Mary kept a shop in Ipswich and Charlotte was the proprietor of a newsagent in York. This was perhaps a less demanding occupation than nursing for older women, although Charlotte did not abandon the profession entirely as she took up a post of nurse/housekeeper for a couple in Andover just two years before she died in 1924. Mary died six years later.[76]

Ann Elizabeth Armson was the seventh child of ten born in Birmingham in 1873. Her father had been a silk ribbon weaver in Warwickshire but had moved to the city to work in a chemical works. Like Mary and Charlotte Lightfoot, Ann's first job was as a domestic servant. After 1891, she began training as a nurse in Birmingham, although it is not clear which hospital she trained at. She completed her training at the Sheffield Infirmary and in 1901 she was working at the workhouse infirmary in the city.

Ann's son, Bernard, was born in 1906 in Wakefield. There is no record of a marriage for Ann or for a baptism for Bernard in the surrounding parishes. Ann lived close to Pinderfield Hospital where she may have worked to support herself and her son. As an unmarried mother in Edwardian England, Ann would have experienced a certain amount of prejudice. This may have prompted her decision to emigrate to Australia in February 1909 where she settled in Maitland, New South Wales. Ann went on to own and run a maternity hospital in Maitland in the 1920s.

Sadly, Ann lost her only son, Bernard, in 1943. He had joined the Australian Air Force, but died in an accident falling down a flight of concrete stairs while clearing out an air-raid shelter in Sydney. Ann died five years later in Sydney aged seventy-five.[77]

Nursing the wealthy

There was an insatiable demand for private hospital-trained nurses in the upper and middle classes, and hospitals were quick to take advantage of this new way to generate extra income. In London, St Thomas's, St Bartholomew's and St George's were among the first hospitals to send trained nurses out to private houses. At The London, it was not until the new nurses' home was opened in 1887 that the hospital could follow the example of the other city institutions. By 1888, a net profit of £1,173 was made from 'the training of nurses from outside institutions, paying probationers and from fees received for private nurses, over and above the expenses of maintaining the houses in Philpot Street'. A few years later, when 'there were 681 applications for private nurses, of which only 339 could be supplied', the net profit to the hospital from private nursing alone was more than £1,000.[78]

At the Cardiff Royal Infirmary in 1884, the matron Miss Pratt instigated a Training School for Probationers and a system of private nursing to the public who could afford it. In 1886, the gross sum received for such private nursing was 'upwards of £350'. Miss Pratt had a vested interest in the success of the private nursing scheme as, under an arrangement with the managers of the hospital, she was to receive 10 per cent commission on all such nursing. The fees in 1888 for continuous night nursing were 30s per week and 35s to non-subscribers.[79]

Nursing in poor law institutions

Nurses in poor law institutions were subject to the orders of the master, matron and medical officer, and to the conditions set by the unions which ran the workhouses. Many unions, mindful of the burden on the ratepayers resisted appointing paid nurses for as long as possible. In the 1850s, the central authority in London was reluctant to insist that unions employ 'professional nurses for work which they regarded as part of the inmates' duties'.[80]

Where workhouse nurses were paid, they received between £12 and £50 per annum, plus board and an allowance of beer or porter. Their main duty was to supervise the large number of unpaid paupers 'who provided the bulk of the Poor Law 'nursing' staff'.[81] Elderly paupers were the backbone of workhouse nursing but many were 'too feeble to lift patients' and those at the Strand 'wanted good Nursing and Nourishment themselves, trembling and coughing all day long…'.[82]

The Nurses' Sitting-Room at The London, 1900. (*The Windsor Magazine*)

There was some increase in the number of paid workhouse nurses after the reform of poor law infirmaries in the 1860s. However, it was not until after 1897 when unions were banned from using paupers as nurses that the number of paid nurses significantly increased. Despite this new rule, paupers were still allowed to work in the infirmaries under the supervision of a trained nurse.

Even if a workhouse paid its nurses, it was extremely rare for them to be hospital trained. In many cases, a scrubber or laundress was promoted to a paid nursing post.[83] For those unions wishing to employ trained nurses in their poor law infirmaries, it was an uphill struggle to attract suitably qualified applicants. Poor law infirmaries did not compare favourably with the expanding voluntary hospitals which offered higher salaries, better working conditions, higher quality training and superior accommodation. As a result, applicants for probationer posts in union workhouses tended to be from those who had lower expectations or who had been rejected by the voluntary hospitals.

The first national nurse training system was introduced in 1885 by the poor law system in Scotland[84] but English and Welsh poor law infirmaries were not so progressive. In a survey by *The Lancet* in the 1890s of fifty English poor law infirmaries, only four had 'nursing arrangements comparable with voluntary hospitals'.[85]

From the 1870s, the Poor Law Board encouraged larger poor law infirmaries to train nurses themselves by appointing probationers. The medical officer and head nurse would provide a year's training. Despite this initiative, there was still a shortage of trained nurses. In 1879, Louisa Twining founded the Association for Promoting Trained Nursing in Workhouse Infirmaries which aimed to finance the training of workhouse nurses.[86]

Towards the end of the nineteenth century, both the training and accommodation for workhouse nurses started to improve. In 1897, the Local Government Board decreed that 'all infirmaries with a staff of three or more nurses had to employ a superintendent nurse' who could only be trained by an infirmary with a resident doctor.[87] The superintendent nurse had to have undergone 'for three years at least a course of instruction in the Medical and Surgical Wards of a Hospital or Infirmary being a Training School for Nurses, and maintaining a Resident Physician or House Surgeon'. She had to hold a midwifery certificate and it was her responsibility to 'superintend, control and instruct the Probationer Nurses in the Infirmary…'.[88] These new rules excluded infirmaries with less than three nurses so 'in 1901 only 63 (of about 300) rural infirmaries had superintendent nurses'.[89] The new superintendent nurse remained subordinate to the workhouse matron.

Lunatic asylum staff

The staff of an asylum were resident and were known as keepers and attendants, not nurses, unless they worked in the hospital section. Attendants needed to be 'active healthy persons, of strength equal to any emergency, which may befall them from an excited or fitful patient'.[90]

Asylum attendants were responsible for the safety, cleanliness and general condition of the patients, and for the ventilation, proper warmth and good order of their respective wards.[91] They were to 'treat their patients kindly and indulgently, and never to strike or speak harshly to them…'.[92] At the Duddeston Asylum, the staff were expected to rise at six o'clock. They were then to 'wash and comb their patients, and observe if there be any soreness or discoloration of the skin in any part of the body.' They were also expected to 'examine the stools and urine of the patients, so as to be able to report their state, and every particular concerning them'.[93]

At Lancaster, the rules stated there should be no less than one attendant for every twenty-five patients who are tranquil or convalescent, and no less than one attendant for every fifteen patients who are 'dirty, violent, or refractory, or dangerous to themselves or others'.[94] This would still seem a high number of patients for one attendant to look after, especially if they were troublesome. At Duddeston, the keepers were not allowed to leave the ward or room for which they were responsible, except on urgent business. If they left, 'any patient thought liable to be violent had to be locked up and, if necessary, chained or tied'.[95]

Looking after the insane as an attendant could be a dangerous job. In 1884 at the Prestwich Asylum, it was reported that 'a sudden and unprovoked attack by a supposed harmless patient upon a Female Attendant' had taken place. It was pointed out that the attack 'might have been attended with fatal consequences' if another patient had not intervened.[96]

Harmless lunatics and imbeciles were often accommodated in poor law institutions, rather than asylums. From the 1860s onwards, unions were forced to provide extra staff to look after the ever increasing numbers housed in workhouses. Many unions employed insufficient paid attendants, relying on assistance from unpaid sane pauper inmates. This lack of paid medical staff mirrored the situation in poor law infirmaries. Pressure was brought to bear on the unions to appoint sufficient staff by the Lunacy Commissioners who visited each workhouse annually to check on the lunatics and imbeciles housed there. However, it could take many years for unions to implement any recommendations.

Notes

Introduction

1. Bynum, W.F., *Science and the Practice of Medicine in the Nineteenth Century*, (1994, Cambridge University Press), p209
2. Cherry, Steven, *Medical Services and the Hospitals in Britain 1860–1939*, (1996, Cambridge University Press), p45

Part 1: THE DEVELOPMENT OF HOSPITALS

Chapter 1 - The Hospitals of the Eighteenth Century

1. Porter, Roy, *Blood & Guts: A Short History of Medicine* (2002, Penguin Books), p137
2. *ibid*
3. *ibid*, p138
4. Maggs, Christopher, 'Profit and Loss and the Hospital Nurse' in Maggs, Christopher (ed.), *Nursing History: The State of the Art* (1987, Croom Helm), p177
5. Porter, op cit, p138
6. Davies, T.G., *Deeds Not Words: A History of the Swansea General and Eye Hospital 1817–1948* (1988, Cardiff University of Wales Press), p13
7. NHS Grampian – Who Was Dr Gray? <http://www.nhsgrampian.org/>
8. Maggs, op cit, p177
9. *ibid*
10. DHC/47 Annual Report 1853, Cardiff Royal Infirmary (Glamorgan Record Office)
11. Maggs, op cit, p177
12. *ibid*
13. Porter, Roy, 'Hospitals and Surgery' in Porter, Roy, (ed.), *The Cambridge Illustrated History of Medicine* (1996, Cambridge University Press), p213
14. *ibid*
15. Hamilton, David, *The Healers: A History of Medicine in Scotland*, (1981, Canongate), p214
16. *ibid*
17. Porter, Roy, *Blood & Guts: A Short History of Medicine* (2002, Penguin Books), pp138–139
18. Porter, Roy, 'Hospitals and Surgery' in Porter, Roy, (ed.), *The Cambridge Illustrated History of Medicine* (1996, Cambridge University Press), p213
19. Hamilton, op cit, p214

20. Porter, op cit, p213
21. *ibid*, p214
22. Porter, Roy, *Blood & Guts: A Short History of Medicine* (2002, Penguin Books), p139
23. *ibid*, p142

Chapter 2 - General Voluntary and Endowed Hospitals

1. HC/GH 1/3/16 Annual Report 1884, General Hospital, Birmingham (Birmingham Archives and Heritage Service)
2. Maggs, op cit, p180
3. *ibid*
4. DHC/48 Annual Report 1848, Cardiff Royal Infirmary (Glamorgan Record Office)
5. Bynum, op cit, p185
6. Maggs, op cit, p183
7. *ibid*, p181
8. *ibid*, p185
9. *ibid*
10. Information provided and researched by Carl Higgs
11. Reinarz, Jonathan, 'Healthcare and the Second City: The Development of the Birmingham Teaching Hospitals in the Nineteenth Century', *Birmingham Historian*, Vol. 26, summer 2004, p17
12. www.smallandspecial.org (Kingston University: Great Ormond Street Hospital NHS Trust)
13. GRHB 1/7/3 Annual Report 1867, Aberdeen Royal Infirmary (Northern Health Services Archives)
14. Maggs, op cit, p181
15. www.smallandspecial.org (Kingston University: Great Ormond Street Hospital NHS Trust)
16. Mitton, Lavinia, *The Victorian Hospital* (2001, Shire Publications), p4
17. Reinarz, op cit, p20
18. *ibid*
19. Abel-Smith, Brian, *The Hospitals 1800–1948: A Study in Social Administration in England and Wales*, (1964, Heinemann), p135
20. Reinarz, op cit, pp20–21
21. *British Medical Journal*, 26 May 1889, p1187
22. Bynum, op cit, p190
23. Abel-Smith, op cit, p135
24. *ibid*
25. Bynum, op cit, p190

26. Quoted in Abel-Smith, op cit, pp64–65
27. Hardy, Anne, *Health and Medicine in Britain Since 1860* (2001, Palgrave Macmillan), p15
28. Cherry, op cit, p23
29. Porter, op cit, p145
30. *ibid*
31. Bynum, op cit, p75
32. Hamilton, David, op cit, pp152–153
33. *ibid*
34. Clark-Kennedy, A. E., *The London: A Study in the Voluntary Hospital System, Volume Two, The Second Hundred Years 1840–1948* (1963, Pitman Medical Publishing Co. Ltd), p104
35. *ibid*
36. McKenzie, Fred A., 'The London Hospital', *The Windsor Magazine*, December 1900, XIII: 49, p56
37. *ibid*
38. Cherry, op cit, p45
39. *ibid*
40. *ibid*
41. *ibid*, p47
42. McKenzie, op cit, p52
43. *ibid*
44. Abel-Smith, op cit, p42
45. *ibid*
46. *ibid*
47. Mitton, op cit, p6
48. Bynum, op cit, p133
49. *ibid*, pp188–189
50. Florence Nightingale quoted in Abel-Smith, op cit, p154
51. *ibid*, p41
52. Mitton, op cit, p6
53. *ibid*

Chapter 3 - Specialist Hospitals

1. Hardy, op cit, p16
2. Cherry, op cit, p45
3. Abel-Smith, op cit, p27
4. Granshaw, Lindsay, *St Mark's Hospital, London: A Social History of a Specialist Hospital* (1985, Oxford University Press), p1
5. *ibid*, p79
6. Porter, op cit, p145
7. Reinarz, op cit, p19
8. Abel-Smith, op cit, p22
9. Reinarz, op cit, p18
10. *ibid*
11. *ibid*
12. Dickens, Charles, 'No Hospital for Incurables', *Household Words*, 24 August 1850, p517
13. *ibid*
14. *ibid*
15. *ibid*
16. Abel-Smith, op cit, p25
17. *ibid*
18. *ibid*, p24
19. Reinarz, op cit, p18
20. Abel-Smith, op cit, p24
21. Reinarz, op cit, p18
22. Mitton, op cit, p17
23. Reinarz, op cit, p23
24. *ibid*
25. *ibid*
26. *ibid*
27. *ibid*
28. Abel-Smith, p106
29. *ibid*, p30
30. *ibid*, p138
31. *ibid*, p28
32. *British Medical Journal*, 29 July 1860, p582 quoted in *ibid*, 30
33. Abel-Smith, *ibid*, p28
34. *Lancet*, Vol.I, 1863 quoted in *ibid*, p29
35. *ibid*
36. Abel-Smith, *ibid*, p30
37. *ibid*, p159
38. *ibid*, p30
39. *ibid*
40. H.C. Cameron quoted in Abel-Smith, *ibid*, p159
41. Sir D'Arcy Power quoted in *ibid*

Chapter 4 – Dispensaries

1. Berridge, Virginia, 'Health and Medicine' in Thompson, F. M.L. (ed.), *The Cambridge Social History of Britain 1750–1950 Volume 3: Social Agencies and Institutions* (1993, Cambridge University Press), p206
2. Davies, T. G., *Deeds Not Words: A History of the Swansea General and Eye Hospital 1817–1948* (1988, Cardiff University of Wales Press), p13
3. Cherry, op cit, p43
4. *ibid*
5. Hamilton, op cit, p217
6. *ibid*
7. *ibid*
8. *ibid*
9. *ibid*, p216
10. *ibid*
11. *ibid*
12. *ibid*
13. *ibid*
14. GRHB 1/15/42 Papers relating to Dispensary & Out-patients, Aberdeen Royal Infirmary (Northern Health Services Archives)
15. Hardy, op cit, p18
16. Cherry, op cit, p42
17. Hardy, op cit, p18
18. *ibid*
19. Bristowe, John Syer and Holmes, Timothy, *Report on the Hospitals of the United Kingdom: Appendix 15 to the Privy Council Medical Officer's Report*, (1863, HMSO), p702
20. Bayliss, Anne & Paul and Jackson, Alan, *Scarborough Hospital and Dispensary: The First Fifty Years 1852–1902*, (2006, A. M. Bayliss), p28
21. *ibid*

Chapter 5 – Children's Hospitals

1. Reinarz, op cit, p21
2. Abel-Smith, op cit, p37
3. *ibid*, p24
4. Walvin, James, *A Child's World: A Social History of English Childhood 1800–1914* (1982, Penguin Books Ltd), p22
5. *ibid*
6. *ibid*
7. *ibid*, p23
8. *ibid*
9. Horn, Pamela, *Labouring Life in the Victorian Countryside* (1987, Alan Sutton Publishing Ltd), p184
10. Abel-Smith, op cit, p39
11. Lomax, Elizabeth, M. R., 'Small and Special: The Development of Hospitals for Children in Victorian Britain', *Medical History*, 1996, Supplement No.16, p18
12. Abel-Smith, op cit, pp24–25
13. Lomax, op cit, p20
14. Abel-Smith, op cit, p38
15. *ibid*, p25
16. www.smallandspecial.org (Kingston University: Great Ormond Street Hospital NHS Trust)
17. www.smallandspecial.org (Kingston University: Great Ormond Street Hospital NHS Trust)
18. www.smallandspecial.org (Kingston University: Great Ormond Street Hospital NHS Trust)
19. Lomax, op cit, p18
20. *ibid*, p18
21. *ibid*, p26
22. Abel-Smith, op cit, p38
23. Cherry, op cit, p45
24. Lomax, op cit, p1
25. Reinarz, op cit, p22
26. *ibid*
27. *ibid*
28. *ibid*
29. *ibid*, p23
30. Gray, H.M.W., 'Royal Hospital for Sick Children', *BMA Handbook & Guide* (1914), p48
31. *ibid*
32. Lomax, op cit, p8
33. *ibid*, p20
34. *ibid*, p8
35. www.smallandspecial.org (Kingston University: Great Ormond Street Hospital NHS Trust)

Chapter 6 – Poor Law Infirmaries

1. Mitton, op cit, p20
2. Peter Murray quoted in Higgs, Michelle, *Life in the Victorian and Edwardian Workhouse* (2007, Tempus Publishing), p70
3. Higgs, *ibid*, p70
4. *ibid*
5. Abel-Smith, op cit, p52
6. *ibid*
7. *ibid*
8. *ibid*
9. *ibid*
10. *ibid*, p53
11. Charles Dickens quoted in Higgs, op cit, p71
12. *ibid*, p70
13. *ibid*
14. Abel-Smith, op cit, p53
15. *ibid*
16. Higgs, op cit, p70
17. *ibid*
18. Abel-Smith, op cit, p50
19. *ibid*, p51
20. Higgs, op cit, p73
21. *ibid*
22. Mitton, op cit, p22
23. Higgs, op cit, p73
24. Mitton, op cit, p22
25. Cherry, op cit, p48
26. Abel-Smith, op cit, pp130–131
27. *ibid*, p131
28. Hardy, op cit, p20
29. Abel-Smith, op cit, pp94–95
30. *ibid*, p95
31. Cherry, op cit, p43
32. *ibid*, p36
33. Hamilton, op cit, p228
34. Abel-Smith, op cit, p215
35. Higgs, op cit, p76
36. *ibid*
37. Cherry, op cit, p48
38. Hardy, op cit, pp19–20
39. Higgs, op cit, p71
40. Cherry, op cit, p48
41. Abel-Smith, op cit, p212
42. *ibid*
43. Cherry, op cit, p48
44. *ibid*, p44
45. Hamilton, op cit, p229

Chapter 7 – Hospitals for Infectious Diseases

1. Bynum, op cit, p66
2. *ibid*
3. *ibid*
4. *ibid*
5. Keith, William, 'Hospital Statistics of Stone in the Bladder', *Edinburgh Medical & Surgical Journal*, 1843, No.158
6. GRHB 1/3/19 Admission & Discharge Registers 1849–1853, Aberdeen Royal Infirmary, (Northern Health Services Archives)
7. Abel-Smith, op cit, p45
8. *ibid*
9. *ibid*
10. Mitton, op cit, p24
11. *ibid*, p25
12. *ibid*
13. Hardy, op cit, p27
14. *ibid*, p161–7
15. Black, Nick, *Walking London's Medical History*,

(2006, The Royal Society of Medicine Press Limited), p102

16. Mitton, op cit, p23
17. Black, op cit, p102
18. Mitton, op cit, p23
19. Lomax, op cit, p11
20. Hay, Matthew, 'The City Hospital for Infectious Diseases', *BMA Handbook & Guide* (1914), p53
21. Abel-Smith, op cit, p126
22. *ibid*
23. *ibid*, p127
24. Cherry, op cit, p49
25. Abel-Smith, op cit, p127
26. *ibid*
27. Report of the Medical Officer of Health, 1893, presented to Cheshire County Council Public Health Committee, quoted in Midwinter, E. C., *Victorian Social Reform* (1968, Longman Group Ltd), p100
28. *ibid*
29. *ibid*

Chapter 8 - Cottage Hospitals

1. Hardy, op cit, p16
2. Emrys-Roberts, Meyrick, *The Cottage Hospitals 1859–1990* (1991, Tern Publications), p1
3. *ibid*, p4
4. *ibid*
5. Abel-Smith, op cit, p102
6. *ibid*
7. HRAC 1/1 1894–1898, Cottage Hospital Organising Committee Minutes, Accrington & District Cottage Hospital Minutes (Lancashire Record Office)
8. *ibid*
9. Abel-Smith, op cit, pp102–3
10. *ibid*, p103
11. Horn, op cit, p189
12. Abel-Smith, op cit, p103
13. *ibid*
14. Horn, op cit, p189
15. *ibid*
16. *ibid*

Chapter 9 – Hospitals for Paying Patients

1. *British Medical Journal*, 22 March 1879, p437
2. *ibid*, 17 May 1879, p791
3. *ibid*, 25 August 1877, pp243–5
4. Abel-Smith, op cit, p142
5. *ibid*, p150
6. *British Medical Journal*, 8 January 1881, p61
7. *ibid*
8. Abel-Smith, op cit, p142
9. *British Medical Journal*, 5 March 1881, p348
10. Abel-Smith, op cit, p148
11. *ibid*, p149
12. *ibid*
13. *ibid*
14. *ibid*
15. *British Medical Journal*, 4 March 1882, p312

Chapter 10 – Convalescent Homes

1. Clark-Kennedy, op cit, p72
2. GRHB 1/7/4 1875–1889, Annual Report 1879, Aberdeen Royal Infirmary (Northern Health Services Archives)
3. www.smallandspecial.org (Kingston University: Great Ormond Street Hospital NHS Trust)
4. Mitton, op cit, p24
5. HB14 2/9, Annual Reports 1883–1894, Glasgow Royal Infirmary (NHS Greater Glasgow and Clyde Board Archives)
6. *ibid*
7. Abel-Smith, op cit, p189
8. *ibid*
9. *ibid*, p150
10. *ibid*, p189–190
11. *British Medical Journal*, 17 January 1903, p147
12. Abel-Smith, op cit, p190
13. *ibid*
14. *ibid*

Chapter 11 – Lunatic Asylums

1. Porter, Roy, 'Mental Illness' in Porter, Roy, (ed.), *The Cambridge Illustrated History of Medicine* (1996, Cambridge University Press), p286
2. *ibid*
3. *ibid*, p289
4. *ibid*, p294
5. *ibid*
6. Porter, Roy, 'Hospitals and Surgery' in Porter, Roy, (ed.), *The Cambridge Illustrated History of Medicine* (1996, Cambridge University Press), p213
7. *ibid*
8. Cherry, op cit, p50
9. Bynum, op cit, p185
10. Williams, L.H., *Abergavenny Asylum* (2006, Unpublished Research), p3
11. Smith, L.D., 'Duddeston Hall and the Trade in Lunacy 1835–65', *Birmingham Historian*, Vol. 8, p20
12. *ibid*
13. Mitton, op cit, p27
14. *ibid*
15. *ibid*
16. Hamilton, p218
17. *ibid*
18. *ibid*
19. *ibid*
20. *ibid*
21. *ibid*
22. Higgs, op cit, p77
23. Bynum, op cit, p185
24. Porter, Roy, 'Mental Illness' in Porter, Roy (ed.), *The Cambridge Illustrated History of Medicine* (1996, Cambridge University Press), p289
25. *ibid*
26. Mitton, op cit, p26
27. Williams, op cit, p15
28. *ibid*

29. *ibid*
30. Cherry, op cit, p50
31. *ibid*
32. Porter, op cit, p294
33. Cherry, op cit, pp50–51

Part 2: GOING TO HOSPITAL

Chapter 12 – Getting Medical Treatment

1. Hardy, op cit, p17
2. *ibid*
3. *ibid*
4. Berridge, op cit, p189
5. *ibid*, p186
6. *ibid*, p188–189
7. Walvin, op cit, p26
8. Horn, op cit, p283
9. *ibid*, p187
10. Berridge, op cit, p191
11. *ibid*
12. quoted in Royston Pike, E., *Human Documents of the Victorian Golden Age*, (1967, George Allen and Unwin), p185
13. Walvin, op cit, p26
14. *ibid*
15. Horn, op cit, p184
16. *ibid*
17. *ibid*
18. Higgs, op cit, p67
19. James Riley quoted in Hardy, op cit, p18
20. *ibid*
21. Higgs, op cit, p67
22. *ibid*
23. Bynum, op cit, p198
24. *ibid*
25. *ibid*, p199
26. Cherry, op cit, p43
27. Hardy, op cit, pp17–18
28. Cherry, op cit, p8
29. *ibid*, p42
30. *ibid*, p25
31. Bynum, op cit, pp33–34
32. Abel-Smith, op cit, p134
33. *ibid*

Chapter 13 – Admission Procedures to Hospital

1. Berridge, op cit, p205
2. Abel-Smith, op cit, inside open page
3. HRBK 4/1 1862–1871, Annual Reports, Blackburn Royal Infirmary (Lancashire Record Office)
4. Abel-Smith, op cit, p38
5. *ibid*
6. Bristowe and Holmes, op cit, p470
7. *ibid*, p702
8. GRHB 1/10/3 Regulations 1882, Aberdeen Royal Infirmary (Northern Health Services Archives)
9. Abel-Smith, op cit, p36

10. *ibid*
11. *ibid*, pp36–37
12. Abel-Smith, op cit, p37
13. *ibid*
14. *ibid*
15. *ibid*, p38
16. *ibid*
17. *ibid*, p155
18. Hardy, op cit, p15
19. GRHB 1/10/15 Poster 1897, Aberdeen Royal Infirmary (Northern Health Services Archives)
20. Abel-Smith, op cit, p45
21. *ibid*, p38
22. *ibid*, pp38–39
23. Higgs, op cit, p75
24. *ibid*
25. *ibid*
26. GRHB 1/7/19 Communications by Hospital Medical and Surgical Staff regarding Out-patients 1879, Aberdeen Royal Infirmary (Northern Health Services Archives)
27. Clark-Kennedy, op cit, pp72–73
28. *ibid*
29. Abel-Smith, op cit, p106
30. *ibid*

Chapter 14 – Out-Patients

1. McKenzie, Fred A., 'The London Hospital', *The Windsor Magazine*, December 1900, XIII: 49, p50
2. DHC/49 Rules & Regulations 1877, Cardiff Royal Infirmary (Glamorgan Record Office)
3. Reinarz, op cit, p17
4. GRHB 1/10/3 Regulations 1882, Aberdeen Royal Infirmary, (Northern Health Services Archives)
5. *ibid*
6. DHC/49 Rules & Regulations 1877, Cardiff Royal Infirmary (Glamorgan Record Office)
7. Frederick Treves quoted in Clark-Kennedy, op cit, p55
8. McKenzie, op cit, p50
9. Clark-Kennedy, op cit, p91
10. McKenzie, op cit, p51
11. *ibid*
12. *ibid*
13. Shorter, Edward, 'Primary Care' in Porter, Roy (ed.), *The Cambridge Illustrated History of Medicine* (1996, Cambridge University Press), p136
14. Anonymous quoted in *ibid*
15. Higgs, op cit, p76
16. GRHB 1/7/4 Annual Report 1880, Aberdeen Royal Infirmary (Northern Health Services Archives)
17. GRHB 1/7/19 Communications by Hospital Medical and Surgical Staff regarding Out-patients 1879, Aberdeen Royal Infirmary (Northern Health Services Archives)
18. *ibid*
19. *ibid*

20. *ibid*
21. Hardy, op cit, p15
22. *ibid*
23. DHC/24 House Committee Minute Book 6 May 1885, Cardiff Royal Infirmary (Glamorgan Record Office)
24. HC/GH 1/1/6/3 House Committee Minutes 13 June 1879, General Hospital, Birmingham (Birmingham Archives and Heritage Service)
25. HC/GH 1/1/6/3 House Committee Minutes 3 October 1879, General Hospital, Birmingham (Birmingham Archives and Heritage Service)
26. HRBK 4/2 Annual Report 1871, Blackburn Infirmary (Lancashire Record Office)

Chapter 15 – In-Patients
1. Abel-Smith, op cit, p41
2. GRHB 1/7/4 Annual Report 1877, Aberdeen Royal Infirmary (Northern Health Services Archives)
3. HRBK 4/1 Annual Report 1867, Blackburn Infirmary (Lancashire Record Office)
4. HC/GH 1/1/6/3 House Committee Minutes 13 February 1880, General Hospital, Birmingham (Birmingham Archives and Heritage Service)
5. DHC/49 Annual Reports 1874–1877, Cardiff Royal Infirmary (Glamorgan Record Office)
6. DHC/51 Annual Reports 1886–1893, Cardiff Royal Infirmary (Glamorgan Record Office)
7. Bristowe & Holmes, op cit, p599
8. Hawker, Ruth 'For the Good of the Patient?', in Maggs, Christopher (ed.), *Nursing History: The State of the Art*, (1987, Croom Helm), p145
9. Abel-Smith, op cit, p43
10. HRBK 4/1 Annual Reports 1852–1871 Blackburn Infirmary (Lancashire Record Office)
11. GRHB 1/10/3 Regulations 1882, Aberdeen Royal Infirmary (Northern Health Services Archives)
12. Hawker, op cit, p145
13. HB14 9/83 Rules & Regulations 1867–1900, Glasgow Royal Infirmary (NHS Greater Glasgow and Clyde Board Archives)
14. GRHB 1/10/3 Regulations 1882, Aberdeen Royal Infirmary (Northern Health Services Archives)
15. GRHB 1/7/4 Annual Report 1884, Aberdeen Royal Infirmary (Northern Health Services Archives)
16. Hawker, op cit, p149
17. *ibid*
18. *ibid*, p150
19. www.smallandspecial.org (Kingston University: Great Ormond Street Hospital NHS Trust)
20. www.smallandspecial.org (Kingston University: Great Ormond Street Hospital NHS Trust)
21. Hawker, op cit, p147
22. *ibid*, p146
23. *ibid*

24. GRHB 1/10/3 Regulations 1882, Aberdeen Royal Infirmary (Northern Health Services Archives)
25. Hawker, op cit, p146
26. Clark-Kennedy, op cit, p72
27. www.smallandspecial.org (Kingston University: Great Ormond Street Hospital NHS Trust)
28. www.smallandspecial.org (Kingston University: Great Ormond Street Hospital NHS Trust)
29. *The Family Physician: A Manual of Domestic Medicine by Physicians and Surgeons of the Principal London Hospitals*, (1884, Cassell & Co. Ltd), Vol. II, p399
30. *ibid*, p397
31. *ibid*, Vol. IV, p890
32. HC/GH 4/2/18, Admission & Discharge Register for Medical In-Patients, General Hospital, Birmingham (Birmingham Archives and Heritage Service)
33. With thanks to Geoff Couling and Paula Couling for providing information and research about their ancestor James Hadley
34. *The Times*, 12 May 1886
35. With thanks to Benjamin Caine for providing information and research about his ancestor Thomas Roberts
36. John Gallacher – Medical Records – Western Infirmary, Glasgow 1903 (Glasgow University Archive)
37. D-HEW 16/5/7 Matilda Jones m.s. Gallacher: Poor Relief Applications Glasgow 1903 (Mitchell Library, Glasgow)
38. With thanks to Ava Connelly for providing information and research about her ancestors John and Matilda Gallacher

Chapter 16 – Accidents and Emergencies
1. Hawker, op cit, pp147–148
2. Frederick Treves quoted in Clark-Kennedy, op cit, pp55–56
3. HC/GH 1/1/6/3, 20 February 1885, House Committee Minutes, General Hospital, Birmingham (Birmingham Archives and Heritage Service)
4. Bayliss, op cit, p39
5. Jenkinson, Jacqueline, Moss, Michael and Russell, Iain, *The Royal: The History of the Glasgow Royal Infirmary, 1794–1994* (1994, Glasgow Royal Infirmary NHS Trust), p63
6. Harrison, J. F. C., *Early Victorian Britain 1832–1851* (1979, Fontana Press), p58
7. *ibid*
8. www.smallandspecial.org (Kingston University: Great Ormond Street Hospital NHS Trust)
9. Lomax, op cit, p18
10. www.smallandspecial.org (Kingston University: Great Ormond Street Hospital NHS Trust)
11. GRHB 1/3/19 Admission & Discharge Register 1849–1853, Aberdeen Royal Infirmary (Northern

Health Services Archives)

12. www.smallandspecial.org (Kingston University: Great Ormond Street Hospital NHS Trust)

13. HC/GH 4/2/17 Admission & Discharge Register for Medical In-Patients 10 March 1862, General Hospital, Birmingham (Birmingham Archives and Heritage Service)

14. HB14/5/5 Ward Day Book – Male Surgical 1863–1865, Glasgow Royal Infirmary (NHS Greater Glasgow and Clyde Board Archives)

15. *ibid*

16. *The Times*, 10 December 1870

17. HC/GH 1/1/2/14 Weekly Board Minutes 1870–1879, General Hospital, Birmingham (Birmingham Archives and Heritage Service)

18. *ibid*

19. *ibid*

Chapter 17 – Conditions in Hospital

1. Bristowe & Holmes, op cit, p606

2. F. Oppert quoted in Abel-Smith, op cit, p42

3. *ibid*

4. Blaker, Nathaniel Paine, *Sussex in Bygone Days: Reminiscences of Nathaniel Paine Blaker, M.R.C.S.*, (1919), Chapter 43, quoted on http://freepages. genealogy.rootsweb.com/~blaker/reminiscences/contents.html

5. HC/GH 1/1/6/3 House Committee Minutes 28 February 1879, General Hospital, Birmingham (Birmingham Archives and Heritage Service)

6. HRBK 4/2 Annual Report 1871 Blackburn Royal Infirmary (Lancashire Record Office)

7. GRHB 1/10/3 Dietary Table 1881 in Regulations 1882, Aberdeen Royal Infirmary (Northern Health Services Archives)

8. HB14 9/49 Report on a Visit to Glasgow Royal Infirmary, 1905 (NHS Greater Glasgow and Clyde Board Archives)

9. DHC/112 'The True Romance of Hospital Work' Cardiff Infirmary Maintenance Fund 1903, Cardiff Royal Infirmary (Glamorgan Record Office)

10. HB14 9/49 Report on a Visit to the General Hospital, Birmingham, 1905 (NHS Greater Glasgow and Clyde Board Archives)

11. F. Oppert quoted in Abel-Smith, op cit, p42

12. GRHB 1/10/3 Regulations 1882, Aberdeen Royal Infirmary (Northern Health Services Archives)

13. Aldis, Arnold S., *Cardiff Royal Infirmary 1883–1983* (1984, University of Wales Press), p11

14. HB14 9/83, Rules & Regulations 1867–1900, Glasgow Royal Infirmary (NHS Greater Glasgow and Clyde Board Archives)

15. Abel-Smith, op cit, p42

16. *ibid*

17. *ibid*, p43

18. *ibid*, p42

19. *ibid*, p55

20. *ibid*, p44

21. *ibid*

22. Blaker, op cit, Chapter 49

23. HB14/6/55–56, Correspondence including the case of the late Duncan Ritchie, 1869, Glasgow Royal Infirmary (NHS Greater Glasgow and Clyde Board Archives)

24. *ibid*

25. *ibid*

26. *ibid*

27. *ibid*

28. *ibid*

29. *ibid*

Chapter 18 – Treatment of Diseases

1. Shorter, op cit, p123

2. *ibid*

3. *ibid*, p124

4. Porter, Roy, 'Hospitals and Surgery' in Porter, Roy (ed.), *The Cambridge Illustrated History of Medicine* (1996, Cambridge University Press), p207

5. *ibid*

6. Shorter, op cit, p122

7. Blaker, op cit, Chapter 43

8. Shorter, op cit, p122

9. Keith, William, 'Hospital Statistics of Stone in the Bladder', *Edinburgh Medical & Surgical Journal*, 1843, No.158, Table II

10. Bristowe & Holmes, op cit, p600

11. Shorter, op cit, p128

12. *ibid*

13. *ibid*

14. *ibid*

15. *ibid*

16. *ibid*

17. *ibid*, p130

18. *ibid*

19. *ibid*, p128

20. *ibid*

21. *ibid*

22. *ibid*

23. Hardy, op cit, p27

24. *ibid*

25. *Family Physician*, op cit, Vol. III, p749

26. *ibid*, p750

27. www.smallandspecial.org (Kingston University: Great Ormond Street Hospital NHS Trust)

28. www.smallandspecial.org (Kingston University: Great Ormond Street Hospital NHS Trust)

29. *Family Physician*, op cit, Vol. III, p794

30. Hardy, op cit, p13

31. *ibid*, p12

32. *ibid*

33. *ibid*, p36

34. *ibid*, p33

35. Cherry, op cit, p12

36. Hardy, op cit, p24

37. Cherry, op cit, p12

38. Hardy, op cit, p24
39. Cherry, op cit, p12
40. Hardy, op cit, p24
41. Bynum, op cit, p205
42. Cherry, op cit, p12
43. *ibid*, p16
44. Hardy, op cit, pp36–37
45. Harrison, op cit, p58
46. Royston Pike, E., *Human Documents of the Age of the Forsytes* (1969, George Allen and Unwin), p254
47. *ibid*
48. *ibid*
49. HC/GH 4/2/18, Admission & Discharge Register for Medical In-patients 1876–1886, General Hospital, Birmingham (Birmingham Archives and Heritage Service)

Chapter 19 – Surgical Cases

1. Hardy, op cit, p28
2. Granshaw, Lindsay, 'Upon This Principle I Have Based A Practice: The Development and Reception of Antisepsis in Britain, 1867–1890' in Pickstone, John V., (ed.), *Medical Innovations in Historical Perspective* (1992, Macmillan), p18
3. *ibid*
4. *ibid*
5. *ibid*
6. Blaker, op cit, Chapter 47
7. HB14/5/5 Ward Day Book for Male Surgical Patients, 1863–1865, Glasgow Royal Infirmary (NHS Greater Glasgow and Clyde Board Archives)
8. DHC/48 Annual Reports 1837–1873, Cardiff Royal Infirmary (Glamorgan Record Office)
9. *ibid*
10. Frederick Treves quoted in Clark-Kennedy, op cit, p71
11. DHC/24 1883–1891, House Committee Minute Book, Cardiff Royal Infirmary (Glamorgan Record Office)
12. Granshaw, op cit, p18
13. *ibid*, p19
14. *ibid*
15. Porter, Roy, *Blood & Guts: A Short History of Medicine* (2002, Penguin Books), p125
16. Granshaw, op cit, p19
17. *ibid*, p23
18. Porter, op cit, p125
19. *ibid*
20. Granshaw, op cit, p23
21. *ibid*
22. *ibid*
23. *ibid*, p30
24. *ibid*, p23
25. *ibid*, p31
26. *ibid*, p32
27. *ibid*
28. *ibid*, p27

29. Blaker, op cit, Chapter 52
30. Cherry, op cit, pp18–19
31. Bynum, op cit, p135
32. *ibid*, pp135–136
33. Granshaw, op cit, p45
34. *ibid*, p46
35. Porter, op cit, p113
36. *ibid*, p115
37. Bynum, op cit, p121
38. *ibid*, p122
39. Porter, op cit, p123
40. Porter, Roy, 'Hospitals and Surgery' in Porter, Roy (ed.), *The Cambridge Illustrated History of Medicine* (1996, Cambridge University Press), p229
41. Bynum, op cit, p122
42. Porter, Roy, *Blood & Guts: A Short History of Medicine*, (2002, Penguin Books), p124
43. Cherry, op cit, pp18–19
44. Porter, op cit, p124
45. Cherry, op cit, pp18–19
46. Porter, Roy, 'Hospitals and Surgery' in Porter, Roy, (ed.), *The Cambridge Illustrated History of Medicine* (1996, Cambridge University Press), p230
47. *ibid*
48. Clark-Kennedy, op cit, p130
49. Cherry, op cit, p19
50. Porter, op cit, p230
51. McKenzie, op cit, pp54–55
52. Hardy, op cit, p28
53. Porter, Roy, *Blood & Guts: A Short History of Medicine* (2002, Penguin Books), p148
54. Blaker, op cit, Chapter 48
55. Porter, op cit, p126
56. Hardy, op cit, p27
57. *ibid*
58. *ibid*, p35
59. *ibid*
60. HC/GH 4/2/36, Admission & Discharge Register for Surgical In-Patients 1879–1885, General Hospital, Birmingham (Birmingham Archives and Heritage Service)
61. *ibid*
62. Hardy, op cit, p5
63. *ibid*, p28
64. *ibid*
65. *British Medical Journal*, 12 January 1903
66. Abel-Smith, op cit, p189

Chapter 20 – Medical Innovations

1. Cherry, op cit, pp17–18
2. *ibid*
3. Shorter, op cit, p140
4. *ibid*
5. *ibid*
6. Hardy, op cit, p25
7. Shorter, op cit, p140
8. Hardy, op cit, p5

9. *ibid*, p25
10. *ibid*
11. *ibid*
12. *ibid*
13. *ibid*, p5
14. *ibid*
15. *Jack's Reference Book*, p348, 1916
16. Weindling, Paul, From Medical Research to Clinical Practice: Serum Therapy for Diphtheria in the 1890s' in Pickstone, John V. (ed.), *Medical Innovations in Historical Perspective* (1992, Macmillan), p73
17. *ibid*
18. *Jack's Reference Book*, op cit, p348
19. Shorter, op cit, p136
20. *ibid*
21. Edward T. Schofield quoted in Shorter, op cit, p137
22. Clark-Kennedy, op cit, p124
23. Hardy, op cit, p26
24. *ibid*
25. Shorter, op cit, p134
26. *ibid*, p135
27. Hardy, op cit, p27
28. Shorter, op cit, p140
29. *ibid*
30. *ibid*
31. Cherry, op cit, p19
32. Clark-Kennedy, op cit, p125
33. *ibid*, p126
34. *ibid*, p131
35. Bayliss, op cit, p79
36. *ibid*
37. Clark-Kennedy, op cit, p130

Chapter 21 – Discharge from Hospital

1. Granshaw, Lindsay, *St Mark's Hospital, London: A Social History of a Specialist Hospital* (1985, Oxford University Press), p87
2. *ibid*
3. HC/GH 1/3/16 Annual Report 1884, General Hospital, Birmingham (Birmingham Archives and Heritage Service)
4. *ibid*
5. *ibid*
6. *ibid*
7. GRHB 1/10/3 Regulations 1882, Aberdeen Royal Infirmary (Northern Health Services Archives)
8. DHC/52 Annual Reports 1894–1900, Cardiff Royal Infirmary (Glamorgan Record Office)
9. Granshaw, op cit, pp87–88
10. HB14 2/9 Annual Reports 1883–1894, Glasgow Royal Infirmary (NHS Greater Glasgow and Clyde Board Archives)
11. McKenzie, op cit, p52
12. *ibid*

Part 3: GOING INTO AN ASYLUM

Chapter 22 – Admission to Asylums

1. Porter, Roy, 'Mental Illness' in Porter, Roy (ed.), *The Cambridge Illustrated History of Medicine* (1996, Cambridge University Press), p297
2. HRRA 31/1/6 Twenty-Eighth Annual Report of the Somerset County Pauper Lunatic Asylum (Lancashire Record Office)
3. Smith, L.D. 'Duddeston Hall and the Trade in Lunacy 1835–65', *Birmingham Historian*, Vol. 8, p18
4. Roberts, A. 1981 section – Farming Out
5. Williams, op cit, p3
6. With thanks to Rina Callingham for providing information and research about her ancestor Llewelyn Bevan
7. Hamilton, op cit, p218
8. Fraser, David (ed.), *The Christian Watt Papers*, (1988, Caledonian Books), pxiii
9. Medical Superintendent's Report 1884, Prestwich Lunatic Asylum (Lancashire Record Office)
10. *ibid*
11. Medical Superintendent's Report 1892, Aberdeen Royal Asylum (Northern Health Services Archives)
12. Porter, op cit, p295
13. QAM 4/7 Rules for Lancaster County Asylum (Lancashire Record Office)
14. Porter, op cit, p295
15. Medical Superintendent's Report 1888, Aberdeen Royal Asylum (Northern Health Services Archives)

Chapter 23 – Pauper and Private Patients

1. Smith, op cit, p17
2. *ibid*
3. *ibid*, p21
4. *ibid*, p17
5. *ibid*, p19
6. Porter, op cit, p289
7. Reid, William, 'The Royal Asylum, Aberdeen', *BMA Handbook & Guide* (1914), pp68–69
8. Williams, op cit, pp4–5
9. *ibid*
10. HO22 83/3/4 Medical Certificate for Mary Ann Royle dated 7 September 1883 (Reproduced with the permission of Gloucestershire NHS Trust and Gloucestershire Archives)
11. HO22 – 70–48 page 87 Patient Records for Mary Ann Royle, County & City of Gloucester Lunatic Asylum (Reproduced with the permission of Gloucestershire NHS Trust and Gloucestershire Archives)
12. With thanks to John Royle for providing information and research about his ancestor Mary Ann Royle

Chapter 24 – Mental Illnesses and Their Causes

1. Medical Superintendent's Report 1881, Aberdeen Royal Asylum (Northern Health Services Archives)
2. *ibid*
3. Male Casebook No.4 (1877–78): LMA Piece H11/HLL/B20/13 (Reproduced with the permission of West London Mental Health NHS Trust)
4. *ibid*
5. With thanks to Dr Christopher J. Hogger for providing information and research about his ancestor Alfred Woodhurst
6. With thanks to Dr Christopher J. Hogger for providing information and research about his ancestor James Woodhurst
7. With thanks to Jill Reeves for providing information and research about her ancestor Arthur Brown
8. DHGL 10/75 Richard Morgan – Case No.7447, Bridgend Asylum (Information reproduced with the permission of Glamorgan Record Office)
9. DHGL 10/75 Richard Morgan – Case No.7447, Bridgend Asylum (Information reproduced with the permission of Glamorgan Record Office)
10. With thanks to John Royle for providing information and research about his ancestor Richard Morgan
11. Fraser, op cit, p106
12. *ibid*, p111
13. *ibid*, p115–116
14. *ibid*, p117
15. *ibid*
16. HRRA 31/1/6 Twenty-Eighth Annual Report of the Somerset County Pauper Lunatic Asylum (Lancashire Record Office)
17. Higgs, op cit, p80
18. *ibid*
19. Smith, Toni, 'Witches, Idiots, Imbeciles and Lunatics', *Your Family Tree*, November 2004, p44
20. *ibid*, p43
21. Stretton, Hesba, 'One of God's Palaces: The Royal Albert Asylum', *Sunday Magazine*, January 1885, p8 (Lancashire Record Office)
22. Williams, op cit, p11
23. *ibid*
24. *ibid*
25. *ibid*
26. Smith, op cit, p45
27. Medical Superintendent's Report 1884, Prestwich Lunatic Asylum (Lancashire Record Office)
28. HRRA 31/1/6 Twenty-Eighth Annual Report of the Somerset County Pauper Lunatic Asylum (Lancashire Record Office)
29. HRRA 30/16 'A Day at the Royal Albert Asylum, from the Manchester Guardian, 21 September 1872 (Lancashire Record Office)
30. *ibid*
31. Stretton, op cit, p8
32. *ibid*, p2
33. *ibid*, p3
34. *ibid*, p5
35. *ibid*, p6
36. *ibid*
37. Bramwell, Byrom, *Studies in Clinical Medicine: A Record of Some of the More Interesting Cases Observed, and Some of the Remarks Made, At the Author's Out-patient Clinic in the Edinburgh Royal Infirmary* (1890, Y.J. Pentland), pp191–192
38. With thanks to Lyn and Alan Howsam for providing information and research about Alan's ancestor John McGregor
39. NHS Greater Glasgow & Clyde, History of Gartnavel Royal Hospital http://www.nhsggc.org.uk/content/default. asp?page=s1065
40. John Davies Patient No.1597, Register of Patients, Bridgend Asylum. (Information reproduced with the permission of Glamorgan Record Office)
41. *ibid*
42. With thanks to Janet Gale for providing information and research about her ancestor John Davies

Chapter 25 – Living Conditions in Asylums

1. Porter, op cit, p295
2. Mitton, op cit, p27
3. Williams, op cit, p4
4. HRRA 31/1/6 Twenty-Eighth Annual Report of the Somerset County Pauper Lunatic Asylum, p31 (Lancashire Record Office)
5. *ibid*
6. *ibid*
7. Smith, L.D., 'Duddeston Hall and the Trade in Lunacy 1835–65', *Birmingham Historian*, Volume 8, p18
8. *ibid*, p19
9. Williams, op cit, p16
10. Medical Superintendent's Report 1881, Aberdeen Royal Asylum (Northern Health Services Archives)
11. HRRA 31/1/6 Twenty-Eighth Annual Report of the Somerset County Pauper Lunatic Asylum (Lancashire Record Office)
12. QAM 5/33 Annual Report 1884, Lancaster County Lunatic Asylum (Lancashire Record Office)
13. QAM 4/7 Rules for Lancaster County Lunatic Asylum (Lancashire Record Office)
14. *ibid*
15. QAM 5/33 Annual Report 1884, Lancaster County Lunatic Asylum (Lancashire Record Office)
16. Higgs, op cit, p82
17. *ibid*

18. *ibid*
19. *ibid*, p83
20. *ibid*, p81
21. *ibid*
22. Abel-Smith, op cit, p54
23. Higgs, op cit, p84

Chapter 26 – Treatment of the Mentally Ill

1. Porter, op cit, p295
2. Williams, op cit, p4
3. *ibid*, p16
4. HRRA 31/1/6 Twenty-Eighth Annual Report of the Somerset County Pauper Lunatic Asylum (Lancashire Record Office)
5. QAM 4/7 Rules for Lancaster County Lunatic Asylum (Lancashire Record Office)
6. Medical Superintendent's Report 1884, Prestwich Lunatic Asylum (Lancashire Record Office)
7. Reid, op cit, p69
8. Porter, op cit, p280
9. *ibid*, p295
10. *ibid*
11. Medical Superintendent's Report 1841, Aberdeen Royal Asylum (With thanks to Stuart Reid for sourcing document)
12. *ibid*
13. Medical Superintendent's Report 1900, Aberdeen Royal Asylum (Northern Health Services Archives)
14. Higgs, op cit, p84
15. *ibid*
16. J4/190/5 Patient No.1324 Case Notes for John Oatley, Wiltshire County Lunatic Asylum (Reproduced with the permission of Wiltshire and Swindon Archives)
17. *ibid*
18. *ibid*
19. With thanks to Ellie Thomas for providing information and research about her ancestor John Oatley
20. MH/Md2/Ap28/76 and MH/Md2/Ap25/15 Case Notes for John Henderson, Kent County Lunatic Asylum (Reproduced with the permission of the Kent & Medway NHS & Social Care Partnership Trust and the Centre for Kentish Studies, Kent Archives)
21. *ibid*
22. CH84/NC3 Case Notes for John Henderson, Malling Place Lunatic Asylum (Reproduced with the permission of the Kent & Medway NHS & Social Care Partnership Trust and the Centre for Kentish Studies, Kent Archives
23. *ibid*
24. *ibid*
25. With thanks to Ellie Thomas for providing information and research about her ancestor John Henderson

Chapter 27 – Recovery

1. Porter, Roy, 'Hospitals and Surgery' in Porter, Roy, (ed.), *The Cambridge Illustrated History of Medicine* (1996, Cambridge University Press), p213
2. Higgs, op cit, pp84–85
3. Medical Superintendent's Report 1841, Aberdeen Royal Asylum
4. Fraser, op cit, p108
5. *ibid*, p124
6. Williams, op cit, p13
7. Medical Superintendent's Report 1900, Aberdeen Royal Asylum (Northern Health Services Archives)

Part 4: MEDICAL STAFF

Chapter 28 – Physicians and Surgeons

1. Berridge, op cit, p180
2. *ibid*
3. *ibid*, p181
4. Cherry, op cit, p29
5. Hamilton, op cit, p148
6. *ibid*
7. Abel-Smith, op cit, p16
8. Bynum, op cit, p50
9. Abel-Smith, op cit, pp17–18
10. *ibid*, p17
11. Bynum, op cit, pp178–179
12. *ibid*
13. Reinarz, op cit, p19
14. *ibid*, p20
15. *ibid*
16. *ibid*
17. Cherry, op cit, p28
18. Porter, op cit, p215
19. Bynum, op cit, p49
20. *ibid*
21. DHC 48 Annual Reports 1837–1873, Cardiff Royal Infirmary (Glamorgan Record Office)
22. Cherry, op cit, pp27–28
23. Abel-Smith, op cit, p2
24. Hardy, op cit, pp23–24
25. *ibid*, p24
26. Bynum, op cit, p181
27. *ibid*
28. Abel-Smith, op cit, p19
29. *ibid*
30. Hardy, op cit, p22
31. Bynum, op cit, p178
32. Hardy, op cit, pp.22–23
33. Bynum, op cit, pp179–180
34. *ibid*, p180
35. Royston Pike, E., *Human Documents of the Age of the Forsytes* (1969, George Allen and Unwin), pp.101–102
36. Cherry, op cit, p30
37. *ibid*, p31
38. Hamilton, op cit, pp207–208

39. Hardy, op cit, p17
40. GRHB 1/10/3 Regulations 1882, Aberdeen Royal Infirmary (Northern Health Services Archives)
41. *ibid*
42. *ibid*
43. *ibid*
44. *ibid*
45. Abel-Smith, op cit, p20
46. *ibid*
47. *ibid*
48. *ibid*, p21
49. Bynum, op cit, p47
50. Abel-Smith, op cit, p21
51. *ibid*
52. *ibid*
53. HC/GH 1/1/2/14 Weekly Board Minutes, 28 October 1870, General Hospital, Birmingham (Birmingham Archives and Heritage Service)
54. HC/GH 1/1/2/14 Weekly Board Minutes, 18 November 1870, General Hospital, Birmingham (Birmingham Archives and Heritage Service)
55. GRHB 1/10/3 Regulations 1882, Aberdeen Royal Infirmary (Northern Health Services Archives)
56. Clark-Kennedy, op cit, p129
57. *ibid*, p130
58. *ibid*, pp130–131
59. *ibid*
60. Bynum, op cit, p47
61. *ibid*, p180
62. *ibid*, p181
63. *ibid*
64. Hardy, op cit, p14
65. *ibid*
66. *ibid*
67. *ibid*, p15
68. *ibid*
69. Higgs, op cit, p120
70. *ibid*
71. *ibid*, p117
72. Cherry, op cit, pp43–44
73. Higgs, op cit, p118
74. *ibid*
75. *ibid*, p122
76. Abel-Smith, op cit, p96
77. *ibid*
78. *ibid*
79. *ibid*
80. With thanks to Richard Waddy for providing information and research about his ancestor Frederick Henry Waddy
81. Berridge, op cit, p180
82. Porter, Roy, *Blood & Guts: A Short History of Medicine* (2002, Penguin Books), p52
83. *ibid*
84. Cherry, op cit, p32
85. *ibid*
86. HB14 2/9, Annual Reports 1883–1894, Glasgow Royal Infirmary (NHS Greater Glasgow and Clyde Board Archives)
87. HB14 6/63 Correspondence including admission of women medical students 1890–1899, Glasgow Royal Infirmary (NHS Greater Glasgow and Clyde Board Archives)
88. Blaker, op cit
89. With thanks to Prue Stokes for providing information and research about her great-grandfather John Taylor Porter
90. With thanks to Prue Stokes for providing information and research about her grandfather, William Smith Porter

Chapter 29 – Matrons

1. Abel-Smith, op cit, p68
2. DHC/2 Minute Book 1841–1855, 3 September 1847, Cardiff Royal Infirmary (Glamorgan Record Office)
3. *ibid*, 8 November 1847
4. DHC/48 Annual Reports 1837–1873, Cardiff Royal Infirmary (Glamorgan Record Office)
5. Maggs, op cit, p186
6. GRHB 1/1/18 Minute Book 1884–1886, Aberdeen Royal Infirmary (Northern Health Services Archives)
7. HB14 2/8 Annual Report 1879, Glasgow Royal Infirmary (NHS Greater Glasgow and Clyde Board Archives)
8. McGann, Susan, 'Strong, Rebecca (1843–1944)', *Oxford Dictionary of National Biography*, (2004, Oxford University Press)
9. 'Nurses of Note – Mrs Rebecca Strong', *British Journal of Nursing*, January 1924
10. Baly, Monica E., 'The Nightingale Nurses: The Myth and the Reality' in Maggs, Christopher (ed.), *Nursing History: The State of the Art* (1987, Croom Helm), p50
11. DHC/48 Annual Reports 1837–1873, Cardiff Royal Infirmary (Glamorgan Record Office)
12. HC/GH 1/1/6/3 House Committee Minutes, 24 February and 21 April 1882, General Hospital, Birmingham (Birmingham Archives and Heritage Service)
13. *ibid*, 16 June 1882
14. *ibid*, 1 September 1882
15. HRBK 4/2 Annual Reports 1865–1877, Blackburn Royal Infirmary (Lancashire Record Office)
16. Baly, op cit, p56
17. Webster, Kenneth Alistair, *Nursing History of Aberdeen*, (1986, Grampian Area Health Board Scholarship), p21
18. Webster, Kenneth, 'Rachel Frances Lumsden of Glenbogie', *Aberdeen Postgraduate Medical Bulletin*, Vol. 22 No.1, 1988, p18
19. GRHB 1/1/18 Minute Book 1884–1886, Aberdeen Royal Infirmary (Northern Health Services Archives)

20. Webster, op cit, p18
21. GRHB 1/1/18 Minute Book 1884–1886, Aberdeen Royal Infirmary (Northern Health Services Archives)
22. Clark-Kennedy, op cit, p94
23. *ibid*, pp94–95
24. *ibid*, p95
25. *ibid*
26. *ibid*, p96
27. Bynum, op cit, p188
28. Abel-Smith, op cit, p68
29. *ibid*
30. *ibid*
31. *ibid*

Chapter 30 – Nurses

1. Bristowe & Holmes, op cit, p485
2. *ibid*
3. J. Delpratt Harris quoted in Hawker, op cit, pp.147–148
4. Frederick Treves quoted in Clark-Kennedy, op cit, p56
5. Hawker, op cit, pp147–148
6. *ibid*, p149
7. 'Nurses of Note – Mrs Rebecca Strong', *British Journal of Nursing*, January 1924
8. Baly, op cit, p37
9. *ibid*
10. *ibid*
11. *ibid*
12. 'Nurses of Note – Mrs Rebecca Strong', *British Journal of Nursing*, January 1924
13. Webster, Kenneth Alistair, *Nursing History of Aberdeen* (1986, Grampian Area Health Board Scholarship), p19
14. *ibid*
15. Baly, op cit, p39
16. 'Nurses of Note – Mrs Rebecca Strong', *British Journal of Nursing*, January 1924
17. Porter, Roy, *Blood & Guts: A Short History of Medicine* (2002, Penguin Books), p147
18. Baly, op cit, p40
19. *ibid*, p41
20. *ibid*, p43
21. Abel-Smith, op cit, p43
22. Clark-Kennedy, op cit, pp57–58
23. GRHB 1/7/4 Annual Reports 1875–1889, Aberdeen Royal Infirmary (Northern Health Services Archives)
24. Clark-Kennedy, op cit, p96
25. *ibid*
26. *ibid*, p97
27. *ibid*
28. Webster, Kenneth, 'Rachel Frances Lumsden of Glenbogie', *Aberdeen Postgraduate Medical Bulletin*, Vol. 22 No.1, 1988, p19
29. DHC/39 Nursing Committee Minute Book 1885–1909, Cardiff Royal Infirmary (Glamorgan Record Office)

30. HC/GH 1/1/9/1 Minutes of the Nursing Committee, 8 December 1899, General Hospital, Birmingham (Birmingham Archives and Heritage Service)
31. HC/GH 1/1/9/1 Minutes of the Nursing Committee, 23 February 1900, General Hospital, Birmingham (Birmingham Archives and Heritage Service)
32. HB14 2/8 Annual Report 1880, Glasgow Royal Infirmary (NHS Greater Glasgow and Clyde Board Archives)
33. *ibid*
34. 'Nurses of Note – Mrs Rebecca Strong', *British Journal of Nursing*, January 1924
35. Clark-Kennedy, op cit, pp122–123
36. *ibid*, p109
37. Porter, op cit, p147
38. Cherry, op cit, p35
39. *ibid*
40. HC/GH 1/1/2/14 Weekly Board Minutes, General Hospital, Birmingham (Birmingham Archives and Heritage Service)
41. Clark-Kennedy, op cit, p109
42. HB14 8/95 Nurses' Timetable & Regulations 1892, Glasgow Royal Infirmary (NHS Greater Glasgow and Clyde Board Archives)
43. *ibid*
44. GRHB 1/7/4 Annual Reports 1875–1889, Aberdeen Royal Infirmary (Northern Health Services Archives)
45. *ibid*
46. HB14 2/8 Annual Report 1880, Glasgow Royal Infirmary (NHS Greater Glasgow and Clyde Board Archives)
47. HB14 8/95 Nurses' Timetable & Regulations 1892, Glasgow Royal Infirmary (NHS Greater Glasgow and Clyde Board Archives)
48. Clark-Kennedy, op cit, p96
49. Maggs, op cit, p185
50. *ibid*
51. *ibid*
52. HB14 2/9 Annual Reports 1883–1894, Glasgow Royal Infirmary (NHS Greater Glasgow and Clyde Board Archives)
53. *ibid*
54. *ibid*
55. Clark-Kennedy, op cit, p99
56. *ibid*
57. Abel-Smith, op cit, p44
58. HB14 2/8 Annual Report 1880, Glasgow Royal Infirmary (NHS Greater Glasgow and Clyde Board Archives)
59. HC/GH 1/1/9/1 Minutes of the Nursing Committee, 14 July 1892, General Hospital, Birmingham (Birmingham Archives and Heritage Service)
60. Clark-Kennedy, op cit, p98
61. Cherry, op cit, p36
62. Baly, op cit, p38

63. *ibid*
64. Clark-Kennedy, op cit, p98
65. GRHB 1/3/19 Admission & Discharge Register 1849–1853, Aberdeen Royal Infirmary (Northern Health Services Archives)
66. Baly, op cit, p39
67. Abel-Smith, op cit, inside front page
68. HC/GH 1/1/9/1 Minutes of the Nursing Committee, 26 April 1895, General Hospital, Birmingham (Birmingham Archives and Heritage Service)
69. Cherry, op cit, p34
70. Bynum, op cit, p188
71. Cherry, op cit, p35
72. *ibid*
73. Clark-Kennedy, op cit, p105
74. Berridge, op cit, p183
75. *ibid*
76. With thanks to David Rawdon for providing information and research about his ancestors Mary and Charlotte Lightfoot
77. With thanks to Wendy Fitzpatrick for providing information and research about her ancestor Ann Elizabeth Armson
78. Clark-Kennedy, op cit, p102
79. DHC/39 Nursing Committee Minute Book 1885–1909, Cardiff Royal Infirmary (Glamorgan Record Office)
80. Higgs, op cit, p131
81. Abel-Smith, op cit, p56
82. *ibid*, p57
83. *ibid*, p56
84. Cherry, op cit, p36
85. *ibid*
86. Higgs, op cit, p134
87. *ibid*, p135
88. *ibid*
89. *ibid*
90. Smith, L. D., 'Duddeston Hall and the Trade in Lunacy 1835–65', *Birmingham Historian*, Volume 8, p19
91. QAM 4/7 Rules for the Lancaster County Asylum (Lancashire Record Office)
92. *ibid*
93. Smith, op cit, p18
94. QAM 4/7 Rules for the Lancaster County Asylum (Lancashire Record Office)
95. Smith, op cit, p19
96. Medical Superintendent's Report 1884, Prestwich Lunatic Asylum (Lancashire Record Office)

Bibliography

Books

Abel-Smith, Brian, *The Hospitals 1800–1948: A Study in Social Administration in England and Wales* (1964, Heinemann)

Aldis, Arnold S., *Cardiff Royal Infirmary 1883–1983* (1984, University of Wales Press)

Baly, Monica E., 'The Nightingale Nurses: The Myth and the Reality' in Maggs, Christopher (ed.), *Nursing History: The State of the Art* (1987, Croom Helm), pp33–59

Bayliss, Anne & Paul and Jackson, Alan, *Scarborough Hospital and Dispensary: The First Fifty Years 1852–1902*, (2006, A.M. Bayliss)

Berridge, Virginia, 'Health and Medicine' in Thompson, F.M.L. (ed.), *The Cambridge Social History of Britain 1750–1950 Volume 3: Social Agencies and Institutions*, (1993, Cambridge University Press), pp171–242

Black, Nick, *Walking London's Medical History* (2006, The Royal Society of Medicine Press Ltd)

Blaker, Nathaniel Paine, *Sussex in Bygone Days: Reminiscences of Nathaniel Paine Blaker, M.R.C.S.* (1919)

Bolwell, John S. and Evans, Andrea, *A History of the County Infirmary, Carmarthen 1848 to 1948 and the NHS and the West Wales General Hospital 1948 to 2004* (2005, Noon Books)

Bramwell, Byrom, *Studies in Clinical Medicine: A Record of Some of the More Interesting Cases Observed, and Some of the Remarks Made, At the Author's Out-patient Clinic in the Edinburgh Royal Infirmary*, (1890, Y.J. Pentland)

Bristowe, John Syer and Holmes, Timothy, *Report on the Hospitals of the United Kingdom: Appendix 15 to the Privy Council Medical Officer's Report* (1863, HMSO)

Bynum, W.F., *Science and the Practice of Medicine in the Nineteenth Century* (1994, Cambridge University Press)

Cherry, Steven, *Medical Services and the Hospitals in Britain 1860–1939* (1996, Cambridge University Press)

Clark-Kennedy, A.E., *The London: A Study in the Voluntary Hospital System Volume Two The Second Hundred Years 1840–1948* (1963, Pitman Medical Publishing Co. Ltd)

Davies, Paul P., *History of Medicine in Great Yarmouth: Hospitals and Doctors* (2003, Paul P. Davies)

Davies, T.G., *Deeds Not Words: A History of the Swansea General and Eye Hospital 1817–1948* (1988, Cardiff University of Wales Press)

Emrys-Roberts, Meyrick, *The Cottage Hospitals 1859–1990* (1991, Tern Publications)

The Family Physician: A Manual of Domestic Medicine by Physicians and Surgeons of the Principal London Hospitals (1884, Cassell & Co. Ltd)

Fraser, David (ed.), *The Christian Watt Papers* (1988, Caledonian Books)

Granshaw, Lindsay, *St Mark's Hospital, London: A Social History of a Specialist Hospital* (1985, Oxford University Press)

Granshaw, Lindsay, 'Upon This Principle I Have Based A Practice: The Development and Reception of Antisepsis in Britain, 1867–1890' in Pickstone, John V. (ed.), *Medical Innovations in Historical Perspective* (1992, Macmillan), pp17–46

Granshaw, Lindsay, 'Fame and fortune by means of bricks and mortar': the medical profession and specialist hospitals in Britain, 1800–1948' in Granshaw, Lindsay and Porter, Roy (ed.), *The Hospital In History* (1989, Routledge), pp199–220

Granshaw, Lindsay and Porter, Roy (ed.), *The Hospital In History* (1989, Routledge)

Gray, H.M.W., 'Royal Hospital for Sick Children', *BMA Handbook & Guide* (1914)

Haden, H. Jack, *The Corbett Hospital: A Centenary History 1893–1993* (1993)

Halliday, Stephen, *The Great Filth: The War Against Disease in Victorian England* (2007, Sutton Publishing)

Hamilton, David, *The Healers: A History of Medicine in Scotland* (1981, Canongate)

Hardy, Anne, *Health and Medicine in Britain Since 1860* (2001, Palgrave Macmillan)

Harrison, J.F.C., *Early Victorian Britain 1832–1851* (1979, Fontana Press)

Harrison, J.F.C., *Late Victorian Britain 1875–1901* (1990, Fontana Press)

Hawker, Ruth 'For the Good of the Patient?', in Maggs, Christopher (ed.), *Nursing History: The State of the Art*, (1987, Croom Helm)

Hay, Matthew, 'The City Hospital for Infectious Diseases', *BMA Handbook & Guide* (1914)

Higgs, Michelle, *Life in the Victorian and Edwardian Workhouse* (2007, Tempus Publishing)

Horn, Pamela, *Labouring Life in the Victorian Countryside* (1987, Alan Sutton Publishing Limited)

Jack's Reference Book (1916, T. C. & E. C. Jack Ltd.)

Jenkinson, Jacqueline, Moss, Michael and Russell, Iain, *The Royal: The History of the Glasgow Royal Infirmary, 1794–1994* (1994, Glasgow Royal Infirmary NHS Trust)

Levack, Iain and Dudley, Hugh (ed.), *Aberdeen Royal Infirmary: The People's Hospital of the North-East* (1992, Bailliere Tindall)

Loudon, Irvine, *The Tragedy of Childbed Fever* (2000, Oxford University Press)

Maggs, Christopher (ed.), *Nursing History: The State of the Art* (1987, Croom Helm)

Maggs, Christopher, 'Profit and Loss and the Hospital Nurse' in Maggs, Christopher (ed.), *Nursing History: The State of the Art* (1987, Croom Helm), pp176–189

McGann, Susan, 'Strong, Rebecca (1843–1944)', *Oxford Dictionary of National Biography* (2004, Oxford University Press)

Midwinter, E.C., *Victorian Social Reform* (1968, Longman Group Ltd)

Miller, C, *Broken Gleams* (1873)

Mitton, Lavinia, *The Victorian Hospital* (2001, Shire Publications)

Newsholme, Arthur, *The Prevention of Tuberculosis* (1908, Methuen & Co.)

Nightingale, Florence, *Notes on Hospitals* (1863)

Pickstone, John V., (ed.), *Medical Innovations in Historical Perspective* (1992, Macmillan)

Porter, Roy, *A Social History of Madness: Stories of the Insane* (1987, George Weidenfeld and Nicolson Ltd)

Porter, Roy, *Blood & Guts: A Short History of Medicine* (2002, Penguin Books)

Porter, Roy, (ed.), *The Cambridge Illustrated History of Medicine* (1996, Cambridge University Press)

Porter, Roy, 'Hospitals and Surgery' in Porter, Roy (ed.), *The Cambridge Illustrated History of Medicine* (1996, Cambridge University Press), pp.202–245

Porter, Roy, 'Mental Illness' in Porter, Roy (ed.), *The Cambridge Illustrated History of Medicine* (1996, Cambridge University Press), pp.278–303

Reid, William, 'The Royal Asylum, Aberdeen', *BMA Handbook & Guide* (1914)

Royston Pike, E., *Human Documents of the Age of the Forsytes* (1969, George Allen and Unwin)

Royston Pike, E., *Human Documents of the Victorian Golden Age* (1967, George Allen and Unwin)

Shorter, Edward, 'Primary Care' in Porter, Roy (ed.), *The Cambridge Illustrated History of Medicine* (1996, Cambridge University Press), pp.118–153

Thompson, F.M.L. (ed.), *The Cambridge Social History of Britain 1750–1950 Volume 3: Social Agencies and Institutions* (1993, Cambridge University Press)

Walvin, James, *A Child's World: A Social History of English Childhood 1800–1914* (1982, Penguin Books Ltd)

Webster, Kenneth Alistair, *Nursing History of Aberdeen* (1986, Grampian Area Health Board Scholarship)

Weindling, Paul, 'From Medical Research to Clinical Practice: Serum Therapy for Diphtheria in the 1890s' in Pickstone, John V. (ed.), *Medical Innovations in Historical Perspective* (1992, Macmillan), pp72–83

Williams, L.H., *Abergavenny Asylum* (2006, Unpublished Research)

Worboys, Michael, 'The Sanatorium Treatment for Consumption in Britain, 1890–1914' in Pickstone, John V. (ed.), *Medical Innovations in Historical Perspective* (1992, Macmillan), pp47–71

Yule, Bill, *Matrons, Medics and Maladies: Inside Edinburgh Royal Infirmary in the 1840s* (1999, Tuckwell Press)

Articles in periodicals

Dickens, Charles, 'No Hospital for Incurables', *Household Words*, 24 August 1850

Keith, William, 'Hospital Statistics of Stone in the Bladder', *Edinburgh Medical & Surgical Journal*, 1843, No.158

Lomax, Elizabeth, M.R., 'Small and Special: The Development of Hospitals for Children in Victorian Britain', *Medical History*, 1996, Supplement No.16

McKenzie, Fred A., 'The London Hospital', *The Windsor Magazine*, December 1900, XIII: 49

'Nurses of Note – Mrs Rebecca Strong', *British Journal of Nursing*, January 1924

Reinarz, Jonathan, 'Healthcare and the Second City: The Development of the Birmingham Teaching Hospitals in the Nineteenth Century', *Birmingham Historian*, Vol. 26, summer 2004, pp16–27

Royall, Arthur, 'Eva Lückes: Too Young and Too Pretty', *Family Tree*, October 2007, pp39–41

Smith, L.D., 'Duddeston Hall and the Trade in Lunacy 1835–65', *Birmingham Historian*, Vol. 8, pp16–22

Smith, Toni, 'Witches, Idiots, Imbeciles and Lunatics', *Your Family Tree*, November 2004, pp42–45

Stretton, Hesba, 'One of God's Palaces: The Royal Albert Asylum', *Sunday Magazine*, January 1885

Webster, Kenneth, 'Rachel Frances Lumsden of Glenbogie', *Aberdeen Postgraduate Medical Bulletin*, Vol. 22 No.1, 1988

Contemporary periodicals and newspapers

The British Journal of Nursing
British Medical Journal
The Graphic
Household Words
The Illustrated London News
The Lancet
Sunday Magazine
The Times
The Windsor Magazine

Websites

Jackson, Lee – The Victorian Dictionary www.victorianlondon.org

Roberts, Andrew 1981 /timeline – Mental Health History Timeline www.mdx.ac.uk/www/study/mlhtim. htm Middlesex University

Small and Special – Kingston University: Great Ormond Street Hospital NHS Trust www.smallandspecial.org

NHS Grampian – Who was Dr Gray? www.nhsgrampian.org

Higginbotham, Peter 'The Workhouse' www.workhouses.org

NHS Greater Glasgow & Clyde, History of Gartnavel Royal Hospital – www.nhsggc.org.uk/content/default. asp?page=s1065

Index